Lecture Notes in Artificial Intelligence 13651

Subseries of Lecture Notes in Computer Science

More information about this subseries at https://link.springer.com/bookseries/1244

Olarik Surinta · Kevin Kam Fung Yuen (Eds.)

Multi-disciplinary Trends in Artificial Intelligence

15th International Conference, MIWAI 2022
Virtual Event, November 17–19, 2022
Proceedings

 Springer

Editors
Olarik Surinta 🆔
Mahasarakham University
Maha Sarakham, Thailand

Kevin Kam Fung Yuen 🆔
Hong Kong Polytechnic University
Hong Kong, China

ISSN 0302-9743   ISSN 1611-3349 (electronic)
Lecture Notes in Artificial Intelligence
ISBN 978-3-031-20991-8   ISBN 978-3-031-20992-5 (eBook)
https://doi.org/10.1007/978-3-031-20992-5

LNCS Sublibrary: SL7 – Artificial Intelligence

This Springer imprint is published by the registered company Springer Nature Switzerland AG
The registered company address is: Gewerbestrasse 11, 6330 Cham, Switzerland

Preface

The Multi-disciplinary International Conference on Artificial Intelligence (MIWAI), formerly called the Multi-disciplinary International Workshop on Artificial Intelligence, is a well-established scientific venue in Artificial Intelligence (AI). The MIWAI series started in 2007 in Thailand as the Mahasarakham International Workshop on Artificial Intelligence and has been held yearly since then. It has emerged as an international workshop with participants from around the world. In 2011, MIWAI was held outside of Thailand for the first time, in Hyderabad, India, so it became the "Multi-disciplinary International Workshop on Artificial Intelligence." Then the event took place in various Asian countries: Ho Chi Minh City; Vietnam (2012); Krabi, Thailand (2013); Bangalore, India (2014); Fuzhou, China (2015); Chiang Mai, Thailand (2016); Bandar Seri Begawan, Brunei (2017); Hanoi, Vietnam (2018); and Kuala Lumpur, Malaysia (2019). In 2018, MIWAI was renamed to the "Multi-disciplinary International Conference on Artificial Intelligence." The event planned for 2020 was postponed, and it was held virtually in 2021 due to the COVID-19 pandemic.

The MIWAI series serves as a forum for AI researchers and practitioners to discuss and deliberate cutting-edge AI research. It also aims to elevate the standards of AI research by providing researchers and students with feedback from an internationally renowned Program Committee.

AI is a broad research area. Theory, methods, and tools in AI sub-areas encompass cognitive science, computational philosophy, computational intelligence, game theory, multi-agent systems, machine learning, natural language processing, representation and reasoning, data mining, speech, computer vision, and deep learning. The above methods have broad applications in big data, bioinformatics, biometrics, decision support systems, knowledge management, privacy, recommender systems, security, software engineering, spam filtering, surveillance, telecommunications, web services, and IoT. Submissions received by MIWAI 2022 were wide-ranging and covered both theory and applications.

This year, the 15th MIWAI was held as a virtual conference during November 17–18, 2022. MIWAI 2022 received 42 full papers from authors in eight countries: France, China, South Korea, India, Malaysia, Philippines, Vietnam, and Thailand. Following the success of previous MIWAI conferences, MIWAI 2022 continued the tradition of a rigorous review process.

In the end, 19 papers were accepted with an acceptance rate of 45.24%. A total of 14 papers were accepted as regular papers and five papers were accepted as short papers. Each submission was carefully reviewed by at least two members of a Program Committee consisting of 78 AI experts from 25 countries, and some papers received up to four reviews when necessary. The reviewing process was double blind. Many of the papers that were excluded from the proceedings showed promise, but the quality of the proceedings had to be maintained. We would like to thank all authors for their submissions. Without their contribution, this conference would not have been possible.

In addition to the papers published in the proceedings, the technical program included a keynote talk and we thank the keynote speaker for accepting our invitation. We are also thankful to the Research Development Institute (RDI), Muban Chombueng Rajabhat University (MCRU), for co-organizing this virtual conference.

We acknowledge the use of the EasyChair conference management system for the paper submission, review, and compilation process. Last but not least, our sincere thanks go to the excellent team at Springer for their support and cooperation in publishing the proceedings as a volume of Lecture Notes in Computer Science.

September 2021   Olarik Surinta
                                                    Kevin Kam Fung Yuen

Organization

Steering Committee

Arun Agarwal — University of Hyderabad, India
Rajkumar Buyya — University of Melbourne, Australia
Patrick Doherty — University of Linköping, Sweden
Rina Dechter — University of California, Irvine, USA
Leon Van Der Torre — University of Luxembourg, Luxembourg
Peter Haddawy — Mahidol University, Thailand
Jérôme Lang — Université Paris-Dauphine, France
James F. Peters — University of Manitoba, Canada
Somnuk Phon-Amnuaisuk — UTB, Brunei
Srinivasan Ramani — IIIT Bangalore, India
C. Raghavendra Rao — University of Hyderabad, India

Honorary Advisor

Sasitorn Kaewman — Mahasarakham University, Thailand

Conveners

Richard Booth — Cardiff University, UK
Chattrakul Sombattheera — Mahasarakham University, Thailand

Program Chairs

Olarik Surinta — Mahasarakham University, Thailand
Kevin Kam Fung Yuen — The Hong Kong Polytechnic University,
Hong Kong SAR, China

Program Committee

Arun Agarwal — University of Hyderabad, India
Grigoris Antoniou — University of Huddersfield, UK
Adham Atyabi — University of Colorado, Colorado Springs and
Seattle Children's Research Institute, USA
Thien Wan Au — Universiti Teknologi Brunei, Brunei
Costin Badica — University of Craiova, Romania
Raj Bhatnagar — University of Cincinnati, USA

Richard Booth	Cardiff University, UK
Zied Bouraoui	CRIL - CNRS and Université d'Artois, France
Gauvain Bourgne	CNRS and Sorbonne Université, LIP6, France
Rapeeporn Chamchong	Mahasarakham University, Thailand
Zhicong Chen	Fuzhou University, China
Suwannit-Chareen Chit	Universiti Utara Malaysia, Malaysia
Phatthanaphong Chomphuwiset	Mahasarakham University, Thailand
Sook Ling Chua	Multimedia University, Malaysia
Todsanai Chumwatana	Rangsit University, Thailand
Abdollah Dehzangi	Morgan State University, USA
Juergen Dix	Clausthal University of Technology, Germany
Nhat-Quang Doan	University of Science and Technology of Hanoi, Vietnam
Abdelrahman Elfaki	University of Tabuk, Saudi Arabia
Lee Kien Foo	Multimedia University, Malaysia
Hui-Ngo Goh	Multimedia University, Malaysia
Chatklaw Jareanpon	Mahasarakham University, Thailand
Himabindu K.	Vishnu Institute of Technology, India
Manasawee Kaenampornpan	Mahasarakham University, Thailand
Ng Keng Hoong	Multimedia University, Malaysia
Kok Chin Khor	Universiti Tunku Abdul Rahman, Malaysia
Suchart Khummanee	Mahasarakham University, Thailand
Ven Jyn Kok	National University of Malaysia, Malaysia
Satish Kolhe	North Maharashtra University, India
Raja Kumar	Taylor's University, Malaysia
Chee Kau Lim	University of Malaya, Malaysia
Chidchanok Lursinsap	Chulalongkorn University, Thailand
Sebastian Moreno	Universidad Adolfo Ibañez, Chile
Sven Naumann	University of Trier, Germany
Atul Negi	University of Hyderabad, India
Thi Phuong Nghiem	USTH, Vietnam
Dung D. Nguyen	Institute of Information Technology, Vietnam Academy of Science and Technology, Vietnam
Thi-Oanh Nguyen	VNU University of Science, Vietnam
Tho Quan	Ho Chi Minh City University of Technology, Vietnam
Srinivasan Ramani	IIIT Bangalore, India
Alexis Robbes	University of Tours, France
Annupan Rodtook	Ramkhamhaeng University, Thailand
Harvey Rosas	University of Valparaiso, Chile
Junmo Kim	KAIST, South Korea

Adrien Rougny	National Institute of Advanced Industrial Science and Technology, Japan
Jose H. Saito	Universidade Federal de São Carlos, Brazil
Nicolas Schwind	National Institute of Advanced Industrial Science and Technology, Japan
Myint Myint Sein	University of Computer Studies, Yangon, Myanmar
Jun Shen	University of Wollongong, Australia
Guillermo R. Simari	Universidad Nacional del Sur, Argentina
Alok Singh	University of Hyderabad, India
Dominik Slezak	University of Warsaw, Poland
Chattrakul Sombattheera	Mahasarakham University, Thailand
Heechul Jung	Kyungpook National University, South Korea
Panida Songrum	Mahasarakham University, Thailand
Frieder Stolzenburg	Harz University of Applied Sciences, Germany
Olarik Surinta	Mahasarakham University, Thailand
Ilias Tachmazidis	University of Huddersfield, UK
Thanh-Hai Tran	MICA, Vietnam
Suguru Ueda	Saga University, Japan
Chau Vo	Ho Chi Minh City University of Technology, Vietnam
Chalee Vorakulpipat	NECTEC, Thailand
Kewen Wang	Griffith University, Australia
Kevin Wong	Murdoch University, Australia
Pornntiwa Pawara	Mahasarakham University, Thailand
Peter Scully	Mahasarakham University, Thailand
Sheng He	Harvard Medical School, USA
Maria do Carmo Nicoletti	UNIFACCAMP, Brazil
Khanista Namee	King Mongkut's University of Technology North Bangkok, Thailand
Sajjaporn Waijanya	Silpakorn University, Thailand
Kraisak Kesorn	Naresuan University, Thailand
Narit Hnoohom	Mahidol University, Thailand
Artitayaporn Rojarath	Mahasarakham University, Thailand
Emmanuel Okafor	Ahmadu Bello University, Nigeria
Sakorn Mekruksavanich	University of Phayao, Thailand
Jantima Polpinij	Mahasarakham University, Thailand
Narumol Choomuang	Muban Chombueng Rajabhat University, Thailand

Publicity Chairs

Olarik Surinta   Mahasarakham University, Thailand
Artitayaporn Rojarath   Mahasarakham University, Thailand

Financial Chair

Olarik Surinta   Mahasarakham University, Thailand

Web Master

Panich Sudkhot   Mahasarakham University, Thailand

Contents

Computing Nash Equilibrium of Crops in Real World Agriculture Domain

Chattrakul Sombattheera[✉]

Multiagent, Intelligent and Simulation Laboratory (MISL), Faculty of Informatics, Mahasarakham University, Khamreang, Kantarawichai, Mahasarakham, Thailand
chattrakul.s@msu.ac.th

Abstract. Since the emergence of game theory as an area of research in artificial intelligence (AI), a lot of progress has been made over the years and is yet to be adopted in agriculture domain. The Department of Agriculture Extension (DOAE), Ministry of Agriculture, Thailand, has launched an innovative AI-based system, namely, Personalized Data (PD), to provide farmers with analyzed data through mobile applications. Among many features, the first and foremost is to provide information to DOAE officer to help decide for appropriate policies. As part of PD, a very important system for analyzing balance between yields and prices of crops, has also been developed. This system deploys Nash Equilibrium as a principle to help find balances among crops so that further policies can be examined and declared. Nash equilibrium has been widely adopted but not many has been applied in agriculture domains and more interestingly through mobile applications for farmers. This paper presents the NE-based system and its analytic results on pragmatic use under real world conditions. The approach used strictly follows Nash equilibrium as a preliminary tool for more complex analysis in later stage. The results show that the computation complexity is exponential. Combinations of 5 crops can take days to find equilibrium. Due to this nature, it is found that combinations of 3 crops is reasonable and bearable to real world usage.

Keywords: Game theory · Non-cooperative game · Nash equilibrium · Agriculture

1 Introduction

Game theory has been used as a powerful tool for making decision for a long time. Since world war II throughout the cold war, game theory has been extensively used in international political strategies. In the 80s and 90s, game theory has been widely adopted in real world business. After John Nash was awarded the so called Nobel Prize in Economics in 1995, game theory has been popularly an area of research in AI. While many areas in AI, including machine learning, in

Supported by the Department of Agriculture Extension of Thailand.

O. Surinta and K. Kam Fung Yuen (Eds.): MIWAI 2022, LNAI 13651, pp. 1–13, 2022.
https://doi.org/10.1007/978-3-031-20992-5_1

particular, has been making good progress. The area of real world applications include agriculture. On the other hand game theory has made a slow progress. Any real world application in agriculture would be a significant progress.

Being aware of advances of AI applications in real world domain, DOAE is courageous to join the band wagon of AI rush. Having maintained large databases, containing multi-terabytes of data, over several decades, DOAE would like to apply AI advances to benefit more than 20 millions of Thai farmers (already registered with its existing mobile application) with analyzed data that the farmers are interested in. Based on this ground, DOAE has launched an AI-based system, namely, Personalized Data (PD), to notify Thai farmers with useful information of their interest. This system is composed of front-end modules for both farmers, via their mobile phones, and DOAE personnel, via desktop computers, and the backend analytic modules, using two AI components. The first one is equipped with machine learning libraries for predicting yields, prices, etc., of crops. The other one is equipped with game theory, both cooperative and non-cooperative, libraries and use the derived results from the first module to strategically analyze and generate helpful information for farmers.

As per the game theory module, the cooperative game libraries help individual farmers to cooperate and leverage their hidden power for enhancing their productivity and negotiation power, and reducing costs. Non-cooperative game theory module, on the other hand, acts as an strategic analyzing tool for making policies. Two simple factors, prices and quantity, combine and produce so many complex scenarios, considering a number of crops for future policies. While most non-cooperative game studies considers only a game of a few players, each of which has a couple of strategies, this non-cooperative module of PD allows for hundreds thousands of million scenarios to be analyzed. This paper presents algorithmic processes used in the fundamental components of this module and fundamental analysis.

The paper is structured as follow. We review works in research on non-cooperative game. Some interesting applications of non-cooperative game in agricultural domains are also reviewed. We then discuss the actual requirements in this project, including calculation for equilibrium non-equilibrium. We then discuss about experiments and results, then conclude, lastly.

2   Related Works

Both Game theory and AI has been extensively used to help make decision. Game theory, particularly, non-cooperative, has been widely adopted in solving real world problems for a long time. The wide range of areas includes, but not limited to, allocating cost [20], water pollutant discharge [19], supply chains [18], purchasing strategies [17], logistics [16], power pricing [15], pricing strategy [14], etc. Due to limited space, we selectively review previous works that use game theory and AI to help decide problems related to agriculture.

Agbo et.al. [3] use game theory, both cooperative and non-cooperative, to help farmers sell their products to their respective cooperatives or local markets. It is found that selling to cooperative affect direct selling to local markets.

Pakrooh et.al. [4] proposed both cooperative and non-cooperative game models to find equilibrium of prices and demands to help decrease CO2 emissions in agriculture sector of Iran, using coefficient functions. It is found that the models can modify different types of energy consumption and provide optimal prices. Nazari et.al. [5] address the problem of conflicts in environmental protection among ground water stakeholders, government and local farmers in Iran, by applying dynamic non-cooperative game theory. It is found that creating transactional relationship help increase farmers' profit and cooperation with government. Si et.al. [6] address the problem of real-time navigation scheduling of agricultural harvesters during rush hours in high season, using non-cooperative game. The results show that the solution helps increase efficiency in scheduling, reliability, and profits for harvesters. Liu et.al. [7] address the problem of allocating resources among countries in multinational river basins. by constructing the fuzzy coalition game model. It is found that the model help solve the problem successfully, providing optimal allocation to all parties. Sedghamiz et.al. [8] propose a model to help solve conflicts among agricultural water users in Iran. The leader-follower bargaining model helps find optimal water and crop area allocation. It is found that the leader incomes do not depend on water allocation, but crop pattern and crop area.

Yazdian et.al. [9] propose a game theoretic finite-differences model to help solve the problems of groundwater level drawdown when the demand for groundwater is too high. It is found that the model can manage the bankruptcy conditions, providing higher profits and reducing groundwater drawndown. Zhang et.al. [10] apply Stackelberg game to solve the problem of three-level green supply chain. It is found that profits of global supply chains and their members can be maximized because members are motivated to respond positively. Barati et.al. [11] address the problem of agricultural fragmentation in Iran using non-cooperative game theoretic approaches in order to find the strategic space of decision makers. It is found that the same strategies should not be applied to all agricultural lands. Monfared et.al. [12] consider a problem of multi-objective optimization among human decision makers, using non-cooperative approaches. Illustrative examples show that Pareto optimal equilibrium can help solve the problem.

As we can see, none of these work focus on exactly the same issue as ours. Many of game theoretic approaches are adopted to solve particular problems, whereas we consider a large search space.

3   Non-cooperative Game

Game theory study problems of conflict and cooperation among independent decision makers. The decision made by one decision makers will affect the others, hence it is known as *inter-related* decision making. In conflict situation, we call it non-cooperative game. It is a convenient way to model strategic interaction problems, e.g. economics, politics, biology, etc.

3.1   Strategic Form Game and Nash Equilibrium

There are a variety of non-cooperative form game. The most commonly known form is *strategic* form game (SFG). In general, SFG consists of a set of players (decision makers), a set of all strategies of all players, a set of payoff (utility) functions for each combination of players' strategies, and a set of information. There is a set of rules providing details how the game is played, e.g., how many players, what players can do, what players will achieve. Modelers study a game to find equilibrium, a steady state of the game where players select their best possible strategies. Suppose there are two players $\{a_1, a_2\}$ and there are strategies $\{s_1^1, s_1^2\}$ and $\{s_2^1, s_2^2\}$ for a_1 and a_2 respectively. There are $2 \times 2 = 4$ strategic profiles, (s_1^1, s_2^1), (s_1^1, s_2^2), (s_1^2, s_2^1) and (s_1^2, s_2^2). For each strategic profile ϕ, the payoff function $v_1(\phi)$ and $v_2(\phi)$ specifies the payoff for a_1 and a_2, respectively.

Agent	Strategies	a_2	
		s_2^1	s_2^2
a_1	s_1^1	$v_1(s_1^1, s_2^1), v_2(s_1^1, s_2^1)$	$v_1(s_1^1, s_2^2), v_2(s_1^1, s_2^2)$
	s_1^2	$v_1(s_1^2, s_2^1), v_2(s_1^2, s_2^1)$	$v_1(s_1^2, s_2^2), v_2(s_1^2, s_2^2)$

The most well known and widely adopted solution concept in non-cooperative game is defined by John Nash, the economics Nobel Winner in 1995. Given n agents and a strategy profile $s = \{s_1, s_2, \ldots, s_n\}$, a Nash equilibrium is a **strategy profile $s*$ with the property that no player i can do better by choosing an action different from s_i*, given that every other player j adheres to s_j*.**

Note that not all games have NE. Although Nash originally proved that every game has an NE, it has been later prove that it is not the case. For decision makers, non-NE cases does not allow any specific planning. This is the case for DOAE that they want to known when they can be certain about planning

3.2   Prisoner Dilemma

We introduce *Prisoner Dilemma* [13], probably, if not, the most widely known SFG, as an example. Two suspects in a crime are held in separate cells. There is enough evidence to convict each one of them for a minor offend, not for a major crime. One of them has to be a witness against the other (finks) for convicting major crime. If both stay quiet, each will be jailed for 1 year. If one and only one finks, he will be freed while the other will be jailed for 4 years. If both fink, they will be jailed for 3 years. Utility function is assigned as following: $v_1(Fink, Quiet) = 4$, $v_1(Quiet, Quiet) = 3$, $v_1(Fink, Fink) = 1$, $v_1(Quiet, Fink) = 0$, $v_2(Quiet, Fink) = 4$, $v_2(Quiet, Quiet) = 3$, $v_2(Fink, Fink) = 1$, and $v_2(Fink, Quiet) = 0$. The game matrix is shown in the table below.

		Prisoner2	
Agent	Strategies	Quiet	Fink
Prisoner1	Quiet	3, 3	0, 4
	Fink	4, 0	1, 1

According to NE, the outcome is this game is $(Fink, Fink)$ and their respective payoff vector is $(1, 1)$. This happens because both agents cannot act Quiet because they could be heavily penalized by the other agent act Fink. Their best strategy is to act Fink.

3.3   Cardinal vs Ordinal Utility

There are two types of utilities: cardinal and ordinal utility. Cardinal utility can be used to specify the value of the strategy the utility is associated with. For example, when we consider a game in order to decide which good to produce. The associated utility is typically profit expected to earn from producing a good. Comparing between two strategies, we can tell how much better or more profit we will achieve from choosing one strategy, compared to another strategy. Given a simple scenario, for example, choosing s_1 will receive 15 dollars and choosing s_2 will receive 10 dollars. We known that s_1 is better than s_2 by 5 dollars.

Ordinal utility, on the other hand, does not really specify how much better or how much more one strategy is, compared to another. We typically use ordinary when we deal with situations where we cannot really associate strategies with money but we can compare between two strategies which one we prefer. When we go for a dinner in a restaurant, for example, we prefer fish to beef because it is healthier. In case fish is not available, we do not mind taking beef instead of pork, because it is tastier. In this case, we can associate 1 to fish, 0 to beef and -1 to pork.

In the context of DOAE analysis, we rather use ordinary utility because of a couple of reasons. First, although we can estimate the prices and yields of crops, there are still a lot of possibilities that prices and yields that can vary a lot. Second, using ordinary utility is enough to suggest what croup is the best, better, or the same, compared to a few other crops.

4   Complexity of the Problem

In general, game theorists study a certain game, composed of strategic profiles and associated outcomes. They are only dealing with a particular, yet inter-related and complex, situation. They will reach a conclusion, having analyzed the game carefully. In our situation, DOAE, wants an analytic tools that can deal with reasonably complex problems over a large possible scenarios. From theoretical perspective, this problem's time complexity is obviously non-polynomial. However, it is also necessary to investigate the complexity in practical perspective. In this section, we will carefully analyze the complexity of DOAE's real world scenarios.

4.1 Typical Cases

Typical normal form games are found in combinations of 2 agents with 2 strategies each. That make 2×2 strategic matrix. From computer science perspective, this is a naive problem because we can write a simple program to find the outcomes of the game almost instantly.

4.2 Relation of Agent Payoffs

Since the actual payoffs in a given game can vary, we shall focus on the relation of agent payoffs in each outcome. In case of 2 agents, the associated payoff vector of each strategic profile can have merely three scenarios: $i)$ $v_1 < v_2$, $ii)$ $v_1 = v_2$, and $iii)$ $v_1 > v_2$, regardless of the actual payoff vectors. In case of 3 agents, The relation of payoffs of agents are more complex. There are 3 cases between v_1 and v_2, similar to the case of 2 agents. Combined with the third agent, there are 3 more cases associated with each of the existing relation, making 9 cases. However, we can consider in more details. By using ordinal utility, we can have $\{-1, 0, 1\}$ associated with any strategy profile. Therefore, there are $3 \times 3 \times 3 = 27$, e.g. $(-1, -1, -1)$, $(-1, -1, 0)$, $(-1, -1, 1)$, ... $(1, 1, -1)$, $(1, 1, 0)$, $(1, 1, 1)$, possible payoff vectors associated with a strategy profile. .

4.3 Case of 3 Agents and 2 Strategies

Suppose there are 2 agents: a_1, a_2 and a_3, each of which has 2 strategies: $(s_{1,1}, s_{1,2})$, $(s_{2,1}, s_{2,2})$, and $(s_{3,1}, s_{3,2})$, respectively. This setting generate $2 \times 2 \times 2 = 8$ combinations of strategic profile. The payoff matrix of this kind of games is shown below.

				a_3					
				$s_{3,1}$			$s_{3,2}$		
a_1	$s_{1,1}$	a_2	$s_{2,1}$	$v_1^{(s_1^1,s_2^1,s_3^1)}$	$v_2^{(s_1^1,s_2^1,s_3^1)}$	$v_3^{(s_1^1,s_2^1,s_3^1)}$	$v_1^{(s_1^1,s_2^1,s_3^2)}$	$v_2^{(s_1^1,s_2^1,s_3^2)}$	$v_3^{(s_1^1,s_2^1,s_3^2)}$
			$s_{2,2}$	$v_1^{(s_1^1,s_2^2,s_3^1)}$	$v_2^{(s_1^1,s_2^2,s_3^1)}$	$v_3^{(s_1^1,s_2^2,s_3^1)}$	$v_1^{(s_1^1,s_2^2,s_3^2)}$	$v_2^{(s_1^1,s_2^2,s_3^2)}$	$v_3^{(s_1^1,s_2^2,s_3^2)}$
	$s_{1,2}$	a_2	$s_{2,1}$	$v_1^{(s_1^2,s_2^1,s_3^1)}$	$v_2^{(s_1^2,s_2^1,s_3^1)}$	$v_3^{(s_1^2,s_2^1,s_3^1)}$	$v_1^{(s_1^2,s_2^1,s_3^2)}$	$v_2^{(s_1^2,s_2^1,s_3^2)}$	$v_3^{(s_1^2,s_2^1,s_3^2)}$
			$s_{2,2}$	$v_1^{(s_1^2,s_2^2,s_3^1)}$	$v_2^{(s_1^2,s_2^2,s_3^1)}$	$v_3^{(s_1^2,s_2^2,s_3^1)}$	$v_1^{(s_1^2,s_2^2,s_3^2)}$	$v_2^{(s_1^2,s_2^2,s_3^2)}$	$v_3^{(s_1^2,s_2^2,s_3^2)}$

However, once take in to account the payoff vector setting mentioned in section above, there are 27 cases of payoff vectors may be associated to each strategic profiles. Since there are 8 strategic profiles, there can be $27^8 = 282,429,536,481$ cases. Given this reasonably large number, we shall carefully investigate this setting.

4.4 Case of 3 Agents and 3 Strategies

Suppose there are 3 agents: a_1, a_2 and a_3, each of which has 3 strategies: $(s_{1,1}, s_{1,2}, s_{1,3})$, $(s_{2,1}, s_{2,2}, s_{2,3})$, and $(s_{3,1}, s_{3,2}, s_{3,3})$, respectively. This setting generate $3 \times 3 \times 3 = 27$ combinations of strategic profile. The payoff matrix of this kind of games is shown below.

			a_3								
				s_3^1			s_3^2			s_3^3	
			$v_1^{(s_1,s_2,s_3)}$	$v_2^{(s_1,s_2,s_3)}$	$v_3^{(s_1,s_2,s_3)}$	$v_1^{(s_1,s_2,s_3)}$	$v_2^{(s_1,s_2,s_3)}$	$v_3^{(s_1,s_2,s_3)}$	$v_1^{(s_1,s_2,s_3)}$	$v_2^{(s_1,s_2,s_3)}$	$v_3^{(s_1,s_2,s_3)}$
a_1	s_1^1 a_2	s_2^1									
		s_2^2									
		s_2^3									
	s_1^2 a_2	s_2^1									
		s_2^2									
		s_2^3									
	s_1^3 a_2	s_2^1									
		s_2^2									
		s_2^3									

Fig. 1. Game matrix of 3 agents, with 3 strategies

However, once take in to account the payoff vector setting mentioned in section above, there are 27 cases of payoff vectors may be associated to each strategic profiles. Since there are 27 strategic profiles, there can be $27^{27} = 443, 426, 488, 243, 037, 769, 948, 249, 630, 619, 149, 892, 803$ cases. Given this extremely large number, it is impossible to investigate this setting.

5 Searching for Nash Equilibrium

In order to help DOAE personnel analyze various scenarios for public policy, it is important that exhaustive search must be carried out in order to ensure that there will be no consequent mistakes. Whereas most works that apply NE in AI community consider merely a game, we cover all cases possible for that reason.

5.1 Control Loops

As we have discuss in previous sections, we want to thoroughly examine all possible cases to look for the number of games with and without Nash equilibrium. This will allow for further analysis on patterns of payoffs in game of this setting, i.e. 3 players, each of which has two strategies. We merely need to cover cases of ordinary relationship among agents' payoffs. Therefore, the range of payoffs is ($-1, 0, 1$). Given three agents and two strategies for each agent, we have $3 \times 3 = 27$ strategy profiles for each of the $2 \times 2 \times 2 = 8$ strategy matrix. To cover these combinations, we can have 8 nested loops, each of which has values ranging from $(-1, -1, -1)$ up to $(1, 1, 1)$. i.e. 27 cases. Therefore, each of these 27 cases can be represented by an integer value. Within the inner-most loop, the integer value of each of the nested loop has to be transformed to an array of integer representing the respective payoff vector. The arrays will be used for examining Nash equilibrium. On the other hand, the array also has to be converted back to its corresponding index for later use in the loops. These little but important algorithms are described in Sect. 5.3.

5.2   Algorithm for Examining Nash Equilibrium

With this algorithm, we can find if the given game is either i) has at least an NE, or ii) does not have any NE. This algorithm takes as input a payoff matrix and exhaustively search for the first NE. If NE does not exist However, we need to exhaustively search for all cases, given much broader search space. In general, we need to go through each agent and check if every other agent can improve its payoff.

Algorithm 1. SolveBruteForce Algorithm

```
int array ne
for i = 1 to noAgent do
    int array profile ← indexToStrategyProfile(i)
    boolean canImprove ← false
    for p = 1 to noAgent do
        for o = 0 to noAgent do
            if o == p then
                continue;
            end if
            double oPayoff ← payoffs[i][o]
            int oStrategy ← profile[o]
            int array testProfile ← Arrays.copyOf(profile, profile.length)
            for t = 1 to strategies[o] do
                if t == oStrategy then
                    continue;
                end if
                testProfile ← t
                int index ← strategyProfileToIndex(testProfile)
                double testPayoff ← payoffs[index][o]
                if testPayoff > oPayoff then
                    canImprove ← true
                    return ne
                end if
            end for
        end for
    end for
    if !canImprove then
        print " * * * NE * * * "
    end if
end for
ne ← testProfile
return ne;
```

Firstly, the algorithm create an integer array ne to store the payoff vector that is in NE. The algorithm enters the first loop, verifying if each agent can improve its payoff. Another int array *profile* is initialized by calling function *indexToStrategyProfile*. We assume *canImprove*, whether this payoff vector can be payoff, is false. The algorithm enters the second loop to check if each agent p can improve its payoff. The third loop is to check of each other player o can improve its payoff. If agent $p = o$ the algorithm skips to the next agent. The payoff *oPayoff* and *oStrategy* are initialized. The strategy profile of *testProfile* of agent o is initialized. The forth loop is to every strategy t of agent o. If strategy t is its own strategy *oStrategy*, the algorithm skips. The agent o's *testProfile* is assigned with strategy t, and is changed to an integer *index* by function *StrategyToProfileIndex* Variable *testPayoff* is initialized with the corresponding value in array *payoffs*. If *testPayoff* is greater than *oPayoff*, agent o can improve its payoff and *canImprove* is set accordingly. We can merely return the *ne* with value *null* right here and terminates the algorithm. If none of the agents can improve its payoff, the algorithm prints a notifying message and the return the Nash equilibrium *ne* profile.

5.3 Supporting Algorithms

There are low level algorithms, including *IndexToStrategyProfile* and *StrategyToIndex*, working In order to convert an integer *index* to an array of strategy *profile*, the *index* is given as an input. There are two more important numbers, *remainder* and *base*. The *base* is the divisor for the digit at the corresponding index. The *profile* is an array of integer of size n (players). There are two loops. In the outer loop, the first thing to do is to initialize *base* to 1. The algorithm then enters the inner loop where *base* is repeatedly multiplied by the number of strategies. After that, it the algorithm is to assign the division result between *remainder* and *base* to the corresponding *profile* element. Also, the *remainder* is to reduced by *base*. The last element of *profile* is assigned with the value of *remainder* after the outer loop.

Algorithm 2. IndexToStrategyProfile Algorithm

```
int index
int array profile[noAgent]
int remainder ← index
for i = 1 to noAgent do
    int base ← 1
    for j = noAgent to 1 do
        base ← base * strategies[j]
    end for
    profile[i] ← remainder/base;
    remainder ← remainder%base;
end for
profile[noAgent] = remainder;
return profile;
```

In order to convert an array of payoff vector to an integer of the corresponding index, as shown in algorithm *StrategyToIndex*, the algorithm takes the array as an input. The integer *index* is initialized to 0. The right most position of the array is the least significant digit, while the left most position of the array is the most significant digit. The *base* value is set to 1. The algorithm iterates through the array from right to left. In each iteration, the value of *index* is increased by the multiplication of the value of *profile*[i] and *base*. Also, the value of *base* is multiplied by the number of strategies.

Algorithm 3. StrategyToIndex

int array *profile*
int *index* ← 0 // strategy profile
int *base* ← 1
for $i = noProfile$ to 1 **do**
    $index ← index + profile[i] * base$
    $base ← base * strategies[i]$
end for
return index;

---

6   Experiments and Results

We are interested in thoroughly investigating the case of 3 agents, each of which has 2 strategies. As previously mentioned, solving a typical game with computer program is naive. We are interested in analyzing a very large scenario.

We examine how quickly our algorithm performs in practice. We carried out the experiments on a reasonably powerful computer, equipped with AMD Ryzen 9 5950X 16-Core Processor, 3.4 GHz, 16 GB Ram and 1 GB HDD.

6.1   Overview Result

Since there are a lot of games can possibly take place and it will take a long time to complete this exhaustively analysis, we need to periodically observe how the results turn out. As previously mentioned, there are $(27^8) = 282,429,536,481$ cases altogether. We count the number of either NE and non-NE from each game and print out the number of both cases every 1,000,000,000 games completed. We found that there are 275,107,342,383 NE cases and 7,322,194,098 non-NE cases. It took 28,834,447 milliseconds to complete or more than 8 h to complete. Since the case of non-NE are the most difficult to plan, we are interesting in finding out when we can be certain that there will be no further non-NE game found. Instead of showing results exact figures, we show percentages of *Elapsed* time, *Counts* of games, counts of *NE* and counts of *non-NE* games in Fig. 2. We can clearly see that non-NE are found until the iterations almost finishes.

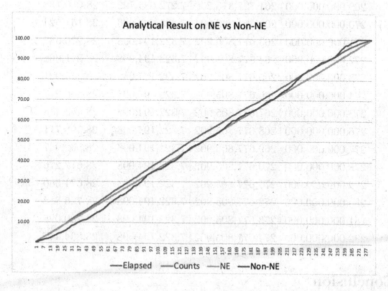

Fig. 2. Progresses of elapsed time, counts, NE and Non-NE in percentage.

6.2 Detailed Results

As we can see from the overview result, the number of Non-NE cases remains the same near the end of the execution. To clearly see that when exactly the non-NE games are not found any more, we present the detailed results in Table 1. Non-NE are found until iteration 270×10^9. From iteration 271×10^9 until finish, there is no further non-NE found anymore. This can be explained that the value of *indices* are high, representing the payoffs of agents are high, i.e. (1,1,1). This implies that there is certainly an equilibrium. However, if we change the way we encode the payoff vector, we may say the different patterns of results. Note that the iteration number presented in the table below is to be

Table 1. Detailed Results The number of Non-NE does not increase after iteration number 272.

Analytical results			
Total counts	NE counts	Non-NE counts	Elapsed time
267,000,000,000	259,763,212,140	7,236,787,860	27,912,654
268,000,000,000	260,743,818,310	7,256,181,690	27,989,634
269,000,000,000	261,727,315,208	7,272,684,792	28,066,138
270,000,000,000	262,694,309,004	7,305,690,996	28,151,524
271,000,000,000	263,677,805,902	7,322,194,098	28,226,687
272,000,000,000	264,677,805,902	7,322,194,098	28,291,608
273,000,000,000	265,677,805,902	7,322,194,098	28,345,901
274,000,000,000	266,677,805,902	7,322,194,098	28,400,218
275,000,000,000	267,677,805,902	7,322,194,098	28,454,478
276,000,000,000	268,677,805,902	7,322,194,098	28,508,711
277,000,000,000	269,677,805,902	7,322,194,098	28,562,947
278,000,000,000	270,677,805,902	7,322,194,098	28,617,276
279,000,000,000	271,677,805,902	7,322,194,098	28,671,560
280,000,000,000	272,677,805,902	7,322,194,098	28,725,814
281,000,000,000	273,677,805,902	7,322,194,098	28,780,098
282,000,000,000	274,677,805,902	7,322,194,098	28,834,447

7   Conclusion

This paper presents underpinning components of non-cooperative game theoretic analytic module of the Personalized Data system of the Department of Agricultural Extension of Thailand that serves 20 millions of farmers in Thailand. While most of non-cooperative game studies focus merely a game at a time and carefully consider strategic profiles and payoff vectors for the outcome of the game, this system considers hundreds of thousands of millions of possible games and analyze for non-NE. It takes just over 8 h to exhaustively complete the search. It is found that there are more than 2.8×10^{11} games altogether. There are 7,322,194,098 games or 2.66% of non-NE. While the algorithms proceeds, both NE and non-NE games are found interchangeably up to iteration 273 or almost 98%.

References

1. Nash, J.: Non-cooperative Game. PhD thesis, Department of Mathematics, Princeton University, Princeton, USA (1950)
2. Von Neumann, J., Morgenstern, O.: Theory of Games and Economic Behaviour. Princeton University Press, Princeton (1963)
3. Agbo, M., Rousselière, D., Salanié, J.: Agricultural marketing cooperatives with direct selling: a cooperative-non-cooperative game. J. Econ. Behav. Organ. **109**, 56–71 (2015)

4. Pakrooh, P., Nematian, J., Pishbahar, E., Hayati, B.: Reforming energy prices to achieve sustainable energy consumption in the agriculture sector of Iran's provinces: using game approach. J. Cleaner Prod. **293**, 126146 (2021)
5. Nazari, S., Ahmadi, A., Rad, S.K., Ebrahimi, B.: Application of non-cooperative dynamic game theory for groundwater conflict resolution. J. Environ. Manag. **270**, 110889 (2020)
6. Si, H., Li, Y., Sun, C., Qiao, H., Xiaohong, H.: A hierarchical game approach on real-time navigation scheduling of agricultural harvesters. Comput. Electron. Agric. **162**, 112–118 (2019)
7. Liu, D., Ji, X., Tang, J., Li, H.: A fuzzy cooperative game theoretic approach for multinational water resource spatiotemporal allocation. Eur. J. Oper. Res. **282**(3), 1025–1037 (2020)
8. Sedghamiz, A., Nikoo, M.R., Heidarpour, M., Sadegh, M.: Developing a non-cooperative optimization model for water and crop area allocation based on leader-follower game. J. Hydrol. **567**, 51–59 (2018)
9. Yazdian, M., Rakhshandehroo, G., Nikoo, M.R., Mooselu, M.G., Gandomi, A.H., Honar, T.: Groundwater sustainability: developing a non-cooperative optimal management scenario in shared groundwater resources under water bankruptcy conditions. J. Environ. Manag. **292**, 112807 (2021)
10. Zhang, C.-T., Liu, L.-P.: Research on coordination mechanism in three-level green supply chain under non-cooperative game. Appl. Math. Model. **37**(5), 3369–3379 (2013)
11. Barati, A.A., Azadi, H., Scheffran, J.: Agricultural land fragmentation in Iran: application of game theory. Land Use Policy **100**, 105049 (2021)
12. Monfared, M.S., Monabbati, S.E., Kafshgar, A.R.: Pareto-optimal equilibrium points in non-cooperative multi-objective optimization problems. Expert Syst. Appl. **178**, 114995 (2021)
13. Rapoport, A., Chammah, A.M.: Prisoner's Dilemma: A Study of Conflict and Cooperation. University of Michigan Press, Ann Arbor, MI (1965)
14. Shojaabadi, S., Talavat, V., Galvani, S.: A game theory-based price bidding strategy for electric vehicle aggregators in the presence of wind power producers. Renew. Energy **193**, 407–417 (2022)
15. Zhao, Z., Zhang, L., Yang, M., Chai, J., Li, S.: Pricing for private charging pile sharing considering EV consumers based on non-cooperative game model. J. Cleaner Prod. **254**, 120039 (2020)
16. Santibanez-Gonzalez, E.D., Diabat, A.: Modeling logistics service providers in a non-cooperative supply chain. Appl. Math. Model. **40**(13–14), 6340–6358 (2016)
17. Wang, J., Dou, X., Guo, Y., Shao, P., Zhang, X.: Purchase strategies for power retailers based on the non-cooperative game. Energy Procedia **158**, 6652–6657 (2019)
18. Jin, Z., Zheng, Q.: An evolutionary game analysis of subsidy strategies in the supply chain of SMEs based on system dynamics. Procedia Comput. Sci. **199**, 1513–1520 (2022)
19. Xie, Q., Xu, Q., Rao, K., Dai, Q.: Water pollutant discharge permit allocation based on DEA and non-cooperative game theory. J. Environ. Manag. **302**, 113962 (2022)
20. Li, Y., Lin, L., Dai, Q., Zhang, L.: Allocating common costs of multinational companies based on arm's length principle and Nash non-cooperative game. Eur. J. Oper. Res. **283**(3), 1002–1010 (2020)

Evolutionary Feature Weighting Optimization and Majority Voting Ensemble Learning for Curriculum Recommendation in the Higher Education

Wongpanya S. Nuankaew[1] (iD), Sittichai Bussaman[1] (iD), and Pratya Nuankaew[2]([⊠]) (iD)

[1] Rajabhat Maha Sarakham University, Maha Sarakham 44000, Thailand
[2] University of Phayao, Phayao 56000, Thailand
pratya.nu@up.ac.th

Abstract. The curriculum recommendation strategies are the engines that drive educational organizations. Therefore, this research has three main goals: 1) to explore the context of deploying text mining technology as a curriculum recommendation application, 2) to develop a prototype model for interaction between curriculum coordinators and interested parties, and 3) to evaluate the performance of the prototype model. Research tools are text mining techniques with the genetic algorithm for evolutionary feature weighting optimization and ensemble learning algorithms, including Naïve Bayes (NB), Neural Network (NN), and k-Nearest Neighbor (k-NN). Data collection is 1,592 transactions, with seven classes via the online chat platform of the Department of Information and Communication Technology at the Faculty of Information Technology, Rajabhat Maha Sarakham University. The results showed that the model developed with the majority voting technique had the highest accuracy of 91.65%, averaging 5% higher than that of the single split model. This research has discovered tools and methods to promote and support educational processes in higher education. Therefore, the adoption of text mining technology should be enabled in the education system to communicate with the learners to meet their needs and reduce the duplication of work.

Keywords: Curriculum recommendation · Ensemble learning · Feature weighting optimization · Majority voting · Metadata analytics

1 Introduction

Today, Information Technology and Internet networks have developed and grown widely. These modern technologies play an increasingly essential role in learners' daily life in all activities and show a marked change in consumer behavior at all educational levels. It reflects that communication channels for students to promote the curriculum proactively should use information technology and the Internet as tools.

Moreover, 21st-Century learners are familiar with using electronic tools and small devices. It is therefore imperative to choose applications and analytical techniques for

O. Surinta and K. Kam Fung Yuen (Eds.): MIWAI 2022, LNAI 13651, pp. 14–25, 2022.
https://doi.org/10.1007/978-3-031-20992-5_2

quick interactions that provide relevant information to the learner. Using agents to communicate through the application channel has attracted attention [1–7]. The process of text mining thus has a more significant impact on communication in the education system [6, 7], the classification of skills in line with Industry 4.0 following the text mining approach [5], and management of predictive maintenance with text mining techniques [3].

Successful research has incentivized, motivated, and intrigued researchers to apply text mining technology to create strategies for introducing the university curriculum. Thus, this research has three primary goals: the first primary goal is to explore the context of deploying text mining technology as a curriculum recommendation tool. The second primary goal is to develop a prototype model for interaction between curriculum coordinators and interested parties. The last primary goal is to evaluate the performance of the prototype model. Research data is 1,592 transactions via the online chat platform of the Department of Information and Communication Technology, at the Faculty of Information Technology, Rajabhat Maha Sarakham University. It is an inquiry and answer to the Bachelor of Science Program in Information Technology. Research tools and processes are divided into two parts: the first part uses text mining techniques to extract critical features. The second part uses ensemble learning algorithms and classification techniques to create forecasting models. The model performance assessment section uses split-validation techniques to divide the test data and uses a confusion matrix to measure the model prototype's performance.

The primary research hypotheses for this research consisted of two hypotheses: H1: Machine learning tools and text mining techniques can extract critical attributes of the interactions between curriculum coordinators and interested parties efficiently and appropriately. H2: The feature weighting optimization and ensemble learning algorithms can optimize model prototypes for efficient and appropriate predictions of interested parties. From the research objectives and hypotheses established, the researchers strongly believe this research will significantly benefit learners and educational institutions in Thailand, where the research process and its results are presented in the following sections.

2 Material and Methods

2.1 Research Definition

The purpose of explaining research definitions is to create mutual understanding between the researchers and the research reader. Research definitions include text mining, and ensemble learning.

Text Mining.
Text mining is searching for new knowledge and discovering the hidden facts in a series of texts. It can be said to be the process of analyzing the meanings nested in the message. Text mining focuses on two types of data: unstructured and semi-structured data. Text mining is a branch of data mining technique that discovers knowledge in databases: KDD. The text mining process focuses on building credibility, which consists of three steps: data selection, data preparation, and data indexing. These three steps acquire attributes

or factors for further forecasting prototyping. Text mining for knowledge acquisition is helpful in several dimensions, including topic detection and tracking, text summarization, text classification, text segmentation, and Q&A.

This research emphasizes on answering questions to provide information to those interested in the educational program of the Department of Information Technology, Faculty of Information Technology, at the Rajabhat Maha Sarakham University, Thailand.

Ensemble Learning

Ensemble learning is a method of machine learning that uses to train multiple classifiers to solve the same problem and combines them to produce better predictions [9]. Ensemble learning reduces the likelihood of incorrect predictions and can expand the area for better approximation. Therefore, it is often used to increase the performance of the model. The majority voting ensemble is used in this research as a method by which the collected data trains are used in models created from different techniques. The data test was then put into the model to predict the outcome and voted the result with the most votes as the final answer.

Classification Technique

The classification techniques in this paper consisted of three techniques that were tested against a classification model based on the popular machine learning method in text classification, including Naïve Bayes (NB), Neural Network (NN), and k-Nearest Neighbor (k-NN) [9]. Naïve Bayes (NB) is the supervised learning technique used for classification that employs the principle of computational probability to infer the desired answer, also known as Bayes' Theorem. This technique is not complicated and often learns the problems that arise to create new classification conditions. The method assumes that the amount of interest depends on the probability distribution known as "Conditional Probability". The result of the selected NB calculation will be the class with the highest probability calculated and will be used as the prediction answer. Neural Network (NN) is a type of prediction network that is often used for forecasting tasks. It can help determine the critical node. It consists of a multilayer neural network, in which each layer receives and calculates the sum of the inputs and the weights of each associated point and forwards those values to the connected nodes in the next layer. k-Nearest Neighbor (k-NN) is calculated as the minimum distance between the data to be classified and the learning set, where K is the number to be chosen as the nearest neighbor. A property and advantage of using the k-NN method are that a group of similar datasets can be obtained.

2.2 Data Collection and Word Segmentation

The data collected was 1,592 question-and-answer conversations about the Bachelor of Science in Information Technology program via an online chat platform of the Department of Information and Communication Technology, at the Faculty of Information Technology, Maha Sarakham Rajabhat University. It was used as data analysis to develop text mining. After collecting the data, the researcher considered and assigned each transaction with a category of classes. It consists of seven types. C1: Registration with 659 transactions, C2: Activities and Preparation in the university with 210 transactions,

C3: Occupation with 182 transactions, C4: Location and Roaming with 187 transactions, C5: Qualification with 112 transactions, C6: Expenses and Scholarships with 132 transactions, and C7: Dormitory with 110 transactions.

The word segmentation process is to separate letters from text to determine the boundaries of each morpheme. This research uses a dictionary approach for collecting data and manipulating word segmentation by following Fig. 1.

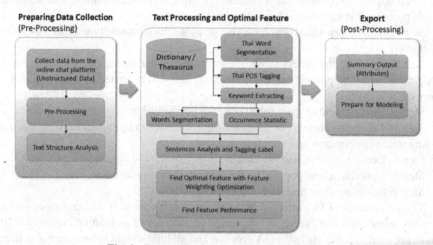

Fig. 1. Data collection and word segmentation

Figure 1 demonstrates the data preparation process by applying management and analysis based on text mining principles. It has three essential steps. The first step is the text import, which is the pre-processing process. In addition, initial text structure analysis. The second step is text processing, whereas the purpose of this step is to create variables for defining the model development attributes. The final step is the text export, whereby the features are summarized through the analysis process and transformed into a modeling-ready state.

2.3   Research Tools

Feature Weighting Optimization

At the end of the data collection and word segmentation process, Bag of Words (BoW) method is used to create the vectors of each word in the data set. Term frequency-Inverse document frequency (TF-IDF) is applied to the weight term of each word. The researchers found that 386 attributes with a massive number of words that needed to be considered were challenging to construct the predictive model. Therefore, finding a process for reducing the number of attributes is necessary. The technique used by the researchers is feature-weighted optimization.

A genetic algorithm (GA) is a metaheuristic optimization and search problem of the evolutionary algorithm (EA). The concept of GA starts with the beginning population as a possible chromosome problem solution and evolution to a better solution. The mainly genetic processes of GA are reproduction, selection, crossover, and mutation. The fitness function is calculated, as in Eq. 1 [8].

$$\text{Fitness} = \text{Accuracy} = \frac{TP + TN}{TP + FN + FP + TN} \tag{1}$$

GA is applied to optimize the feature weighting and reduce the number of attributes in this process. It is summarized as follows:

Step 1: Generate an initial population is a possible chromosome base on the operation parameters.

Step 2: Evaluate the fitness value of each chromosome in the population in Eq. 1. The fitness values help to choose the individuals that will be mated in the reproduction process.

Step 3: Select parent to mate for finding the best solution.

Step 4: The fitness chromosomes have a bigger chance to be chosen for reproduction in the crossover operators and mutation operators.

Step 5: Decode and evaluate the fitness.

Step 6: Generate a new population for the new parent generations.

Step 7: Select survivor and find the best solution.

The parameters of GA are setting mutation rate (value = 0.10), crossover (value = 0.80), population size (value = 50), maximum number of generation (value = 250), which are used to calculate in the GA process, and all final weight values are normalized between the range 0 to 1. After feature weighting optimization, it is necessary to test the feature optimally. Evaluation of the feature weighting optimization is used by Support Vector Machines (SVMs) with spilled validation (70:30). The researchers found 223 optimized features with a weight of each attribute greater than 0.97. It tested the efficiency of weighting optimization for the features, as the efficiency is shown in Table 1.

Table 1. Summary of the efficiency of weighting optimization features and use all features

Class	All features			Weighing optimization features		
	Precision	Recall	F1	Precision	Recall	F1
C1: Registration	96.52	97.98	97.24	98.00	98.99	98.49
C2: Activities and Preparation in the university	93.55	92.06	92.80	95.31	96.83	96.06
C3: Occupation	96.43	98.18	97.30	96.43	98.18	97.30
C4: Location and roaming	88.71	98.21	93.22	98.25	100	99.12
C5: Qualification	96.43	79.41	87.10	93.75	88.24	90.91
C6: Expenses and scholarship	94.74	90.00	92.31	100.00	95.00	97.44
C7: Dormitory	96.88	93.94	95.39	100.00	96.97	98.46
Accuracy	94.99			**97.49**		

From Table 1, the researchers found that the feature-weighted optimization method yielded higher overall accuracy and further contributed to the higher accuracy of each class. Therefore, preprocessing for feature manipulation is essential to the text mining process.

Model Development

There are two phases for model development. Phase one is the development of the voting component. The purpose of this phase is to create a voting tool. It consists of three classifiers: Naïve Bayes (NB), Neural Network (NN), and k-Nearest Neighbor (k-NN). The process is to develop a submodule with all three classifiers and apply it to the second phase of the majority voting.

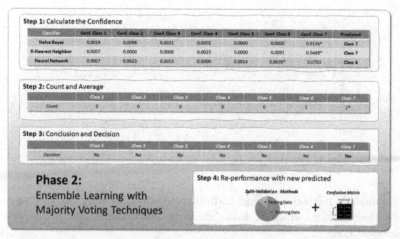

Fig. 2. Prototype model development process and model performance testing

The second phase combines the models developed in the first phase using a majority voting technique to establish the most efficient model. There are four steps: The first step is calculating the confidence value and using the vote to count on the answer (class) with each classifier. The second step is to calculate the voting result based on the class with the highest mean that the class will use to answer that transaction. The third step is to draw conclusions and make decisions. The class with the highest mean is assigned to the prediction answer in that transaction. The final step is to test the voting results of each transaction to determine the effectiveness of the majority voting model. The process of this second phase is presented in Fig. 2. In addition, the results of the model performance analysis in this section are shown in Table 2.

Model Performance Measurement

Model performance measurement aims to find the best performance and deliver the prototype model. This research used the 70:30 data split-validation to develop and test the model, where the researchers conducted the model assessment with a confusion matrix. The basis of the measures in the confusion matrix table consists of four parts.

TP: True Positive, FP: False Positive, FN: False Negative, and TN: True Negative, as shown in Fig. 3. In addition, the indicator of the confusion matrix consists of four indicators: accuracy, precision, recall, and f1-score.

All four indicators are used as tools to determine the quality and properties of the model. The accuracy value results from all correct prediction calculations divided by the total number of transactions. The precision value is the result of calculating the accurate prediction in the predicted class divided by the total number of transactions in the predicted class. The recall value is the result of calculating the correct prediction in the class divided by the total number of transactions in the actual class. The F1-score is the harmonic mean between precision and recall as a single metric that measures model performance. The calculations for each indicator are presented in Fig. 3.

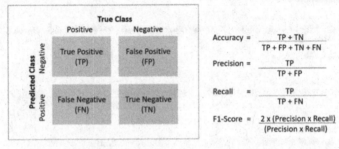

Fig. 3. The elements and calculations in the confusion matrix

This model's methodology and performance indicators were used to assess the model's performance, which is summarized in the research results and research discussion section.

3   Research Results

3.1   Model Performance Classified by Technique

The model performance evaluation results classified by each technique, showing the best model compared to each classifier, are shown in Table 2.

Table 2. Comparison of model performance classified by technique

Class	k-Nearest Neighbor			Naïve Bayes			Neural Network		
	Prec	Rec	F1	Prec	Rec	F1	Prec	Rec	F1
C1	85.00	92.12	88.42	82.30	93.47	87.53	91.04	90.15	90.59
C2	86.89	81.54	84.13	84.62	73.33	78.57	64.13	80.82	71.52
C3	87.93	89.47	88.70	97.87	83.64	90.20	88.52	91.53	90.00
C4	90.00	90.00	90.00	84.21	90.57	87.27	87.10	90.00	88.52
C5	90.91	66.67	76.92	90.32	80.00	84.85	59.09	34.21	43.33
C6	84.62	78.57	81.48	88.57	75.61	81.58	70.59	76.60	73.47
C7	84.62	75.86	80.00	92.31	77.42	84.21	68.18	48.39	56.60
Accuracy	**86.34**			85.87	·		81.02		

From Table 2, the model with the highest accuracy was the k-Nearest Neighbor (k-NN) model with an accuracy of 86.34%. The model with the second highest accuracy was the Naïve Bayes (NB) model with an accuracy of 85.87%. The last model was Neural Network (NN) model with an accuracy of 81.02%.

3.2 Majority Voting Prototype Model

The performance of majority voting prototype model is shown in Table 3, where the model performance analysis with confusion matrix is also shown in Table 4.

Table 3. The majority voting prototype model performance

Class	Majority Voting Prototype Model		
	Precision	Recall	F1-Score
C1: Registration	86.73	98.99	92.46
C2: Activities and Preparation in the university	87.30	87.30	87.30
C3: Occupation	100.00	94.55	97.20
C4: Location and roaming	100.00	91.07	95.33
C5: Qualification	95.83	67.65	79.31
C6: Expenses and scholarship	97.30	90.00	93.51
C7: Dormitory	100.00	78.79	88.14
Accuracy	91.65		

Table 3 show that the model developed with the majority voting technique had greater accuracy than the single prediction model, with an accuracy of 91.65%. It has an average

Table 4. Majority voting prototype model performance

Majority Voting Prototype Model Performance: Accuracy = 91.65							
	True C1	True C2	True C3	True C4	True C5	True C6	True C7	Class Prec
Pred. C1	196	7	3	3	8	3	6	86.73
Pred. C2	2	55	0	2	3	0	1	87.30
Pred. C3	0	0	52	0	0	0	0	100.00
Pred. C4	0	0	0	51	0	0	0	100.00
Pred. C5	0	0	0	0	23	1	0	95.83
Pred. C6	0	1	0	0	0	36	0	97.30
Pred. C7	0	0	0	0	0	0	26	100.00
Class Rec	98.99	87.30	94.55	91.07	67.65	90.00	78.79	

increase in accuracy of 5%. Therefore, the majority voting model is reasonably chosen with the model performance test results shown in Table 4.

In this section, the researchers found that the development of the model with the majority voting technique had a positive impact on the model development, with the researchers found that the model obtained had an accuracy increase of approximately 5% over the previous model, with an accuracy of 91.65%, which was appropriate for further exploitation.

4   Research Discussion

The discussion in this section focuses on research objectives. This research was successful in all objectives. It consists of three main goals: 1) to explore the context of deploying text mining technology as a curriculum recommendation application, 2) to develop a prototype model for interaction between curriculum coordinators and interested parties, and 3) to evaluate the performance of the prototype model.

The context of educational data mining technology applications is becoming increasingly popular [10–14]. Using text mining to support education is part of improving the quality of education [3, 6, 15]. In the context of using text mining through online chat platforms, feature selection for outcome forecasting is a research competitive area [16–18]. This research has developed a feature selection process, as shown in Fig. 1, and applied the feature selection quality improvement process with the feature weighting optimization technique, as shown in the results in Table 1. The researchers found that the appropriate features for this research consisted of 223 features that were significant for the development of the curriculum recommendation in higher education.

In the part of the second and third objectives, the researchers acted in parallel. The researchers selected three machine learning techniques to develop a prototype model. It consists of Naïve Bayes (NB), Neural Network (NN), and k-Nearest Neighbor (k-NN). Regarding model performance evaluation, the researchers used data split-validation techniques to test the prototype and the confusion matrix assessment process to measure the quality of the prototype model. The model development results with all three techniques showed that the model developed by the k-Nearest Neighbor (k-NN) method had the highest accuracy with 86.34% accuracy. The Naïve Bayes (NB) method is as accurate as 85.87%, which has the second highest accuracy. The last model is the Neural Network (NN), with 81.02% accuracy, as shown in Table 2. Moreover, researchers believe the model could be developed with more precision. Therefore, it was decided and applied the majority voting technique to improve the prototype. The results of the model development by using a majority voting technique to improve the prototype showed a very high increase in the model's accuracy, with an accuracy of 91.65%, as shown in Table 3 and Table 4. Significantly for the improvement of the model, it was found that the model had a very high increase in accuracy of about 5%.

Based on the research findings and discussion of the results, the researchers concluded that this research is consistent with the first hypothesis that machine learning tools can extract critical attributes for creating strategies for curriculum recommendation in higher education. The evidence supporting the conclusion is the outcome of the first objective. In addition, the conclusions from the results of the second and third objectives support the second research hypothesis. The researchers found that using the feature weighting optimization and ensemble learning algorithms could improve the model's efficiency better than the previous model. Therefore, researchers mentioned that the research objectives have been achieved and can be used to support the research results to promote the quality of education in higher education, with all research findings answering all research hypotheses.

5 Conclusion

This research has aims to apply the body of knowledge and artificial intelligence technology as a tool to support the development of education quality in higher education. There are three main objectives. The researchers extracted 223 critical attributes analyzed by the feature weighting optimization technique for the first objective. In addition, the researchers found that the feature selection test for determining the number of features had very high accuracy, with an accuracy of 97.49%, as shown in Table 1. The second objective was to develop a prototype model and the final objective was to determine the effectiveness of the model where the last two objectives are performed simultaneously.

The researchers developed the prototype model in two phases. The first phase was the development of the voting component. The researchers used three classifiers as an indicator of the vote: k-Nearest Neighbor (k-NN), Naïve Bayes (NB), and Neural Network (NN). The practical model of each classifier is summarized in Table 2. However, the researchers believed it could improve the higher-performing model, leading to a second phase in which the model was developed with a majority voting technique. The researchers found that it had increased efficiency with an accuracy of 91.65% and an average accuracy increase of approximately 5% over previous models.

All research results reflect the success of the research in which the researchers demonstrate a step-by-step process. Therefore, the researchers believe that the results of this research help apply text mining to improve the quality of education. However, some limitations and recommendations will be an issue in future research studies. As this research process took place during the COVID-19 pandemic, the impact of government regulators, including changing lifestyles, could affect research findings. Therefore, in the future, the data collection period should be extended under normal circumstances to compare with the results of this research.

Acknowledgements. This research project was supported by the Thailand Science Research and Innovation Fund and the University of Phayao (Grant No. FF65-UoE006). The authors would like to thank all of them for their support and collaboration in making this research possible.

Conflict of Interest. The authors declare no conflict of interest.

References

1. Masood Khan, A., Rahat Afreen, K.: An approach to text analytics and text mining in multilingual natural language processing. Materials Today: Proceedings. (2021). https://doi.org/10.1016/j.matpr.2020.10.861
2. Jung, H., Lee, B.G.: Research trends in text mining: Semantic network and main path analysis of selected journals. Expert Systems with Applications. **162**, 113851 (2020). https://doi.org/10.1016/j.eswa.2020.113851
3. Nota, G., Postiglione, A., Carvello, R.: Text mining techniques for the management of predictive maintenance. Procedia Computer Science. **200**, 778–792 (2022). https://doi.org/10.1016/j.procs.2022.01.276
4. Zarindast, A., Sharma, A., Wood, J.: Application of text mining in smart lighting literature - an analysis of existing literature and a research agenda. Int. J. Info. Manage. Data Insights **1**, 100032 (2021). https://doi.org/10.1016/j.jjimei.2021.100032
5. Chiarello, F., Fantoni, G., Hogarth, T., Giordano, V., Baltina, L., Spada, I.: Towards ESCO 4.0 – Is the European classification of skills in line with industry 4.0? A text mining approach. Technological Forecasting and Social Change. **173**, 121177 (2021). https://doi.org/10.1016/j.techfore.2021.121177
6. Urushima, A.Y.F., Tokuchi, N., Hara, S.: Text mining assessment of sustainability learning topics at higher education in Japan. In: 2021 9th International Conference on Information and Education Technology (ICIET), pp. 91–97 (2021). https://doi.org/10.1109/ICIET51873.2021.9419584
7. Liu, W.: Collaborative innovation of online ideological education platform with data mining and text recognition algorithms. In: 2021 5th International Conference on Computing Methodologies and Communication (ICCMC), pp. 1372–1375 (2021). https://doi.org/10.1109/ICCMC51019.2021.9418306
8. Tao, P., Sun, Z., Sun, Z.: An improved intrusion detection algorithm based on GA and SVM. Ieee Access **6**, 13624–13631 (2018). https://doi.org/10.1109/ICDAR.2001.953980
9. Onan, A., Korukoğlu, S., Bulut, H.: A multiobjective weighted voting ensemble classifier based on differential evolution algorithm for text sentiment classification. Expert Systems with Applications. **62**, 1–16 (2016). https://doi.org/10.1016/j.eswa.2016.06.005
10. Antonenko, P.D., Toy, S., Niederhauser, D.S.: Using cluster analysis for data mining in educational technology research. Education Tech Research Dev. **60**, 383–398 (2012). https://doi.org/10.1007/s11423-012-9235-8

11. Baker, R.S.J.D., Inventado, P.S.: Educational data mining and learning analytics. In: Larusson, J.A., White, B. (eds.) Learning Analytics: from Research to Practice. Springer, New York, NY (2014)
12. Jeong, H., Biswas, G.: Mining student behavior models in learning-byTeaching environments. In: Educational Data Mining, pp. 127–136 (2008)
13. Nuankaew, P., Teeraputon, D., Nuankaew, W., Phanniphong, K., Imwut, S., Bussaman, S.: Perception and attitude toward self-regulated learning in educational data mining. In: 2019 6th International Conference on Technical Education (ICTechEd6), pp. 1–5 (2019). https://doi.org/10.1109/ICTechEd6.2019.8790875
14. Nuankaew, P., Nuankaew, W.S.: Student performance prediction model for predicting academic achievement of high school students. Student Performance Prediction Model for Predicting Academic Achievement of High School Students **11**, 949–963 (2022). https://doi.org/10.12973/eu-jer.11.2.949
15. Yuensuk, T., Limpinan, P., Nuankaew, W., Nuankaew, P.: Information systems for cultural tourism management using text analytics and data mining techniques. Int. J. Interact. Mob. Technol. **16**, 146–163 (2022). https://doi.org/10.3991/ijim.v16i09.30439
16. Chen, J., Huang, H., Tian, S., Qu, Y.: Feature selection for text classification with naïve bayes. Expert Systems with Applications. **36**, 5432–5435 (2009). https://doi.org/10.1016/j.eswa.2008.06.054
17. Jovic, A., Brkic, K., Bogunovic, N.: A review of feature selection methods with applications. In: 2015 38th International Convention on Information and Communication Technology, Electronics and Microelectronics (MIPRO), pp. 1200–1205 (2015). https://doi.org/10.1109/MIPRO.2015.7160458
18. Ramaswami, M., Bhaskaran, R.: A study on feature selection techniques in educational data mining (2009). https://doi.org/10.48550/ARXIV.0912.3924

Fuzzy Soft Relations-Based Rough Soft Sets Classified by Overlaps of Successor Classes with Measurement Issues

Aiyared Iampan[1] (ID) and Rukchart Prasertpong[2(✉)] (ID)

[1] Fuzzy Algebras and Decision-Making Problems Research Unit, Department of Mathematics, School of Science, University of Phayao, Mae Ka, Mueang, Phayao 56000, Thailand
[2] Division of Mathematics and Statistics, Faculty of Science and Technology, Nakhon Sawan Rajabhat University, Nakhon Sawan 60000, Thailand
`rukchart.p@nsru.ac.th`

Abstract. In this paper, a new class for data classification in rough set theory is defined as an overlap of successor classes. This kind of rough approximation is proposed via fuzzy soft relations. Depending on the class of fuzzy soft relation, this paper defines the upper and lower rough approximations of a soft set. At this point, the fundamental of rough soft sets and definable soft sets is proposed. Then, some related theories are proved. In the aftermath, the notion of accuracy and roughness measures of soft sets in terms of rough set theory is studied combined with the concept of distance measures.

Keywords: Fuzzy soft relation · Rough set · Soft set · Rough soft set

1 Introduction

For a given non-empty universal set V and an equivalence relation E on V, a pair (V, E) is denoted as a Pawlak's approximation space, and $[v]_E$ is denoted as an equivalence class of $v \in V$ induced by E. Now, let (V, E) be a given Pawlak's approximation space and let X be a subset of V. The set

$$\overline{E}(X) := \{v \in V : [v]_E \cap X \neq \emptyset\}$$

is said to be an *upper approximation* of X within (V, E). The set

$$\underline{E}(X) := \{v \in V : [v]_E \subseteq F(a)\}$$

is said to be a *lower approximation* of X within (V, E). A difference $\overline{E}(X) - \underline{E}(X)$ is said to be a *boundary region* of X within (V, E). Three sets are obtained the following interpretation.

- The upper approximation $\overline{E}(X)$ of X contains all objects which possibly belong to X. At this point, a complement of $\overline{E}(X)$ is said to be a *negative region* of X within (V, E).

© The Author(s), under exclusive license to Springer Nature Switzerland AG 2022
O. Surinta and K. Kam Fung Yuen (Eds.): MIWAI 2022, LNAI 13651, pp. 26–39, 2022.
https://doi.org/10.1007/978-3-031-20992-5_3

- The lower approximation $\underline{E}(X)$ of X consists of all objects which surely belong to X. In this way, such the set is said to be a *positive region* of X within (V, E).
- $\overline{E}(X) - \underline{E}(X)$ is a set of all objects, which can be classified neither as X nor as non-X using E.

In what follows, a pair $(\overline{E}(X), \underline{E}(X))$ is said to be a *rough set* of X within (V, E) if $\overline{E}(X) - \underline{E}(X)$ is a non-empty set. In this way, X is said to be a rough set. X is said to be a *definable* (or an *exact*) *set* within (V, E) if $\overline{E}(X) - \underline{E}(X)$ is an empty set.

As mentioned above, it is a classical theory proposed by Pawlak [1] in 1982. Observe that the notion of a Pawlak's rough set theory is classified by all equivalence classes via an equivalence relation. At this point, it has been extended to arbitrary binary relations and fuzzy relations. In 2019, Prasertpong and Siripitukdet [2] proposed the fundamental of rough sets induced by fuzzy serial relations. It is classified by overlaps of successor classes with respect to level in a closed unit interval under a fuzzy serial relation. This class is defined as follows. Let R be a fuzzy serial relation from V to W and $\alpha \in [0, 1]$ [0, 1]. For an element $v \in V$, the set

$$[v]_R^S := \{w \in W : R(v, w) \geq \alpha\}$$

is said to be a *successor class* of v with respect to α–level based on R. For $v \in V$,

$$[v]_R^{OS} := \{v' \in V : [v]_R^S \cap [v']_R^S \neq \emptyset\}$$

is called an *overlap of the successor class* of v with respect to α–level based on R.

As an extension of Zadeh's fuzzy relations [3], the notion of Zhang's fuzzy soft relations [4] is a mathematical tool for dealing with uncertainty problems. Then, in this research, an overlap of the successor class is considered in terms of fuzzy soft relations to rough approximations. In Sect. 3, the contributions of the section are as follows.

- We extend the concept of fuzzy serial relations by the sense of fuzzy soft relations. That is, a fuzzy soft serial relation over two universes is proposed. An overlap of successor classes via fuzzy soft serial relations is defined. Some related properties are investigated.
- We propose the notion of upper and lower rough approximations of a soft set based on overlaps of successor classes. We introduce the concept of rough soft sets and definable soft sets, and a corresponding example is provided. The relationships between such the softs and fuzzy soft relations are verified.
- As a novel rough soft set theory of the section, we further study the argument to accuracy and roughness measures of soft sets in terms of Pawlak's rough set theory. The relationship between a roughness measure and a distance measure is discussed.

In the end, the work is summarized in Sect. 4.

2 Preliminaries

In this section, let us first review some basic concepts which wi/ll be necessary for subsequent sections. Throughout this paper, K, V, and W denote non-empty sets.

2.1   Some Basic Notions of Fuzzy Sets

Definition 2.1.1 [5]. f is said to be a *fuzzy subset (or fuzzy set)* of V if it is a function from V to the closed unit interval $[0, 1]$. In this way, $FP(V)$ is denoted as a collection of all fuzzy subsets of V.

Definition 2.1.2 [5]. Let f and g be fuzzy subsets of V. $f \prec g$ is denoted by meaning $f(v) \le g(v)$ for all $v \in V$.

Definition 2.1.3 [3]. An element in $FP(V \times W)$ is said to be a *fuzzy relation* from V to W. An element in $FP(V \times V)$ is a fuzzy relation on V if W is replaced by V. Given a fuzzy relation R from V to W and $v \in V$, $w \in W$, the value $R(v, w)$ in $[0, 1]$ is the *membership grade* of the relation between v and w based on R. If R is a given fuzzy relation from V to W, where $V = \{v_1, v_2, v_3, \dots, v_p\}$ and $W = \{w_1, w_2, w_3, \dots, w_q\}$, then every membership grade under R is represented by the $p \times q$ matrix form as

$$
\begin{pmatrix}
R(v_1, w_1) & R(v_1, w_2) & R(v_1, w_3) & \dots & R(v_1, w_q) \\
R(v_2, w_1) & R(v_2, w_2) & R(v_2, w_3) & \dots & R(v_2, w_q) \\
R(v_3, w_1) & R(v_3, w_2) & R(v_3, w_3) & \dots & R(v_3, w_q) \\
\vdots & \vdots & \vdots & \dots & \vdots \\
R(v_p, w_1) & R(v_p, w_2) & R(v_p, w_3) & \dots & R(v_p, w_q)
\end{pmatrix}.
$$

Definition 2.1.4 [6]. Let $R \in FP(V \times W)$. R is said to be a *fuzzy serial relation* if for all $v \in V$, there exists $w \in W$ such that $R(v, w) = 1$.

Definition 2.1.5 [3]. Let $R \in FP(V \times V)$.

(1) R is said to be a *fuzzy reflexive relation* if $R(v, v) = 1$ for all $v \in V$.
(2) R is said to be a *fuzzy transitive relation* if it satisfies $R(v_1, v_2) = \sup_{v \in V}(R(v_1, v) \wedge R(v, v_2))$ for all $v_1, v_2 \in V$.
(3) R is said to be a *fuzzy symmetric relation* if $R(v_1, v_2) = R(v_2, v_1)$ for all $v_1, v_2 \in V$.
(4) R is said to be a *fuzzy equivalence relation* if it is a fuzzy reflexive relation, a fuzzy transitive relation, and a fuzzy symmetric relation.

Definition 2.1.6 [7]. Let $R \in FP(V \times V)$. R is said to be a *fuzzy antisymmetric relation* if for all $v_1, v_2 \in V$, $R(v_1, v_2) > 0$ and $R(v_2, v_1) > 0$ imply $v_1 = v_2$.

2.2   Some Basic Notions of Soft Sets and Fuzzy Soft Relations

Definition 2.2.1 [8]. Throughout this work, $P(V)$ denotes a power set of V. Let A be a non-empty subset of K. If F is a mapping from A to $P(V)$, then (F, A) is said to be a *soft set* over V with respect to A. As the understanding of the soft set, V is said to be a universe of all alternative objects of (F, A), and K is said to be a set of all parameters of (F, A), where the parameter is an attribute, a characteristic or a statement of the alternative object of V. For any element $a \in A$, $F(a)$ is considered as a set of a-approximate elements (or a-alternative objects) of (F, A).

Definition 2.2.2 [9]. Let A be a non-empty subset of K.

(1) A *relative null soft set* over V with respect to A is denoted by $\mathcal{N}_{\emptyset_A} := (\emptyset_A, A)$, where $\emptyset_A$ is a set valued-mapping given by $\emptyset_A(a) = \emptyset$ for all $a \in A$.
(2) For a soft set $\mathscr{F} := (F, A)$ over V with respect to A, a *support* of $\mathscr{F}$ is denoted by $Supp(\mathcal{F})$, where $Supp(\mathcal{F}) := \{a \in A : F(a) \neq \emptyset\}$.
(3) A *relative whole soft set* over V with respect to A is denoted by $\mathcal{V}_{V_A} := (V_A, A)$, where V_A is a set valued-mapping given by $V_A(a) = V$ for all $a \in A$.

Definition 2.2.3 [9]. Let $\mathscr{F} := (F, A)$ and $\mathcal{G} := (G, B)$ be two soft sets over a common alternative universe with respect to non-empty subsets A and B of K, respectively. $\mathscr{F}$ is a soft subset of $\mathcal{G}$ if $A \subseteq B$ and $F(a) \subseteq G(a)$ for all $a \in A$. We denote by $\mathcal{F} \Subset \mathcal{G}$.

Definition 2.2.4 [9]. Let $\mathscr{F} := (F, A)$ and $\mathcal{G} := (G, B)$ be two soft sets over a common alternative universe with respect to non-empty subsets A and B of K, respectively.

(1) A *restricted intersection* of $\mathscr{F}$ and $\mathcal{G}$, denoted by $\mathscr{F} \cap_r \mathcal{G}$ is defined as a soft set (H, C), where $C = A \cap B$ and $H(c) = F(c) \cap G(c)$ for all $c \in C$.
(2) A *restricted union* of $\mathscr{F}$ and $\mathcal{G}$, denoted by $\mathscr{F} \cup_r \mathcal{G}$ is defined as a soft set (H, C), where $C = A \cap B$ and $H(c) = F(c) \cup G(c)$ for all $c \in C$.
(3) An *extended intersection* of $\mathscr{F}$ and $\mathcal{G}$, denoted by $\mathscr{F} \cap_e \mathcal{G}$ is defined as a soft set (H, C), where $C = A \cup B$ and $H(c) = \begin{cases} F(c) & if \ \ c \in A - B \\ G(c) & if \ \ c \in B - A \\ F(c) \cap G(c) & if \ \ c \in A \cap B \end{cases}$ for all $c \in C$.
(4) An *extended union* of $\mathscr{F}$ and $\mathcal{G}$, denoted by $\mathscr{F} \cup_e \mathcal{G}$ is defined as a soft set (H, C), where $C = A \cup B$ and $H(c) = \begin{cases} F(c) & if \ \ c \in A - B \\ G(c) & if \ \ c \in B - A \\ F(c) \cup G(c) & if \ \ c \in A \cap B \end{cases}$ for all $c \in C$.
(5) A *restricted difference* of $\mathscr{F}$ and $\mathcal{G}$, denoted by $\mathscr{F} -_r \mathcal{G}$ is defined as a soft set (H, C), where $C = A \cap B$ and $H(c) = F(c) - G(c)$ for all $c \in C$.

Definition 2.2.5 [10]. Let A be a non-empty subset of K. If F is a mapping from A to $FP(V)$, then (F, A) is said to be a *fuzzy soft set* over V with respect to A.

Definition 2.2.6 [10]. Let $\mathscr{F} := (F, A)$ and $\mathscr{F} := (G, B)$ be two fuzzy soft sets over a common alternative universe with respect to non-empty subsets A and B of K, respectively. $\mathscr{F}$ is a fuzzy soft subset of $\mathcal{G}$ if $A \subseteq B$ and $F(a) \prec G(a)$ for all $a \in A$.

Definition 2.2.7 [4]. Let A be a non-empty subset of K. If F is a mapping from A to $FP(V \times W)$, then (F, A) is said to be a *fuzzy soft relation* over $V \times W$.

Definition 2.2.8 [4]. Let A be a non-empty subset of K, and let $\mathcal{R} := (R, A)$ be a fuzzy soft relation over $V \times V$.

(1) $\mathcal{R}$ is called a *fuzzy soft reflexive relation* if $R(a)$ is a fuzzy reflexive relation for all $a \in A$.
(2) $\mathcal{R}$ is called a *fuzzy soft transitive relation* if $R(a)$ is a fuzzy transitive relation for all $a \in A$.
(3) $\mathcal{R}$ is called a *fuzzy soft symmetric relation* if $R(a)$ is a fuzzy symmetric relation for all $a \in A$.
(4) $\mathcal{R}$ is called a *fuzzy soft equivalence relation* if it is a fuzzy soft reflexive relation, a fuzzy soft transitive relation, and a fuzzy soft symmetric relation.

3   Main Results

In this section, we propose the concept of a successor class and an overlap of the successor classes based on fuzzy soft relations. The related theories are verified. Then, upper and lower rough approximations of a soft set are proposed under the classification of all overlaps of the successor classes. Of course, the notion of rough soft set is defined. A corresponding example is provided. Furthermore, the measurement issue is discussed via rough set theory.

Throughout this section, the set A and B denote two non-empty subsets of V.

3.1   Overlaps of Successor Classes via Fuzzy Soft Relations

In this subsection, we construct a new class for rough approximations of a soft set. Such the class is called the overlaps of successor classes based on fuzzy soft relations.

Definition 3.1.1 Let $\mathcal{R} := (R, A)$ be a fuzzy soft relation over $V \times W$ and $\alpha \in [0, 1]$. For an element $v \in V$, the set

$$[v]^S_{\mathcal{R}, \alpha} := \{w \in W : R(a)(v, w) \geq \alpha, \forall a \in A\}$$

is called a *successor class* of v with respect to α–level based on $\mathcal{R}$. We denote by $[V]^S_{\mathcal{R}, \alpha}$ the collection of $[v]^S_{\mathcal{R}, \alpha}$ for all $v \in V$.

Example 3.1.1 Let
$V = \{v_i \in \mathbb{R} : i \in \mathbb{N}, \ 1 \leq i \leq 6\}$ and $W = \{w_i \in \mathbb{R} : i \in \mathbb{N}, 1 \leq i \leq 5\}$. We define a fuzzy relation $\theta \in FP(V \times W)$ by the matrix representation as

$$\begin{pmatrix} 0.6 & 0.3 & 0.7 & 0.9 & 0.4 \\ 0.2 & 0.4 & 0.8 & 0.1 & 0.3 \\ 0.7 & 0.4 & 0.2 & 0.2 & 0.4 \\ 0.4 & 0.8 & 0.2 & 0.1 & 0.3 \\ 0.2 & 0.9 & 0.1 & 0.3 & 0.2 \\ 0.3 & 0.2 & 0.4 & 0.4 & 0.6 \end{pmatrix}.$$

Suppose that $\mathcal{R} := (R, A)$ is a fuzzy soft relation over $V \times W$ defined by $R(a) = \theta$ for all $a \in A$. Then, the successor class of each element in V with respect to 0.5–level based on R is presented by

$$[v_1]^S_{\mathcal{R}, 0.5} = \{w_1, w_3, w_4\}, [v_2]^S_{\mathcal{R}, 0.5} = \{w_3\}, [v_3]^S_{\mathcal{R}, 0.5} = \{w_1\},$$

$[v_4]^S_{\mathcal{R}, 0.5} = \{w_2\}, [v_5]^S_{\mathcal{R}, 0.5} = \{w_2\}$, and $[v_6]^S_{\mathcal{R}, 0.5} = \{w_5\}$. This is a corresponding example of Definition 3.1.1.

Definition 3.1.2 Let $\mathcal{R} := (R, A)$ be a fuzzy soft relation over $V \times W$. $\mathcal{R}$ is called a *fuzzy soft serial relation* if $R(a)$ is a fuzzy serial relation for all $a \in A$.

Remark 3.1.1 A fuzzy soft serial relation over $V \times V$ is a generalization concept of a fuzzy soft reflexive relation over $V \times V$.

Proposition 3.1.1 If $\mathcal{R} := (R, A)$ is a fuzzy soft serial relation over $V \times W$ and $\alpha \in [0, 1]$, then $[v]^S_{\mathcal{R}, \alpha} \neq \emptyset$ for all $v \in V$.

Proof. Assume that $\mathcal{R}$ is a fuzzy soft serial relation over $V \times W$ and $\alpha \in [0, 1]$. Now, we let $v \in V$. Then, there exists $w \in W$ such that

$$R(a)(v, w) = 1 \geq \alpha$$

for all $a \in A$. Therefore $w \in [v]^S_{\mathcal{R}, \alpha}$. It follows that $[v]^S_{\mathcal{R}, \alpha} \neq \emptyset$.

Definition 3.1.3 Let $\mathcal{R} := (R, A)$ be a fuzzy soft serial relation over $V \times W$ and $\alpha \in [0, 1]$. For an element $v \in V$, the set

$$[v]^{OS}_{\mathcal{R}, \alpha} := \{v' \in V : [v]^S_{\mathcal{R}, \alpha} \cap [v']^S_{\mathcal{R}, \alpha} \neq \emptyset\}$$

is called an *overlap of successor class* of v with respect to α–level based on $\mathcal{R}$ We shall denote by $[V]^{OS}_{\mathcal{R}, \alpha}$ the collection of $[v]^{OS}_{\mathcal{R}, \alpha}$ for all $v \in V$.

Example 3.1.2 Based on Example 3.1.1, we observe that

$$[v_1]^{OS}_{\mathcal{R}, 0.5} = \{v_1, v_2, v_3\}, [v_2]^{OS}_{\mathcal{R}, 0.5} = \{v_1, v_2\}, [v_3]^{OS}_{\mathcal{R}, 0.5} = \{v_1, v_3\},$$

$[v_4]^{OS}_{\mathcal{R}, 0.5} = \{v_4, v_5\}, [v_5]^{OS}_{\mathcal{R}, 0.5} = \{v_4, v_5\}$, and $[v_6]^{OS}_{\mathcal{R}, 0.5} = \{v_6\}$. Observe that it is a corresponding example of Definition 3.1.3.

Proposition 3.1.2 If $\mathcal{R} := (R, A)$ is a fuzzy soft serial relation over $V \times W$ and $\alpha \in [0, 1]$, then $v \in [v]^{OS}_{\mathcal{R}, \alpha}$ for all $v \in V$.

Proof. Suppose that $\mathcal{R}$ is a fuzzy soft serial relation over $V \times W$ and $\alpha \in [0, 1]$. Then, by Proposition 3.1.1, we have $[v]^S_{\mathcal{R}, \alpha} \neq \emptyset$ for all $v \in V$. Let $v \in V$. Then $[v]^S_{\mathcal{R}, \alpha} \cap [v]^S_{\mathcal{R}, \alpha} \neq \emptyset$. This implies that $v \in [v]^{OS}_{\mathcal{R}, \alpha}$.

Proposition 3.1.3 Let $\mathcal{R} := (R, A)$ be a fuzzy soft serial relation over $V \times V$ and $\alpha \in [0, 1]$. If $\mathcal{R}$ is a fuzzy soft reflexive relation, then $[v]^S_{\mathcal{R}, \alpha} \subseteq [v]^{OS}_{\mathcal{R}, \alpha}$ for all $v \in V$.

Proof. Suppose that $\mathcal{R}$ is a fuzzy soft reflexive relation and $v \in V$. Assume that $v' \in [v]^S_{\mathcal{R},\alpha}$. Then, we get that $v' \in V$. Thus $R(a)(v',v') = 1 \geq \alpha$ for all $a \in A$. Whence $v' \in [v']^S_{\mathcal{R},\alpha}$. Hence $[v]^S_{\mathcal{R},\alpha} \cap [v']^S_{\mathcal{R},\alpha} \neq \emptyset$. Then $v' \in [v]^{OS}_{\mathcal{R},\alpha}$. It follows that $[v]^S_{\mathcal{R},\alpha} \subseteq [v]^{OS}_{\mathcal{R},\alpha}$.

Proposition 3.1.4 If $\mathcal{R} := (R,A)$ is a fuzzy soft equivalence relation over $V \times V$ and $\alpha \in [0,1]$, then $[v]^S_{\mathcal{R},\alpha}$ and $[v]^{OS}_{\mathcal{R},\alpha}$ are identical for all $v \in V$.

Proof. By Proposition 3.1.3, we obtain that $[v]^S_{\mathcal{R},\alpha}$ is a subset of $[v]^{OS}_{\mathcal{R},\alpha}$ for all $v \in V$. Let $v \in V$ be given. Suppose that $v' \in [v]^{OS}_{\mathcal{R},\alpha}$. Then $[v]^S_{\mathcal{R},\alpha} \cap [v']^S_{\mathcal{R},\alpha} \neq \emptyset$. Thus, there exists $v'' \in V$ such that $v'' \in [v]^S_{\mathcal{R},\alpha} \cap [v']^S_{\mathcal{R},\alpha}$. It is true that $R(a)(v,v'') \geq \alpha$ and $R(a)(v',v'') \geq \alpha$ for all $a \in A$. Since $\mathcal{R}$ is a fuzzy soft symmetric relation, we have $R(a)(v'',v') \geq \alpha$ for all $a \in A$. Since $\mathcal{R}$ is a fuzzy soft transitive relation, we get that

$$R(a)(v,v') \geq \sup_{v''' v \in V} (R(a)(v,v''') \wedge R(a)(v'''v,v'))$$
$$\geq R(a)(v,v'') \wedge R(a)(v'',v')$$
$$\geq \alpha \wedge \alpha$$
$$= \alpha$$

for all $a \in A$. Hence $v' \in [v]^S_{\mathcal{R},\alpha}$. Thus $[v]^{OS}_{\mathcal{R},\alpha} \subseteq [v]^S_{\mathcal{R},\alpha}$. Hence $[v]^S_{\mathcal{R},\alpha} = [v]^{OS}_{\mathcal{R},\alpha}$.

Next, we shall introduce the notion of fuzzy soft antisymmetric relations in terms of fuzzy soft relations on a single universe.

Definition 3.1.4 Let $\mathcal{R} := (R,A)$ be a fuzzy soft relation over $V \times V$. $\mathcal{R}$ is called a *fuzzy soft antisymmetric relation* if $R(a)$ is a fuzzy antisymmetric relation for all $a \in A$.

Example 3.1.3 Let $V = \{v_i \in \mathbb{R} : i \in \mathbb{N}$ and $1 \leq i \leq 6\}$. Suppose that $\theta \in FP(V \times V)$ is a fuzzy relation defined by the square matrix representation as.

$$\begin{pmatrix} 1 & 1 & 1 & 0 & 0 & 1 \\ 0 & 1 & 0 & 0 & 0 & 0 \\ 0 & 0 & 1 & 0 & 0 & 0 \\ 0 & 0 & 0 & 1 & 0 & 0 \\ 0 & 0 & 0 & 0 & 1 & 0 \\ 0 & 0 & 0 & 0 & 0 & 1 \end{pmatrix}.$$

Assume that $\mathcal{R} := (R,A)$ is a fuzzy soft relation over $V \times V$ defined by $R(a) = \theta$ for all $a \in A$. Then, it is easy to check that $\mathcal{R}$ is a fuzzy soft antisymmetric relation over $V \times V$. In fact, for all $a \in A, v, v' \in V, R(a)(v,v') > 0$ and $R(a)(v',v) > 0$ imply $v = v'$. This is a corresponding example of Definition 3.1.4.

Proposition 3.1.5 Let $\mathcal{R} := (R,A)$ be a fuzzy soft serial relation over $V \times V$ and $\alpha \in (0,1]$. If $[V]^S_{\mathcal{R},\alpha}$ is the partition of V and $\mathcal{R}$ is a fuzzy soft reflexive relation and a fuzzy soft antisymmetric relation over $V \times V$, then the following statements are equivalent.

(1) $v = v'$ for all $v, v' \in V$.

(2) $[v]^{OS}_{\mathcal{R},\alpha} = [v']^{OS}_{\mathcal{R},\alpha}$ for all $v, v' \in V$.

(3) $v \in [v']^{OS}_{\mathcal{R},\alpha}$ for all $v, v' \in V$.

Proof. It is clear that (1) implies (2). According to Proposition 3.3, we obtain that (2) implies (3). In order to prove that (3) implies (1), we let $v, v' \in V$ be such that $v \in [v']^{OS}_{\mathcal{R},\alpha}$. Then $[v]^{S}_{\mathcal{R},\alpha} \cap [v']^{S}_{\mathcal{R},\alpha} \neq \emptyset$. Hence $[v]^{S}_{\mathcal{R},\alpha} = [v']^{S}_{\mathcal{R},\alpha}$. Since $\mathcal{R}$ is a fuzzy soft reflexive relation, it is easy to prove that $v \in [v]^{S}_{\mathcal{R},\alpha}$ and $v' \in [v']^{S}_{\mathcal{R},\alpha}$. Thus $v \in [v']^{S}_{\mathcal{R},\alpha}$ and $v' \in [v]^{S}_{\mathcal{R},\alpha}$. Therefore $R(a)(v', v) \geq \alpha > 0$ and $R(a)(v, v') \geq \alpha > 0$ for all $a \in A$. As $\mathcal{R}$ is a fuzzy soft antisymmetric relation, we obtain that $v = v'$.

3.2   Rough Soft Sets Based on Overlaps of Successor Classes

As rough set theory based on a non-partition classification, in this subsection, the foundation of roughness of soft sets induced by all overlaps of successor classes is proposed via fuzzy soft relations. This concept is generated by upper and lower rough approximations. That is, it is constructed by two distinct classes classified by all overlaps of successor classes. Then, some related properties are investigated under the novel notion.

Definition 3.2.1 If $\alpha \in [0, 1]$ and $\mathcal{R} := (R, K)$ is a fuzzy soft relation over $V \times W$ related to $[V]^{OS}_{\mathcal{R},\alpha}$, then $(V, W, [V]^{OS}_{\mathcal{R},\alpha})$ is called an *approximation space* based on $[V]^{OS}_{\mathcal{R},\alpha}$.

Definition 3.2.2 Let $(V, W, [V]^{OS}_{\mathcal{R}:=(R,K),\alpha})$ be a given approximation space, and let $\mathscr{F} := (F, A)$ be a soft set over V. An upper rough approximation of $\mathscr{F}$ within $(V, W, [V]^{OS}_{\mathcal{R},\alpha})$ is denoted by $\overline{\mathscr{F}}\big|^{OS}_{\mathcal{R},\alpha} := (\overline{F}\big|^{OS}_{\mathcal{R},\alpha}, A)$, where

$$\overline{F}\big|^{OS}_{\mathcal{R},\alpha}(a) := \left\{ v \in V : [v]^{OS}_{\mathcal{R},\alpha} \cap F(a) \neq \emptyset \right\}$$

for all $a \in A$. A lower rough approximation of $\mathscr{F}$ within $(V, W, [V]^{OS}_{\mathcal{R},\alpha})$ denoted by $\underline{\mathscr{F}}\big|^{OS}_{\mathcal{R},\alpha} := (\underline{F}\big|^{OS}_{\mathcal{R},\alpha}, A)$, where

$$\underline{F}\big|^{OS}_{\mathcal{R},\alpha}(a) := \left\{ v \in V : [v]^{OS}_{\mathcal{R},\alpha} \subseteq F(a) \right\}$$

for all $a \in A$. A boundary region of $\mathscr{F}$ within $(V, W, [V]^{OS}_{\mathcal{R},\alpha})$ is denoted by $\mathscr{F}]^{OS}_{\mathcal{R},\alpha} := (F]^{OS}_{\mathcal{R},\alpha}, A)$, where

$$\mathscr{F}]^{OS}_{\mathcal{R},\alpha} = \overline{\mathscr{F}}\big|^{OS}_{\mathcal{R},\alpha} -_r \underline{\mathscr{F}}\big|^{OS}_{\mathcal{R},\alpha}.$$

As introduced above, such sets are obtained the following interpretation.

(1) $\overline{F}\big|^{OS}_{\mathcal{R},\alpha}(a)$ is a set of all elements, which can be possibly classified as $F(a)$ using $\mathcal{R}$ (are possibly in view of $\mathcal{R}$) for all $a \in A$. In this way, a complement of $\overline{F}\big|^{OS}_{\mathcal{R},\alpha}(a)$ is said to be a *negative region* of $F(a)$ within $(V, W, [V]^{OS}_{\mathcal{R},\alpha})$ for all $a \in A$.

(2) $\underline{F}\big|_{\mathcal{R},\alpha}^{OS}(a)$ is a set of all elements, which can be certain classified as $F(a)$ using $\mathcal{R}$ (are certainly $F(a)$ in view of $\mathcal{R}$) for all $a \in A$. In this way, such the set is said to be a *positive region* of $F(a)$ within $(V, W, [V]_{\mathcal{R},\alpha}^{OS})$ for all $a \in A$.

(3) $F]_{\mathcal{R},\alpha}^{OS}(a)$ is a set of all elements, which can be classified neither as $F(a)$ nor as non-$F(a)$ using $\mathcal{R}$ for all $a \in A$.

As introduced above, for all $a \in A$, if $F]_{\mathcal{R},\alpha}^{OS}(a) \neq \emptyset$, then $(\overline{F}\big|_{\mathcal{R},\alpha}^{OS}(a), \underline{F}\big|_{\mathcal{R},\alpha}^{OS}(a))$ is called a rough (or an inexact) set of $F(a)$ within $(V, W, [V]_{\mathcal{R},\alpha}^{OS})$ and we call $F(a)$ a *rough set*. For all $a \in A$, if $F]_{\mathcal{R},\alpha}^{OS}(a) = \emptyset$, then $F(a)$ is called a *definable* (or an *exact*) *set* within $(V, W, [V]_{\mathcal{R},\alpha}^{OS})$. The soft set $\mathscr{F}$ is called a *definable soft set* within $(V, W, [V]_{\mathcal{R},\alpha}^{OS})$ if $\mathscr{F}]_{\mathcal{R},\alpha}^{OS} = \mathcal{N}_{\emptyset_A}$; otherwise $\mathscr{F}$ is called a *rough soft set* within $(V, W, [V]_{\mathcal{R},\alpha}^{OS})$.

In the following, we shall introduce a corresponding example of Definition 3.2.2.

Example 3.2.1 Define an approximation space $(V, W, [V]_{\mathcal{R}:=(R,K),\,0.5}^{OS})$ based on the data from Example 3.1.1, where $\mathcal{R} := (R, K) = (R, A)$. Suppose that $\mathscr{F} := (F, A)$ is a soft set over V defined by.

$$F(a) = \{v_1, v_3, v_5\}$$

for all $a \in A$. Then, by Example 3.1.2, it is true that

$$\overline{F}\big|_{\mathcal{R},0.5}^{OS}(a) = \{v_i : i \in \mathbb{N} \text{ and } 1 \leq i \leq 5\},$$

$$\underline{F}\big|_{\mathcal{R},0.5}^{OS}(a) = \{v_3\}, \text{ and}$$

$$F]_{\mathcal{R},0.5}^{OS}(a) = \{v_1, v_2, v_4, v_5\}$$

for all $a \in A$. Therefore $\mathscr{F}$ is a rough soft set within $(V, W, [V]_{\mathcal{R},0.5}^{OS})$. Observe that upper and lower approximations are necessary for approximated soft sets. In addition, negative and positive regions exist in $(V, W, [V]_{\mathcal{R}:=(R,K),\,0.5}^{OS})$.

Remark 3.2.1 Let $(V, W, [V]_{\mathcal{R}:=(R,K),\,\alpha}^{OS})$ be a given approximation space, and let $\mathscr{F} := (F, A)$ be a soft set over V. Then, it is easy to see that $\underline{\mathscr{F}}\big|_{\mathcal{R},\alpha}^{OS} \Subset \mathscr{F} \Subset \overline{\mathscr{F}}\big|_{\mathcal{R},\alpha}^{OS}$. This is a relationship between upper and lower approximations in general.

The following three results are a straightforward consequence of Definition 3.2.2.

Proposition 3.2.1 Let $(V, W, [V]_{\mathcal{R}:=(R,K),\,\alpha}^{OS})$ be a given approximation space. If $\mathscr{F} := (F, A)$ is a soft set over V, then we have the following statements.

(1) If $\mathscr{F} = \mathcal{V}_{V_A}$, then $\mathscr{F}$ is equal to $\underline{\mathscr{F}}\big|_{\mathcal{R},\alpha}^{OS}$ and $\overline{\mathscr{F}}\big|_{\mathcal{R},\alpha}^{OS}$. Moreover, $\mathscr{F}$ is a definable soft set within $(V, W, [V]_{\mathcal{R},\alpha}^{OS})$.

(2) If $\mathscr{F} = \mathcal{N}_{\emptyset_A}$, then $\mathscr{F}$ is equal to $\underline{\mathscr{F}}\big|_{\mathcal{R},\alpha}^{OS}$ and $\overline{\mathscr{F}}\big|_{\mathcal{R},\alpha}^{OS}$. Moreover, $\mathscr{F}$ is a definable soft set within $(V, W, [V]_{\mathcal{R},\alpha}^{OS})$.

Proposition 3.2.2 Let $(V, W, [V]_{\mathcal{R}:=(R,K),\,\alpha}^{OS})$ be a given approximation space, and let $\mathscr{F} := (F, A)$ and $\mathscr{G} := (G, B)$ be soft sets over V. Then, we have the following statements.

(1) $\overline{\mathscr{F} \cup_r \mathscr{G}}\big|_{\mathcal{R},\alpha}^{OS} = \overline{\mathscr{F}}\big|_{\mathscr{F},\alpha}^{OS} \cup_r \overline{\mathscr{G}}\big|_{\mathcal{R},\alpha}^{OS}.$

(2) $\overline{\mathscr{F} \cup_e \mathscr{G}}\big|_{\mathcal{R},\alpha}^{OS} = \overline{\mathscr{F}}\big|_{\mathcal{R},\alpha}^{OS} \cup_e \overline{\mathscr{G}}\big|_{\mathcal{R},\alpha}^{OS}.$

(3) $\underline{\mathscr{F} \cap_r \mathscr{G}}\big|_{\mathcal{R},\alpha}^{OS} = \underline{\mathscr{F}}\big|_{\mathcal{R},\alpha}^{OS} \cap_r \underline{\mathscr{G}}\big|_{\mathcal{R},\alpha}^{OS}.$

(4) $\underline{\mathscr{F} \cap_e \mathscr{G}}\big|_{\mathcal{R},\alpha}^{OS} = \underline{\mathscr{F}}\big|_{\mathcal{R},\alpha}^{OS} \cap_e \underline{\mathscr{G}}\big|_{\mathcal{R},\alpha}^{OS}.$

(5) $\overline{\mathscr{F} \cap_r \mathscr{G}}\big|_{\mathcal{R},\alpha}^{OS} \Subset \overline{\mathscr{F}}\big|_{\mathcal{R},\alpha}^{OS} \cap_r \overline{\mathscr{G}}\big|_{\mathcal{R},\alpha}^{OS}.$

(6) $\overline{\mathscr{F} \cap_e \mathscr{G}}\big|_{\mathcal{R},\alpha}^{OS} \Subset \overline{\mathscr{F}}\big|_{\mathcal{R},\alpha}^{OS} \cap_e \overline{\mathscr{G}}\big|_{\mathcal{R},\alpha}^{OS}.$

(7) $\underline{\mathscr{F}}\big|_{\mathcal{R},\alpha}^{OS} \cup_r \underline{\mathscr{G}}\big|_{\mathcal{R},\alpha}^{OS} \Subset \underline{\mathscr{F} \cup_r \mathscr{G}}\big|_{\mathcal{R},\alpha}^{OS}.$

(8) $\underline{\mathscr{F}}\big|_{\mathcal{R},\alpha}^{OS} \cup_e \underline{\mathscr{G}}\big|_{\mathcal{R},\alpha}^{OS} \Subset \underline{\mathscr{F} \cup_e \mathscr{G}}\big|_{\mathcal{R},\alpha}^{OS}.$

Proposition 3.2.3 Let $(V, W, [V]_{\mathcal{R}:=(R,K),\,\alpha}^{OS})$ be a given approximation space, and let $\mathscr{F} := (F, A)$ and $\mathscr{G} := (G, B)$ be soft sets over V. If $\mathcal{F} \Subset \mathcal{G}$, then $\underline{\mathscr{F}}\big|_{\mathcal{R},\alpha}^{OS} \Subset \underline{\mathscr{G}}\big|_{\mathcal{R},\alpha}^{OS}$ and $\overline{\mathscr{F}}\big|_{\mathcal{R},\alpha}^{OS} \Subset \overline{\mathscr{G}}\big|_{\mathcal{R},\alpha}^{OS}.$

Proposition 3.2.4 Let $(V, W, [V]_{\mathcal{R}:=(R,K),\,\alpha}^{OS})$ and let $(V, W, [V]_{\mathcal{S}:=(S,K),\,\beta}^{OS})$ be given two approximation spaces with property that $\mathcal{R} \Subset \mathcal{S}$ and that $\alpha \geq \beta$. If $\mathscr{F} := (F, A)$ is a soft set over V, then $\underline{\mathscr{F}}\big|_{\mathcal{S},\beta}^{OS} \Subset \underline{\mathscr{F}}\big|_{\mathcal{R},\alpha}^{OS}$ and $\overline{\mathscr{F}}\big|_{\mathcal{R},\alpha}^{OS} \Subset \overline{\mathscr{F}}\big|_{\mathcal{S},\beta}^{OS}.$

Proof. Suppose that $\mathscr{F}$ is a soft set over V. We shall show that $\underline{\mathscr{F}}\big|_{\mathcal{S},\beta}^{OS} \Subset \underline{\mathscr{F}}\big|_{\mathcal{R},\alpha}^{OS}$. Let $a \in A$ be given. Suppose $v \in \underline{F}\big|_{\mathcal{S},\beta}^{OS}(a)$. Then $[v]_{\mathcal{S},\beta}^{OS} \subseteq F(a)$. Now, we must to prove that $[v]_{\mathcal{R},\alpha}^{OS} \subseteq [v]_{\mathcal{S},\beta}^{OS}$. Assume that $v' \in [v]_{\mathcal{R},\alpha}^{OS}$. Then $[v]_{\mathcal{R}\alpha}^{S} \cap [v']_{\mathcal{R}\alpha}^{S} \neq \emptyset$. There exists $v'' \in V$ such that $v'' \in [v]_{\mathcal{R},\alpha}^{S} \cap [v']_{\mathcal{R},\alpha}^{S}$. Whence $R(k)(v, v'') \geq \alpha$ and $R(k)(v', v'') \geq \alpha$ for all $k \in K$. From the hypothesis, we get that.

$$S(k)(v, v'') \geq R(k)(v, v'') \geq \alpha \geq \beta$$

and

$$S(k)(v', v'') \geq R(k)(v', v'') \geq \alpha \geq \beta$$

for all $k \in K$. It follows that $v'' \in [v]^S_{\mathcal{S},\beta} \cap [v']^S_{\mathcal{S},\beta}$. Then $[v]^S_{\mathcal{S},\beta} \cap [v']^S_{\mathcal{S},\beta} \neq \emptyset$.
Thus $v' \in [v]^{OS}_{\mathcal{S},\beta}$. Hence $[v]^{OS}_{\mathcal{R},\alpha} \subseteq [v]^{OS}_{\mathcal{S},\beta} \subseteq F(a)$. Therefore $v \in \underline{F}\big|^{OS}_{\mathcal{R},\alpha}(a)$. Thus
$\underline{F}\big|^{OS}_{\mathcal{S},\beta}(a) \subseteq \underline{F}\big|^{OS}_{\mathcal{R},\alpha}(a)$. This implies that $\underline{\mathscr{F}}\big|^{OS}_{\mathcal{S},\beta} \Subset \underline{\mathscr{F}}\big|^{OS}_{\mathcal{R},\alpha}$. The remain argument is
straightforward, so we omit it.

Proposition 3.2.5 Let $(V, V, [V]^{OS}_{\mathcal{R}=(R,K),\alpha})$ be a given approximation space with property that $\alpha \in (0, 1]$, $[V]^S_{\mathcal{R},\alpha}$ is the partition of V, and $\mathcal{R}$ is a fuzzy soft reflexive relation and a fuzzy soft antisymmetric relation. If $\mathscr{F} := (F, A)$ is a soft set over V, then $\mathscr{F}$ is a definable soft set within $(V, W, [V]^{OS}_{\mathcal{R},\alpha})$.

Proof. Assume that $\mathscr{F}$ is a soft set over V. Then, by Remark 3.2.1, we obtain that
$\underline{\mathscr{F}}\big|^{OS}_{\mathcal{R},\alpha} \Subset \overline{\mathscr{F}}\big|^{OS}_{\mathcal{R},\alpha}$. Let $a \in A$. Suppose that $v \in \overline{F}\big|^{OS}_{\mathcal{R},\alpha}(a)$. Then $[v]^{OS}_{\mathcal{R},\alpha} \cap F(a) \neq \emptyset$.
Thus, there exists $v' \in V$ such that $v' \in [v]^{OS}_{\mathcal{R},\alpha}$ and $v' \in F(a)$. By Proposition 3.1.5, we
have $v = v'$. We must prove that $[v]^{OS}_{\mathcal{R},\alpha} \subseteq F(a)$. Let $v'' \in [v]^{OS}_{\mathcal{R},\alpha}$. From Proposition
3.1.5, we have $v = v''$. Hence $v'' = v' \in F(a)$, which implies that $[v]^{OS}_{\mathcal{R},\alpha} \subseteq F(a)$.
Therefore $v \in \underline{F}\big|^{OS}_{\mathcal{R},\alpha}(a)$. Thus, it is true that $\overline{F}\big|^{OS}_{\mathcal{R},\alpha}(a) \subseteq \underline{F}\big|^{OS}_{\mathcal{R},\alpha}(a)$. It follows that
$\overline{\mathscr{F}}\big|^{OS}_{\mathcal{R},\alpha} \Subset \underline{\mathscr{F}}\big|^{OS}_{\mathcal{R},\alpha}$. Thus $\underline{\mathscr{F}}\big|^{OS}_{\mathcal{R},\alpha}$ is equal to $\overline{\mathscr{F}}\big|^{OS}_{\mathcal{R},\alpha}$. Consequently, $\mathscr{F}$ is a definable
soft set within $(V, V, [V]^{OS}_{\mathcal{R},\alpha})$.

3.3   Measurement Issues

In this subsection, we shall study to accuracy and roughness measures of soft sets in terms of Pawlak's rough set theory [1]. Now, let X be a subset of V.

An *accuracy measure* of X based on (V, E), denoted by $X|_E$, is defined by

$$X|_E := \frac{card(\underline{E}(X))}{card(\overline{E}(X))}.$$

A *roughness measure* of X based on (V, E), denoted by $X||_E$, is defined by

$$X||_E := 1 - X|_E.$$

In what follows, the concept of rough set theory-based accuracy and roughness measurements via fuzzy soft relation is proposed below.

Definition 3.3.1 Let $(V, W, [V]^{OS}_{\mathcal{R}:=(R,K),\alpha})$ be an approximation space, and let $\mathscr{F} := (F, A)$ be a soft set over V. For $a \in A$, an *accuracy measure* of $F(a)$ based on $(V, W, [V]^{OS}_{\mathcal{R}:=(R,K),\alpha})$, denoted by $F(a)|^{OS}_{\mathcal{R},\alpha}$, is defined by

$$F(a)|^{OS}_{\mathcal{R},\alpha} := \frac{card(\underline{F}\big|^{OS}_{\mathcal{R},\alpha}(a))}{card(\overline{F}\big|^{OS}_{\mathcal{R},\alpha}(a))}.$$

In generality, observe that $F(a)|_{\mathcal{R},\alpha}^{OS} \in [0, 1]$ for all $a \in A$. Then, for all $a \in A$, a *roughness measure* of $F(a)$ based on $(V, W, [V]_{\mathcal{R}:=(R,K),\alpha}^{OS})$, denoted by $F(a)||_{\mathcal{R},\alpha}^{OS}$, is defined by

$$F(a)||_{\mathcal{R},\alpha}^{OS} := 1 - F(a)|_{\mathcal{R},\alpha}^{OS}.$$

Example 3.3.1 Based on Example 3.2.1, we compute that

$$F(a)|_{\mathcal{R},0.5}^{OS} := \frac{card(\underline{F}|_{\mathcal{R},0.5}^{OS}(a))}{card(\overline{F}|_{\mathcal{R},0.5}^{OS}(a))} = \frac{1}{5} = 0.2$$

and

$$F(a)||_{\mathcal{R},0.5}^{OS} := 1 - F(a)|_{\mathcal{R},0.5}^{OS} = 1 - 0.2 = 0.8$$

for all $a \in A$, i.e., the accuracy measure of $F(a)$ is 0.2 and the roughness measure of $F(a)$ is 0.8 for all $a \in A$.

Proposition 3.3.1 Let $(V, W, [V]_{\mathcal{R}:=(R,K),\alpha}^{OS})$ and Let $(V, V, [V]_{\mathcal{S}:=(S,K),\beta}^{OS})$ be given two approximation spaces with property that $\mathcal{R} \Subset \mathcal{S}$ and that $\alpha \geq \beta$. If $\mathscr{F} := (F, A)$ is a soft set over V, then $F(a)|_{\mathcal{R},\alpha}^{OS} \geq F(a)|_{\mathcal{S},\beta}^{OS}$ for all $a \in Supp(\mathscr{F})$.

Proof. Suppose that $\mathscr{F} := (F, A)$ is a soft set over V and $a \in Supp(\mathscr{F})$. Then, by Remark 3.2.1, we have $\overline{F}|_{\mathcal{R},\alpha}^{OS}(a) \neq \emptyset$. From Proposition 3.2.4, it follows that

$$card(\overline{F}|_{\mathcal{R},\alpha}^{OS}(a)) \leq card(\overline{F}|_{\mathcal{S},\beta}^{OS}(a)) \text{ and } card(\underline{F}|_{\mathcal{R},\alpha}^{OS}(a)) \geq card(\underline{F}|_{\mathcal{S},\beta}^{OS}(a)).$$

Now

$$F(a)|_{\mathcal{S},\beta}^{OS} := \frac{card(\underline{F}|_{\mathcal{S},\beta}^{OS}(a))}{card(\overline{F}|_{\mathcal{S},\beta}^{OS}(a))} \leq \frac{card(\underline{F}|_{\mathcal{R},\alpha}^{OS}(a))}{card(\overline{F}|_{\mathcal{S},\beta}^{OS}(a))} \leq \frac{card(\underline{F}|_{\mathcal{R},\alpha}^{OS}(a))}{card(\overline{F}|_{\mathcal{R},\alpha}^{OS}(a))} =: F(a)|_{\mathcal{R},\alpha}^{OS}.$$

Proposition 3.3.2 $(V, V, [V]_{\mathcal{R}:=(R,K),\alpha}^{OS})$ be a given approximation space with property that $\alpha \in (0, 1]$, $[V]_{\mathcal{R}\alpha}^{S}$ is the partition of V, and $\mathcal{R}$ is a fuzzy soft reflexive relation and a fuzzy soft antisymmetric relation. If $\mathscr{F} := (F, A)$ is a soft set over V, then $F(a)|_{\mathcal{R},\alpha}^{OS} = 1$ for all $a \in Supp(\mathscr{F})$. Furthermore, $F(a)||_{\mathcal{R},\alpha}^{OS} = 0$ for all $a \in Supp(\mathscr{F})$.

Proof. Suppose that $\mathscr{F} := (F, A)$ is a soft set over V and $a \in Supp(\mathscr{F})$. Then $\overline{F}|_{\mathcal{R},\alpha}^{OS}(a) \neq \emptyset$ due to Remark 3.2.1. From Proposition 3.2.5, it follows that $card(\underline{F}|_{\mathcal{R},\alpha}^{OS}(a)) = card(\overline{F}|_{\mathcal{R},\alpha}^{OS}(a))$. Thus $F(a)|_{\mathcal{R},\alpha}^{OS} := \frac{card(\underline{F}|_{\mathcal{R},\alpha}^{OS}(a))}{card(\overline{F}|_{\mathcal{R},\alpha}^{OS}(a))} = 1$. It is true that $F(a)||_{\mathcal{R},\alpha}^{OS} := 1 - F(a)|_{\mathcal{R},\alpha}^{OS} = 1 - 1 = 0$.

In the following, we further consider the fact related to the distance measurement of Marczewski and Steinhaus [11]. Let X and Y be given subsets of V. The distance measure of X and Y is defined as follows.

A *symmetric difference* between X and Y, denoted by $X \bigtriangleup Y$, is defined by

$$X \bigtriangleup Y = (X \cup Y) - (X \cap Y).$$

A *distance measure* of X and Y, denoted by $DM(X, Y)$, is defined by

$$DM(X, Y) = \begin{cases} \dfrac{card(X \bigtriangleup Y)}{card(X \cup Y)} & if \quad card(X \cup Y) > 0, \\ 0 & if \quad card(X \cup Y) = 0. \end{cases}$$

As mentioned above, we further study the argument under the relationship between distance measures and roughness measures as the following.

Proposition 3.3.3 Let $(V, W, [V]^{OS}_{\mathcal{R}:=(R,K), \alpha})$ be a given approximation space. If $\mathscr{F} := (F, A)$ is a soft set over V, then $DM(\overline{F}|^{OS}_{\mathcal{R}, \alpha}(a), \underline{F}|^{OS}_{\mathcal{R}, \alpha}(a)) = F(a)||^{OS}_{\mathcal{R}, \alpha}$. For all $a \in Supp(\mathscr{F})$.

Proof. Suppose that $\mathscr{F} := (F, A)$ is a soft set over V and $a \in Supp(\mathcal{F})$. Then, by Remark 3.2.1, we have $\overline{F}|^{OS}_{\mathcal{R}, \alpha}(a) \neq \emptyset$. Now

$$DM\left(\overline{F}|^{OS}_{R,\alpha}(a), \underline{F}|^{OS}_{R,\alpha}(a)\right) := \frac{card(\overline{F}|^{OS}_{R,\alpha}(a) \cup \underline{F}|^{OS}_{R,\alpha}(a))}{card(\overline{F}|^{OS}_{R,\alpha}(a) \cup \underline{F}|^{OS}_{R,\alpha}(a))}$$

$$= \frac{card(\overline{F}|^{OS}_{R,\alpha}(a) \cup \underline{F}|^{OS}_{R,\alpha}(a))}{card(\overline{F}|^{OS}_{R,\alpha}(a) \cup \underline{F}|^{OS}_{R,\alpha}(a))} - \frac{card(\overline{F}|^{OS}_{R,\alpha}(a) \cap \underline{F}|^{OS}_{R,\alpha}(a))}{card(\overline{F}|^{OS}_{R,\alpha}(a) \cup \underline{F}|^{OS}_{R,\alpha}(a))}$$

$$= 1 - \frac{card(\underline{F}|^{OS}_{R,\alpha}(a))}{card(\overline{F}|^{OS}_{R,\alpha}(a))}$$

$$= 1 - F(a)|^{OS}_{R,\alpha} =: F(a)||^{OS}_{R,\alpha}$$

as required.

Example 3.3.2 According to Example 3.2.1, we observe that

$$card(\underline{F}|^{OS}_{\mathcal{R},0.5}(a)) \cup card(\overline{F}|^{OS}_{\mathcal{R},0.5}(a)) = 5 \text{ and } card(\underline{F}|^{OS}_{\mathcal{R},0.5}(a)) \cap card(\overline{F}|^{OS}_{\mathcal{R},0.5}(a)) = 1.$$

Then, we compute that $DM(\overline{F}|^{OS}_{\mathcal{R},0.5}(a), \underline{F}|^{OS}_{\mathcal{R},0.5}(a)) = F(a)||^{OS}_{\mathcal{R},0.5}$. In fact,

$$DM(\overline{F}|^{OS}_{\mathcal{R},0.5}(a), \underline{F}|^{OS}_{\mathcal{R},0.5}(a)) = \frac{5-1}{5} = \frac{4}{5} = 0.8 = F(a)||^{OS}_{\mathcal{R},0.5}$$

due to Example 3.3.1.

As mentioned above, we observe that the notion of these measurements is related to the novel rough soft set model in the previous subsection. Moreover, we see that the distance measure of upper and lower approximations is a roughness measure. It is exhibited in Example 3.3.2.

4 Conclusions

The concept of fuzzy soft serial relations was defined. Then, an overlap of successor classes was proposed as a new class. We introduced a new rough soft set theory. That is, upper and lower rough approximations of a soft set were provided via all overlaps of successor classes under fuzzy soft serial relations. Then, we got that a soft set is definable if a fuzzy soft relation is reflexive and antisymmetric. Finally, we obtained that a roughness measure and a distance measure are identical.

As the novel rough soft set theory, in the future, we shall further study the notion to deal with decision-making problems.

Acknowledgments. We would like to thank the editor-in-chief and reviewers for their helpful suggestions. We would like to thank supporter organizations like Division of Mathematics and Statistics, Faculty of Science and Technology, Nakhon Sawan Rajabhat University, Thailand. We would also like to thank supporter organizations like Fuzzy Algebras and Decision-Making Problems Research Unit, Department of Mathematics, School of Science, University of Phayao, Thailand.

References

1. Pawlak, Z.: Rough sets. Int. J. Inf. Comput. Secur. **11**, 341–356 (1982)
2. Prasertpong, R., Siripitukdet, M.: Rough set models induced by serial fuzzy relations approach in semigroups. Eng. Lett. **27**, 216–225 (2019)
3. Zadeh, L.A.: Similarity relations and fuzzy orderings. Inf. Sci. **3**, 117–200 (1971)
4. Zhang, Y.H., Yuan, X.H.: Soft relation and fuzzy soft relation. In: Cao, B.Y., Nasseri, H. (eds) Fuzzy Information & Engineering and Operations Re-search & Management. Advances in Intelligent Systems and Computing, vol 211. Springer, Berlin, Heidelberg (2014)
5. Zadeh, L.A.: Fuzzy sets. Inf. Control **8**, 338–353 (1965)
6. Wu, W.Z., Mi, J.S., Zhang, W.X.: Generalized fuzzy rough sets. Inf. Sci. **151**, 263–282 (2003)
7. Chakraborty, M.K., Sarkar, S.: Fuzzy antisymmetry and order. Fuzzy Sets Syst. **21**, 169–182 (1987)
8. Molodtsov, D.: Soft set theory-first results. Comput. Math. Appl. **37**, 19–31 (1999)
9. Ali, M.I., Feng, F., Liu, X.Y., Min, W.K., Shabir, M.: On some new operations in soft set theory. Comput. Math. Appl. **57**, 1547–1553 (2009)
10. Maji, P.K., Biswas, R., Roy, A.R.: Fuzzy soft sets. Journal of Fuzzy Mathematics **9**, 589–602 (2001)
11. Marczewski, E., Steinhaus, H.: On a certain distance of sets and the corresponding distance of functions. Colloq. Math. **6**, 319–327 (1958)

Helmet Detection System for Motorcycle Riders with Explainable Artificial Intelligence Using Convolutional Neural Network and Grad-CAM

Suradej Intagorn[1], Suriya Pinitkan[1(✉)], Mathuros Panmuang[2], and Chonnikarn Rodmorn[3]

[1] Department of Mathematics, Statistics, and Computer Science, Faculty of Liberal Arts and Science, Kasetsart University, Kamphaeng Saen Campus, Nakhon Pathom, Thailand
suriya.p@ku.th
[2] Department of Educational Technology and Communications, Faculty of Technical Education, Rajamangala University of Technology, Thanyaburi, Pathum Thani, Thailand
[3] Department of Applied Statistics, Faculty of Applied Science, King Mongkut's University of Technology North Bangkok, Bangkok, Thailand

Abstract. Motorcycle accidents are one of the most common causes of injury and death in road users. This research has applied convolutional neural network (CNN) and explainable AI to detect motorcyclist without helmet and explain why CNN made that decision. The concept is based on deep learning and CNN principles applied to automatically detect motorcycle riders without helmet from images using three baseline classifiers: support vector machine, random forest and logistic regression to compare with deep convolutional neural network and measure accuracy with accuracy and F1-Score. The results revealed that CNN's F1-Score was 0.8326, which was the highest among all predictive models.

Keywords: Helmet · Explainable AI · Convolutional neural network

1 Introduction

Road traffic accidents are a serious problem faced by all countries, especially in urban areas where traffic congestion is a major cause of injury and loss of life and property. Motorcycle accidents are among the most common causes of injury and death among motorcyclists [1] According to the WHO 2018 report, Thailand has the highest road fatality rate in Southeast Asia at 32.7 per 100,000 population [2] This is mainly due to motorcyclists not wearing helmets and violating road signs or signals. This cause can be controlled or prevented if government agencies are strict and have systems that can be used to help detect offenders.

Currently, there are work to install warning signs and CCTV cameras around urban areas, especially in Bangkok where there are more than 60,000 CCTV cameras and the goal in the future will increase to 200,000 [3] However, no system has been developed that can access CCTV images for processing in various fields, including detecting offenders without helmets. Therefore, preventive and corrective actions should be taken. One way

O. Surinta and K. Kam Fung Yuen (Eds.): MIWAI 2022, LNAI 13651, pp. 40–51, 2022.
https://doi.org/10.1007/978-3-031-20992-5_4

to prevent and help reduce the rate of injuries and fatalities of motorcyclists is to wear a helmet while riding or riding a motorcycle. It can be seen that wearing a helmet is an effective way to reduce mortality and reduce the likelihood of head injury. According to research on the system for identifying the use of a helmet using the YOLO V5 and V3 technique, the improved algorithm's detection accuracy increased by 2.44% with the same detection rate as compared to the traditional YOLO V3 in the test set. The development of this model will improve helmet detection and guarantee safe building, which has significant practical implications. [4] From the YOLO V5 experiment findings, YOLOv5s can detect objects at an average speed of 110 frames per second. Meet all real-time detection demands. The mAP of YOLOv5x reaches 94.7% using the trainable target detector's pre-training weight, demonstrating the potency of the helmet detection-based YOLOv5. [5] Other image processing methods will be used in this study, though, to get distinct outcomes.

Based on the aforementioned problems, this research applied Image Processing techniques to process images and applied Deep Learning and Convolution Neural Network (CNN) techniques. CNN, despite its good performance, has a complex internal structure and cannot be understood by humans. Thus, this research has applied the principles of Explainable AI to help machine learning users understand the reasons why the system makes such predictions, especially when the prediction system fails. The approaches utilized are aimed at allowing the machine to learn and recognize features so that it can react quickly when it discovers someone who is not wearing a helmet and alerts the appropriate authorities in real time. As a result, this research will benefit law enforcement and reduce accidents to some extent.

2   Related Works

2.1   Helmet Detection

Motorcycle helmetless detection system research more studies are available. Since the YOLO family of algorithms, which have extremely high precision and speed, have been employed in several scene detection tasks, the majority of them are utilizing the YOLO technique. We suggest a safety helmet detection technique to create a digital safety helmet monitoring system, similar to the work of Zhou, Zhao, and Nie [5], who used a YOLOv5 model with various parameters for training and testing. The comparison and analysis of the four models. According to experimental findings, YOLOv5s's average detection speed is 110 FPS. Meet all real-time detection criteria in full. The mAP of YOLOv5x reaches 94.7% using the trainable target detector's pre-training weight, demonstrating the potency of the helmet detection-based YOLOv5. According to Dasgupta, Bandyo-padhyay, and Chatterji's research [1], CNN approaches are also employed for detection. The foundation for identifying motorcycle riders who don't wear helmets is suggested in this research. The state-of-the-art method for object recognition, YOLO model, and its incremental version, YOLOv3, are used in the proposed approach's initial step to detect motorbike riders. A Convolutional Neural Network (CNN) based architecture has been suggested for the second stage of motorbike rider helmet recognition. In compared to other CNN-based techniques, the suggested model's evaluation on traffic recordings yielded encouraging results.

2.2 Deep Learning and Convolution Neural Network

Today, neural networks are employed in a variety of applications because they provide the notion of quick learning and can also enable deep learning approaches to reach the best validity through machine training. Based on research by Stefanie, Oliver and Frieder [6] who studied machine learning to achieve rapid classification using neural network techniques to classify Speech Recognition and Car Driving Maneuvers. In addition, Traore, Kamsu-Foguem and Tangara [7] also presented applications of deep convolution neural network (CNN) for image recognition. The results showed that on future microscopes, the categorization process could be integrated into a mobile computing solution. In pathogens diagnosis, CNN can increase the accuracy of hand-tuned feature extraction, implying some human errors. With 200 Vibrio cholera photos and 200 Plasmodium falciparum images for the training dataset and 80 images for testing data, the CNN model obtained a classification accuracy of 94%. Based on the concepts of Deep Learning and CNN in this research, image processing was applied to detect behavior of non-helmeted motorcyclists.

2.3 Histograms of Oriented Gradient (HOG)

HOG is represented by Dalal and Triggs [8]. It is often used in object detection and classification problems. HOG calculates the magnitude and gradient vector for each pixel, then generates a histogram for further classification features. HOG is used in a number of problems, such as its use as an extraction feature for the problem of classifying rice types in [9].

2.4 Object Detection

Detecting the behavior of non-helmet motorcyclists rely on the principle of Object Detection, since the motorcyclist is one of the objects in the image. Object Detection is a computer technology that uses the principles of Computer Vision and Image Processing used in AI (Artificial Intelligence) to detect a specific type of object. In general, the objective of Object Detection is at finding and classifying actual items in a single image and labeling them with rectangles to demonstrate the certainty of their existence. [10] A large number of studies have now applied the principles of Object Detection to detect objects such as research by Thipsanthia, Chamchong and Songram [11] that have applied the YOLOv3 technique to detecting and recognizing Thai traffic signs in real-time environments. The dataset was designed and distributed for existing traffic detection and recognition. With 50 classes of road signs and 200 badges in each class, a total of 9,357 images are compared across two architectures (YOLOv3 and YOLOv3 Tiny). The experiment demonstrates that YOLOv3's mean average precision (mAP) is better than YOLOv3 Tiny's (80.84%), while YOLOv3's speed is marginally better than YOLOv3's.

2.5 Convolutional Neural Network

Convolutional Neural Network simulates the human vision of space in small parts and merges groups of spaces together to see what is being seen. An application of CNN to image classification found that if able to greatly enhance many CNN models On ImageNet, for example, improve ResNet-50's top-1 validation accuracy from 75.3% to 79.29%. Therefore, if it is improved image classification accuracy leads to improved transfer learning performance in other application domains such as object identification and semantic segmentation, according to the researchers [12]. In addition, Deep Convolutional Neural Networks were used to classify rice cultivars using Image Classification techniques. Fifteen hundred rice cultivars were chosen for the experiment in the photographic separation of paddy cultivars, and three Classification Algorithms methodologies were employed to compare classification efficiency and alter parameters. The results of the experiments and testing of the model performance showed that the VGG16 model had the highest accuracy of 85% [13]. Therefore, the research had to adjust various parameters to be appropriate and able to recognize the image as accurately as possible.

2.6 Explainable AI

Explainable AI is a concept that requires the machine to have a process of understanding so that the result can be explained and understood. In other words, they want people to understand the idea of a machine, or for a machine to think and explain human language. According to research by Pawar, O'Shea, Rea and O'Reilly [14], Explainable AI (XAI) is a field where strategies are created to explain AI system predictions and has applied XAI to employ to analyze and diagnose health data, as well as a potential approach for establishing responsibility. In the field of healthcare, transparency, outcome tracing, and model improvement are all important.

2.7 Grad-CAM

Grad-CAM: is to visualize what the model sees, such as checking the grain of rice to see what type of rice it is. The model serves to make predictions, which, in principle, is necessary to understand where the model is considering the correct point or not. Grad-CAM computes a heat-map $g \in R^{nxm}$ It shows which parts of the input image are highlighted $x \in R^{NxM}$ have mostly influenced the classifier score in favor of the class c (upper-case letters indicate sizes that are larger than lowercase one). Let y_c denote the score the class c and ak $\in R^{nxm}$, $k = 1,...K$, the activation maps matching to the last convolutional layer's k-th filter. A weighted average of a^k, $k = 1,...K$, is used to establish the Grad-CAM he class c. followed by a ReLU activation: [15]

$$g_c = ReLU\left(\sum_k \alpha_c^k \, a^k\right), \tag{1}$$

where the importance weights $\{\alpha_c^k\}$ are defined as the average derivatives of y_c with respect to each pixel (i,j) in the activation a^k:

$$\alpha_c^k = \frac{1}{nm} \sum_i \sum_j \frac{\partial y_c}{\partial a^k(i,j)} \tag{2}$$

Several researches uses Grad-CAM to verify results and make the model more interpretable such as breast cancer classification [16].

3 Methodology

3.1 Data Collection and Preprocessing

The data was collected in 24 video files from mobile phone cameras from the roadside. Each video file has a different camera angle and location. The video file is preprocessed into an image file as shown in Fig. 1 in the first row. These video files were then pre-processed using a ready-made library called ImageAI for object detection of people and motorcycles as shown in Fig. 1 in the second row. The object detection model is YOLOv3. Two custom object classes are person and motorcycle. Then automatically crop the image of the motorcyclist. If there is more than one motorcyclist in the picture, the system will extract the image according to the number of riders. The image of the motorcyclist that has been extracted is labeled Helmet, NoHelmet or UnDetermined i.e. wearing a helmet, not wearing a helmet and unable to tell. Preprocessing from ImageAI sometimes has extraction errors, i.e., motorcyclist's head is not visible, so we define them as the UnDetermined class.

| Helmet | NoHelmet | UnDetermined |

Fig. 1. Sample images in the dataset of different classes.

In the video file, the number of helmet-wearers outnumbered the non-wearers, but in this dataset, the number of riders in the 2 classes was chosen to be approximately same. Each rider is randomly selected 1–3 images at different distances and angles.

This data is randomly divided into two parts, the training set and the test set. The training set will be 85% of the total data and the test set to 15% of the total data set. Training set is used to teach the classifier while test set is used to test the performance of the classifier Table 1 summarizes the amount of data in each class.

Table 1. The amount of images in the dataset.

Class	Training set (85%)	Test set (15%)	Total (100%)
Helmet	1097	194	1291
NoHelmet	1077	191	1268
UnDetermined	728	129	857

3.2 Deep Convolution Neural Network

Training deep neural network from scratch requires large amounts of data to avoid overfitting problem which may not be applicable to our small dataset [17]. Thus, we use a technique called transfer learning which borrows some layers from well-trained deep neural network such as [18]. The primary purpose of transfer learning is to reduce the amount of learning parameters, which in turn reduces the amount of learning data that doesn't cause overfitting.

The borrowed layers are from a CNN called VGG16 [18]. Our network borrows the first layer to the Block5_pool layer which are convolution and pulling layers from VGG16. The main purpose of this layer set is to extract the visual features of images. In-depth details of VGG16 can be found in [18].

We used a total of two dense layers, 256 neurons each, with a ReLU (Rectified Linear Unit) activation function and a L1 regularization = 0.001. The first dropout layer is added between these two dense layers with a probability of drop out = 0.5. The regularization and dropout layer are used to reduce overfitting. Parameters of these dense layers are optimized from the training set. The main purpose of these layers is to combine visual features extracted from the previous layer with appropriate weights and be able to learn nonlinear decision boundaries for helmet detection.

The last part is also dense layer, but the activation function is softmax. The purpose of this layer is to predict the probabilities in each category. The final output is the class with the highest probability. This layer has the same number of neurons as the image class, which is 3 (Helmet, NoHelmet and UnDetermined). The deep neural network structure is visualized by using Keras utility as shown in Fig. 2.

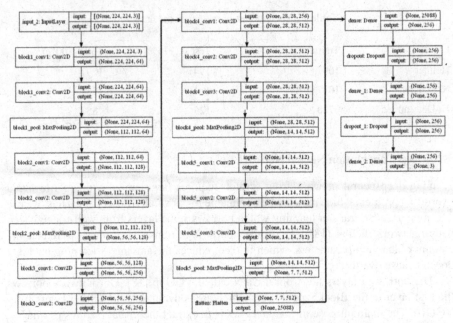

Fig. 2. The deep neural network structure: The layers in the first and second columns are pretrained layers from VGG16. The layers in the third column are trained by the training set detailed in Table 1.

4 Experiment Setup and Results

We benchmark classifiers based on accuracy and macro f1-score metrics, with the deep convolutional neural network compared to three baselines: support vector machine, random forest and logistic regression. The data for each class used is relatively balanced, except for UnDetermined which is lower than the other two classes. The data used for testing were data from the test set which was 15% of the total data set.

The deep convolutional neural network in Fig. 2 uses pretrained layers from VGG16 [18] for feature extraction and trains only the classification layers. Therefore, the image will be resized to 224x224 due to make it compatible with the dimensions of VGG16.

The learning curve of the CNN model are shown in Fig. 3 and Fig. 4

All preprocessing steps are same for both the proposed model and baseline except size of image and the feature extraction. The algorithm for feature extraction of all baselines is Histograms of Oriented Gradient (HOG) descriptors, images for baselines are resized to 64x128 (64 pixels wide and 128 pixels tall) according to the original paper [8]. The hyper parameters for the other HOGs are also same as the default detector in [8] (9 orientation bins 16×16pixel blocks of four 8×8pixel cells). Each image is converted to a HOG feature vector of size 3780.

All baseline classifiers and evaluations are used from the sklearn library [19]. All hyper parameters use the default library value except random_state which is all set to 0 for reproducible result (Tables 4, 5, and 6).

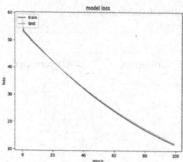
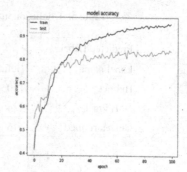

Fig. 3. The loss curve of the CNN model

Fig. 4. The accuracy curve of the CNN model

Table 2. Accuracy, precision, recall and F-Score of classifiers.

Classifiers	Accuracy	Precision	Recall	F-Score
Deep Convolutional Network	**0.8365**	**0.831**	**0.8347**	**0.8326**
Logistic Regression	0.6945	0.6982	0.6997	0.6982
Support Vector Machine	0.7645	0.7748	0.7656	0.7695
Random Forest	0.6439	0.6872	0.6284	0.6417

Table 3. Confusion matrix of deep convolutional network.

	Predicted Label		
True Label	Label name	Helmet	NoHelmet	UnDetermined
	Helmet	169	14	11
	NoHelmet	17	155	19
	UnDetermined	5	18	106

Table 4. Confusion matrix of logistic regression.

	Predicted Label		
True Label	Label name	Helmet	NoHelmet	UnDetermined
	Helmet	140	43	11
	NoHelmet	46	121	24
	UnDetermined	8	25	96

Table 5. Confusion matrix of support vector machine.

	Predicted Label			
True	Label name	Helmet	NoHelmet	UnDetermined
Label	Helmet	150	38	6
	NoHelmet	34	143	14
	UnDetermined	5	24	100

Table 6. Confusion matrix of random forest.

	Predicted Label			
True	Label name	Helmet	NoHelmet	UnDetermined
Label	Helmet	140	51	3
	NoHelmet	56	126	9
	UnDetermined	22	42	65

Table 2 summarizes the accuracy and f1score of each classifiers, with Deep convolutional neural network predicting the most accurate: accuracy = 0.8365 and F1-score = 0.8326, SVM is the highest-performing baseline for, with accuracy = 0.7645 and F1-score = 0.7695.

The confusion matrix shows the number of images predicted in each class for each true label. For example, the first row in the second table states that there are 194 images in the Helmet class in the test set (169 + 14 + 11). The Deep Convolutional Neural Network (CNN) correctly predicted 169 images to Helmet class, but incorrectly predicted 14 images to NoHelmet class and 11 images to UnDetermined class. Therefore, the values on the diagonal line are the number of images correctly predicted and the values where the other position is guessing wrong. The values in Table 3 show that the number of Helmet images that CNN incorrectly predict as NoHelmet and Undertermined are approximately same which are 14 and 11 respectively. The result of NoHelmet images is same tendency with Helmet images. For UnDetermined images, the number of incorrect prediction as NoHelmet is more than as Helmet approximately three times which are 18 and 5 respectively.

4.1 Visualization and Explainable AI

Although predictive accuracy is one of the most important aspects of classifiers, it is also important to understand why classifiers make such decisions. Accuracy = 0.8326 cannot be said whether the classifiers' decisions are reasonable or not. Although there are previous works about automated helmet detection using CNN such as [1], their system cannot give explanation about why their system make such decisions.

Deep convolutional network and three baselines make decisions based on high dimensional features that are difficult to understand for humans. In practical implementation, if we find that the classifier is making the wrong decision, the system should be able to tell the reason why it made that decision so that the developer can provide additional tutorial examples in case the decision is wrong.

Deep convolutional neural network, in addition to high accuracy, can also perform visualization, such as an algorithm called Grad-Cam [20] The result of the algorithm is to give numbers representing the importance of each pixel for predicted class. We visualize these number of those pixels in a heatmap and overlay on the input image.

Grad-Cam results should be consistent with human understanding. For example, to determine whether a helmet is being worn or not, the numbers representing importance around the helmet should be high. The Jet colormap technique for color representation of the weight numbers. Therefore, the important regions that CNN focus in the image has highlighted in red tint (Table 7).

Table 7. Grad-cam visualization for deep convolutional neural network.

True Label	Label name	Predicted Label		
		Helmet	NoHelmet	UnDetermined
	Helmet			
	NoHelmet			
	UnDetermined			

In the first row and first column, CNN puts the correct highlight on the helmet area. In the second row and first column, CNN highlight around head area. However, the motorcyclist worn a cap, not a helmet, so the prediction is incorrect. In the third row and first column, we cannot see the head of the riders, so it is labeled as UnDetermined, but CNN probably assumed that the storage box was a helmet and therefore predicted it as a Helmet. Therefore, CNN in this experiment accurately focuses on the helmet pixels for most images in the Helmet class, but still confuses objects with helmet-like ones, such as caps and motorcycle trunks. Therefore, adding these examples, such as a person wearing a cap, to the training set may improve accuracy in these cases.

Predicting the NoHelmet class, CNN correctly focus the head without helmet area. However, many of the images show that CNN looked at not just the head but also the rider's skin, possibly because in this dataset, the non-helmeted photos tend to be wearing short sleeves and shorts. It seems that CNN instead of just making predictions based on the riders' head without helmet, is also examining the skin pixel in the arms and legs. Therefore, although the prediction accuracy of class NoHelmet is 81% (155/(17 + 155 + 19)), but qualitatively, we find that CNN's pixel focus is still inaccurate. Therefore, adding the samples, for example, a person wearing a helmet but wearing a short sleeve shirt and shorts to the class helmet, for example, should help CNN to better focus in the NoHelmet images.

In UnDetermined class, since the the rider's head is not visible, CNN focuses on other parts of the image such as the bike or the scene. If there is an item close to the helmet, the total weight of the neuron used to predict the Helmet class will be higher, causing the prediction to be the Helmet class instead such as the example in the third row and first column.

5   Conclusion

Motorcycle accidents are one of the most common causes of injury and death in road users. This is mainly due to motorcyclists not wearing helmets and violating traffic signs or signals. Based on the aforementioned problems, this research has applied Convolution Neural Network (CNN) and Grad-Cam techniques. Three baseline classifiers have been used which are support vector machine, random forest and logistic regression to compare with deep convolutional neural network. The evaluation metrics are accuracy and F1-Score. The results of the research revealed that CNN's F1-Score = 0.8326, Logistic Regression = 0.6989, Support Vector Machine = 0.7695 and Random Forest = 0.6417. The highest predictive model accuracy was CNN. Grad-CAM is also used to determined where the CNN is looking in the input image which makes the model more interpretable.

References

1. Dasgupta, M., Bandyopadhyay, O., Chatterji, S.: Automated helmet detection for multiple motorcycle riders using CNN. In: Conference on Information and Communication Technology (CICT), pp.1–4. IEEE, Banff, AB, Canada (2019)
2. World Health Organization: Global status report on road safety 2018. Geneva, France (2018)
3. Bangkok Metropolitan Administration (BMA): Project for studying and analyzing the enterprise architecture in information technology for working processes according to the main mission of Bangkok, phase 1. BMA, Bangkok (2021)
4. Wu, F., Jin, G., Gao, M., HE, Z., and Yang, Y.: Helmet detection based on improved YOLO V3 deep model. In: 2019 IEEE 16th International Conference on Networking, Sensing and Control (ICNSC), pp. 363–368. IEEE, Banff, AB, Canada (2019)
5. Zhou, F., Zhao, H., and Nie, Z.: Safety helmet detection based on YOLOv5, In: 2021 IEEE International Conference on Power Electronics, Computer Applications (ICPECA), pp. 6–11. IEEE, Shenyang, China (2021)

6. Krause, S., Otto, O., Stolzenburg, F.: Fast Classification Learning with Neural Networks and Conceptors for Speech Recognition and Car Driving Maneuvers. In: Chomphuwiset, P., Kim, J., Pawara, P. (eds.) MIWAI 2021. LNCS (LNAI), vol. 12832, pp. 45–57. Springer, Cham (2021). https://doi.org/10.1007/978-3-030-80253-0_5

7. Traore, B.B., Kamsu-Foguem, B., Tangara, F.: Deep convolution neural network for image recognition. Eco. Inform. **48**, 257–268 (2018)

8. Dalal, N., Triggs, B.: Histograms of oriented gradients for human detection. In: 2005 IEEE computer society conference on computer vision and pattern recognition (CVPR'05). vol. 1, pp. 886–893. Ieee (2005)

9. Nguyen-Quoc, H., Hoang, V.T.: Rice seed image classifiation based on hog descriptor with missing values imputation. Telkomnika **18**(4), 1897–1903 (2020)

10. Zhao, Z.-Q., Zheng, P., Xu, S.-T., Wu, X.: Object detection with deep learning: a review. IEEE Trans. Neural Netw. Learn. Sys. **30**(11), 3212–3232 (2019)

11. Thipsanthia, P., Chamchong, R., Songram, P.: Road Sign Detection and Recognition of Thai Traffic Based on YOLOv3. In: Chamchong, R., Wong, K.W. (eds.) MIWAI 2019. LNCS (LNAI), vol. 11909, pp. 271–279. Springer, Cham (2019). https://doi.org/10.1007/978-3-030-33709-4_25

12. He, T., Zhang, Z., Zhang, H., Zhang, Z., Xie, J., Li, M.: Bag of tricks for image classification with convolutional neural networks. In: Proceedings of the IEEE/CVF Conference on Computer Vision and Pattern Recognition (CVPR), California, pp. 558–567 (2019)

13. Panmuang, M., Rodmorn, C., Pinitkan, S.: Image processing for classification of rice varieties with deep convolutional neural networks. In: 16th International Joint Symposium on Artificial Intelligence and Natural Language Processing (iSAI-NLP), pp. 1–6, Ayutthaya, Thailand (2021)

14. Pawar, U., O'Shea, D., Rea, S., and O'Reilly, R.: Explainable AI in Healthcare. In: International Conference on Cyber Situational Awareness, Data Analytics and Assessment (CyberSA), 1–2 Dublin, Ireland (2020)

15. Morbidelli, P., Carrera, D., Rossi, B., Fragneto, P., and Boracchi, G.: Augmented Grad-CAM: Heat-maps super resolution through augmentation. In: IEEE International Conference on Acoustics, Speech and Signal Processing (ICASSP), pp. 4067–4071, Barcelona, Spain (2020)

16. Masud, M., Eldin Rashed, A.E., Hossain, M.S.: Convolutional neural network-based models for diagnosis of breast cancer. Neural Computing and Applications pp. 1–12 (2020)

17. Xia, S., et al.: Transferring ensemble representations using deep convolutional neural networks for small-scale image classifiation. IEEE Access **7**, 168175–168186 (2019)

18. Simonyan, K., Zisserman, A.: Very deep convolutional networks for large-scale image recognition. arXiv preprint arXiv:1409.1556 (2014)

19. Pedregosa, F., et al.: Scikit-learn: machine learning in python. J. Mach. Learn. Res. **12**, 2825–2830 (2011)

20. Selvaraju, R.R., Cogswell, M., Das, A., Vedantam, R., Parikh, D., Batra, D.: Gradcam: visual explanations from deep networks via gradient-based localization. In: Proceedings of the IEEE international conference on computer vision. pp. 618–626 (2017)

Hierarchical Human Activity Recognition Based on Smartwatch Sensors Using Branch Convolutional Neural Networks

Narit Hnoohom[1] , Nagorn Maitrichit[1] , Sakorn Mekruksavanich[2] ,
and Anuchit Jitpattanakul[3(✉)]

[1] Image, Information and Intelligence Laboratory, Department of Computer Engineering,
Faculty of Engineering, Mahidol University, Nakorn Pathom, Thailand
`narit.hno@mahidol.ac.th, nagorn.mat@student.mahidol.ac.th`
[2] Department of Computer Engineering, School of Information and Communication
Technology, University of Phayao, Phayao, Thailand
`sakorn.me@up.ac.th`
[3] Intelligent and Nonlinear Dynamic Innovations Research Center, Department of Mathematics,
Faculty of Applied Science, King Mongkut's University of Technology North Bangkok,
Bangkok, Thailand
`anuchit.j@sci.kmutnb.ac.th`

Abstract. Human activity recognition (HAR) has become a popular research topic in artificial intelligence thanks to the development of smart wearable devices. The main goal of human activity recognition is to efficiently recognize human behavior based on available data sources such as videos and images, including sensory data from wearable devices. Recently, HAR research has achieved promising results using learning-based approaches, especially deep learning methods. However, the need for high performance is still an open problem for researchers proposing new methods. In this work, we investigated the improvement of HAR by hierarchical classification based on smartwatch sensors using deep learning (DL) methods. To achieve the research goal, we introduced branch convolutional neural networks (B-CNNs) to accurately recognize human activities hierarchically and compared them with baseline models. To evaluate the deep learning models, we used a complex HAR benchmark dataset called WISDM-HARB dataset that collects smartwatch sensor data from 18 physical activities. The experimental results showed that the B-CNNs outperformed the baseline convolutional neural network (CNN) models when the hierarchical connection between classes was not considered. Moreover, the results confirmed that branch CNNs with class hierarchy improved the recognition performance with the highest accuracy of 95.84%.

Keywords: Deep learning · Branch convolutional neural network · Class hierarchy · Hierarchical human activity recognition

1 Introduction

Human activity recognition has become popular in artificial intelligence. Recently, promising results in HAR research have led to several applications in healthcare and

O. Surinta and K. Kam Fung Yuen (Eds.): MIWAI 2022, LNAI 13651, pp. 52–60, 2022.
https://doi.org/10.1007/978-3-031-20992-5_5

other related fields, such as tracking athletic performance, monitoring rehabilitation, and detecting misbehavior. Advances in activity data collection and the development of smart wearables have accelerated progress in HAR research as more activity data become available. Smartphones and smartwatches are two convenient wearable devices that people worldwide use daily and contain sensors such as gyroscopes, accelerometers, and magnetometers.

In the study on HAR during the past decade, machine learning (ML) and DL methods have been suggested as methods that can build on top of each other. However, ML has limitations in feature extraction since it depends on human experts to find characteristic features from raw sensor data. The automatic feature extraction of DL approaches has solved this limitation by using convolutional operators as the first process of recognition models.

From the literature, deep learning approaches for HAR have been developed based on CNNs and long short-term memory neural networks. Some models have inspired new architectures proposed for computer vision, image processing, and natural language processing research, such as InceptionTime, Temporal Transformer, and ResNet. However, the recognition performance of these models was limited because the class hierarchy of human activities was unknown.

Activity recognition models use CNNs and one-hot vectors for activity labels. Traditional activity recognition models ignore cross-activity connections because one-hot encoding addresses each class independently. Nevertheless, there are hierarchical connections between actual activities, and these connections are based on similarities in sensor data [1, 2].

This work focuses on the hierarchical recognition of human activities with branched convolutional neural networks based on smartwatch sensor data. We introduced a deep learning model inspired by VGG architecture, which has proven effective in image classification. To evaluate how well the proposed hierarchical model performs, we used a public benchmark dataset consisting of smartwatch sensor data for 18 complex human activities. We conducted experiments to find out the effects of the class hierarchy. The experimental results showed that the branched convolutional neural networks improved the recognition performance of HAR.

The remaining parts of this paper are divided into five sections. Section 2 presents the current work that is of importance. Section 3 describes the details of the branch convolutional neural network model used. Section 4 details our experimental results. Section 5 describes conclusions and challenging future works.

2 Related Works

DL is a popular technique to overcome the limitations of traditional ML models as DL can automatically extract features, which means less human effort. Several DL models for HAR have been presented, which provided promising results and innovative learning methods. Most of the proposed models are based on CNNs.

The development of a CNN model in [3] allows the direct acquisition of raw 3D accelerometer data without requiring complicated pretreatment. Preprocessing was performed using the sliding window approach, and the accelerometer data were normalized.

According to the author's suggestion, the model was validated using the WISDM dataset as a reference. The proposed model achieved high accuracy while keeping the computational cost minimum. A multi-channel CNN was proposed as a solution to the difficulty of activity recognition within the framework of physical activity programs [4]. Sixteen Otago training activities were self-collected in this experiment. Each sensor was connected to its own CNN channel to collect raw inertia data for the different activities. The results showed that combining numerous sensors can yield better results than one alone.

In [5], a deep HAR model is presented that transforms motion sensor data into spectral images. Each CNN model adopts the image sequences generated by the accelerometer and gyroscope. The final class of human activity is then predicted using the combined results of the trained CNNs. In this experiment, the RWHAR dataset was used. There were a total of eight activities. The proposed model could perform static and dynamic activities with F-scores of 0.78 and 0.87, respectively. This model could process image input directly, as claimed by the authors. Although the model's generalization was promising, the accuracy was not good compared to other benchmark DL models. In [6], three strategies for exploiting the temporal information contained in a set of windows are discussed. In the first strategy, the average of the windows is computed, which is then fed into the CNN model. The sequence of the windows is fed to a competing CNN, which then determines the activity class based on the averages in the second strategy. The third and final strategy is very similar to the second strategy.

Nevertheless, the final prediction is made by combining the learned features using a global average pooling layer. It has been shown that the accuracy of activity detection can be improved by using an ensemble of CNNs instead of a single CNN classifier. Zhu et al. [7] presented a CNN-based framework for HAR using multiple smartphone-based sensors. The proposed framework consisted of an ensemble of two different CNN models. The results of each CNN model were integrated using weighted voting to predict unidentified activities. The model achieved an accuracy of 0.962%. Zehra et al. [8] presented an ensemble model combining three different CNN models. The performance of the ensemble model outperformed each CNN model. This experiment shows the generalizability of the ensemble learning model as it increases the learning effect of the weak learner and strengthens the model as a whole. In [9], they proposed a CNN model with two channels for activity recognition. The proposed model improved the recognition accuracy by using frequency and power features derived from sensor signals. A UCI-HAR dataset was used to validate the model, which yielded an accuracy of 0.953. The drawback of this approach was that certain features needed to be extracted to improve the activity detection based on sensor data. The performance of the CNN model was enhanced by including a module to measure the importance of feature attention [10]. Three acceleration channels are concurrent to three convolutional layers with varied filter widths for local feature extraction. The model was validated using a WISDM dataset, which achieved an accuracy of 0.964%.

3 The Sensor-Based HAR Framework

This study proposed a sensor-based HAR framework consisting of four primary processes: data acquisition, pre-processing, data generation, and model training and classification, as shown in Fig. 1.

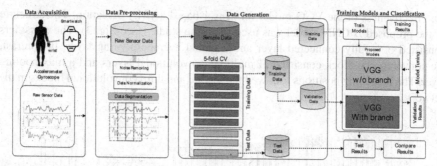

Fig. 1. The HAR framework was developed using sensors from smartwatches and employed in this work.

3.1 WISDM-HARB Dataset

In this study, we used data from the WISDM dataset and the UCI repository, which contains raw sensor data from multiple smartphones (Samsung Galaxy S5 and Google Nexus 5/5X) and data from a smartwatch (LG G Watch).

Smartwatch-based sensor data were collected from 51 subjects on their dominant hand for 18 different types of physical activities that occur in daily life. Each activity was performed independently for 3 min at a frequency of approximately 20 Hz. This indicates that the transitions from one activity to the next were not constant but were recorded separately. The following human activities were used in this study: stair climbing, jogging, sitting, standing, typing, tooth brushing, eating a sandwich, pasta, or chips, eating soup, drinking from a cup, playing, kicking, clapping, dribbling, writing, and folding clothes.

3.2 Data Pre-processing

During data preprocessing, raw sensor data were processed by noise reduction and standardization. The preprocessed sensor data were then segmented utilizing sliding windows with a fixed width of 10 s and an overlap ratio of 50%.

3.3 Branch Convolutional Neural Network

Figure 3 shows the structure of the branch convolutional neural networks (B-CNNs). Based on a class hierarchy, the B-CNNs separate a model into several paths and arrange them, beginning with the class hierarchy's top level. Similar to conventional CNN models (see Fig. 2), the B-CNN classifies based on class values generated by the SoftMax, with each level of classification completed separately.

The branching location in the B-CNN model is represented by a convolutional block consisting of multiple convolutional layers and a pooling layer. Multiple branching patterns are feasible because the structure of a typical CNN model includes several hierarchically connected convolutional blocks.

This study used two model types: the standard CNN model and the B-CNN model. Both models were built on top of the VGG model [12]. Hasegawa et al. [13] have proved

the effectiveness of the VGG model for sensor-based activity detection. The structure
of the proposed B-CNN model was used in all the studies (see Fig. 3). The classifiers
consisted of a fully connected layer and a global average pooling layer. In contrast,
the convolutional block consisted of multiple convolutional layers and a max-pooling
layer. The branching positions followed the second and third convolutional blocks in the
network.

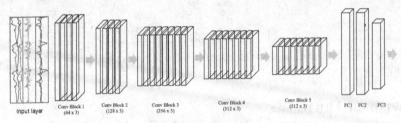

Fig. 2. Model structure of the traditional CNN model.

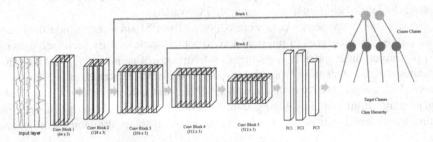

Fig. 3. Model structure of the B-CNN.

3.4 Performance Measurement Criteria

In a 5-fold cross-validation procedure, four standard evaluation metrics such as accuracy,
recall, precision, and F1-score are created to evaluate the performance of the proposed
B-CNN model. The mathematical formulas for the four metrics are given below:

$$Accuracy = \frac{TP + TN}{TP + TN + FP + FN} \tag{1}$$

$$Precision = \frac{TP}{TP + FP} \tag{2}$$

$$Recall = \frac{TP}{TP + FN} \tag{3}$$

$$F1 - score = 2 \times \frac{Precision \times Recall}{Precision + Recall} \tag{4}$$

These four metrics were used to quantify the effectiveness of HAR. The recognition was a true positive (TP) for the class under consideration and a true negative for all other courses. Misclassified sensor data may result in a false positive (FP) recognition for the class under consideration. Sensor data that should belong to another class may be misclassified, resulting in a false negative (FP) recognition of that class.

4   Experiments and Results

This section describes the experimental setup and shows the experimental results used to evaluate the baseline CNN model and the B-CNN model for HAR using smartwatch sensor data.

4.1   Experiments

In this study, all experiments were conducted on the Google Colab Pro using a Tesla V100. The Python programming (Python 3.6.9) and various libraries (Keras 2.3.1, TensorFlow 2.2.0, Scikit-Learn, Pandas 1.0.5, and Numpy 1.18.5) were used to perform the experiments. Four DL models (VGG11, VGG13, VGG16, and VGG19) were used as the CNN base models. To investigate the effects of class hierarchy, we introduced four branch CNNs (B-VGG11, B-VGG13, B-VGG16, and B-VGG19).

4.2   Experimental Results

The average F1-score and average accuracy of our proposed method compared with the baseline method are shown in Table 1. The CNN model with the VGGs is represented by four VGG models (VGG11, VGG12, VGG16, and VGG19) in the table, while the

Table 1. Performance metrics of baseline CNN models Compared with B-CNN models.

Model	Performance		
	Accuracy	Loss	F1-score
Without branch			
VGG11	94.21459% (±0.32225%)	0.33451 (±0.03307%)	94.24582% (±0.32874%)
VGG13	94.28213% (±0.30030%)	0.32312 (±0.02564%)	94.30187% (±0.3242%)
VGG16	94.82927% (±0.34160%)	0.25753 (±0.02173%)	94.83729% (±0.33920%)
VGG19	95.06570% (±0.29745%)	0.25663 (±0.02436%)	95.08818% (±0.29632%)
With branch			
B-VGG11	94.99814% (±0.26362%)	0.28716 (±0.02357%)	95.01542% (±0.26509%)
B-VGG13	95.21459% (±0.20554%)	0.27463 (±0.01788%)	95.10001% (±0.20408%)
B-VGG16	95.21459% (±0.19530%)	0.20238 (±0.01132%)	95.85986% (±0.19677%)
B-VGG19	94.21459% (±0.27056%)	0.21345 (±0.02246%)	95.68116% (±0.27193%)

B-CNN branch-added CNN model is represented by four branch VGGs (B-VGG11, B-VGG13, B-VGG16, and B-VGG19).

Table 1 shows that the branch VGGs performed better than the baseline VGG. The B-VGG16 achieved the best performance with the highest accuracy of 95.84%.

From Figs. 4 and 5, considering confusion matrices of VGG16 and B-VGG16, it can be noticed that the classification performance of B-VGG16 on eating-related activities was higher than the results of the baseline VGG16. Therefore, the results indicated that the class hierarchy strategy could improve classification performance.

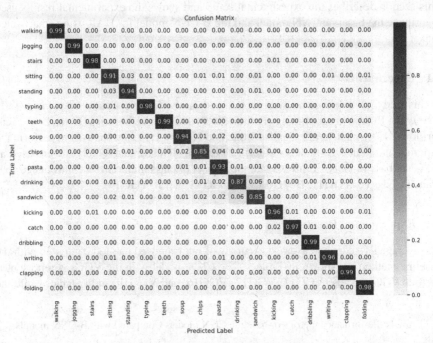

Fig. 4. A confusion matrix of the VGG16.

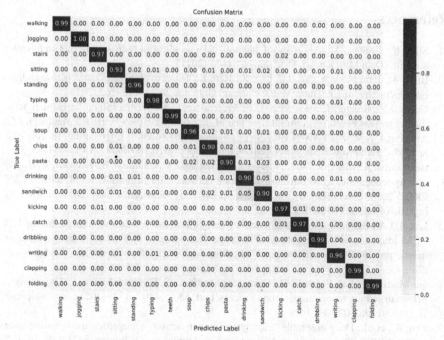

Fig. 5. A confusion matrix of the B-VGG16.

5 Conclusions

In this work, we studied hierarchical activity recognition based on smartwatch sensors. We proposed a B-CNN model to classify hierarchical human activity recognition to achieve the research goal. The B-CNN was trained with our proposed method utilizing the newly established class hierarchy. Therefore, the proposed B-CNN approach was able to classify data based on hierarchical connections between classes. According to the experimental results in Table 1, the branch VGGs achieved better performance than the baseline VGG due to the benefits of the B-CNN architecture. The results demonstrated that the proposed B-CNN model was suitable for identifying activities based on smartwatch sensors.

For future work, we plan to apply the class hierarchy strategy in other types of deep learning networks such as ResNet, Inception Time, Temporal Transformer, etcetera.

Acknowledgments. The authors gratefully acknowledge the financial support provided by the Thammasat University Research fund under the TSRI, Contract No. TUFF19/2564 and TUFF24/2565, for the project of "AI Ready City Networking in RUN", based on the RUN Digital Cluster collaboration scheme. This research project was supported by the Thailand Science Research and Innovation fund, the University of Phayao (Grant No. FF65-RIM041), and supported by National Science, Research and Innovation (NSRF), and King Mongkut's University of Technology North Bangkok, Contract No. KMUTNB-FF-66-07.

References

1. Silla, C., Freitas, A.: A survey of hierarchical classification across different application domains. Data Min. Knowl. Disc. **22**(1), 31–72 (2011)
2. Bilal, A., Jourabloo, A., Ye, M., Liu, X., Ren, L.: Do convolutional neural networks learn class hierarchy? IEEE Trans. Visual Comput. Graphics **24**(1), 152–162 (2018)
3. Coelho, Y., Rangel, L., dos Santos, F., Frizera-Neto, A., Bastos-Filho, T.: Human activity recognition based on convolutional neural network. In: Costa-Felix, R., Machado, J.C., Alvarenga, A.V. (eds.) XXVI Brazilian Congress on Biomedical Engineering. IP, vol. 70/2, pp. 247–252. Springer, Singapore (2019). https://doi.org/10.1007/978-981-13-2517-5_38
4. Bevilacqua, A., MacDonald, K., Rangarej, A., Widjaya, V., Caulfield, B., Kechadi, T.: Human activity recognition with convolutional neural networks. In: Brefeld, U., et al. (eds.) ECML PKDD 2018. LNCS (LNAI), vol. 11053, pp. 541–552. Springer, Cham (2019). https://doi.org/10.1007/978-3-030-10997-4_33
5. Lawal, I.A., Bano, S.: Deep human activity recognition using wearable sensors. In: the 12th ACM International Conference on PErvasive Technologies Related to Assistive Environments, pp. 45–48. Association for Computing Machinery, New York, NY, United States (2019)
6. Gil-Martín, M., San-Segundo, R., Fernández-Martínez, F., Ferreiros-López, J.: Time analysis in human activity recognition. Neural Process. Lett. **53**(6), 4507–4525 (2021). https://doi.org/10.1007/s11063-021-10611-w
7. Zhu, R., et al.: Deep ensemble learning for human activity recognition using smartphone. In: 2018 IEEE 23rd International Conference on Digital Signal Processing (DSP), pp. 1–5. IEEE, Shanghai, China (2018)
8. Zehra, N., Azeem, S.H., Farhan, M.: Human activity recognition through ensemble learning of multiple convolutional neural networks. In: 2021 55th Annual Conference on Information Sciences and Systems (CISS), pp. 1–5. IEEE, Baltimore, MD, USA (2021)
9. Sikder, N., Chowdhury, M.S., Arif, A.S.M., Nahid, A.-A.: Human activity recognition using multichannel convolutional neural network. In: 2019 5th International Conference on Advances in Electrical Engineering (ICAEE), pp. 560–565. IEEE, Dhaka, Bangladesh (2019)
10. Zhang, H., Xiao, Z., Wang, J.: A novel IoT-perceptive human activity recognition (HAR) approach using multihead convolutional attention. IEEE Internet Things J. **7**(2), 1072–1080 (2020)
11. Weiss, G.M., Yoneda, K., Hayajneh, T.: Smartphone and smartwatch-based biometrics using activities of daily living. IEEE Access **7**, 133190–133202 (2019)
12. Simonyan, K., Zisserman, A.: Very deep convolutional networks for large-scale image recognition. In: the 3rd International Conference on Learning Representations (ICLR), pp. 1–14. San Diego, CA, USA (2015)
13. Hasegawa, T., Koshino, M.: Representation learning by convolutional neural network for smartphone sensor based activity recognition. In: the 2019 2nd International Conference on Computational Intelligence and Intelligent Systems, pp. 99–104 (2019)

Improving Predictive Model to Prevent Students' Dropout in Higher Education Using Majority Voting and Data Mining Techniques

Pratya Nuankaew[1] , Patchara Nasa-Ngium[2] , and Wongpanya S. Nuankaew[2(✉)]

[1] University of Phayao, Phayao 56000, Thailand
[2] Rajabhat Maha Sarakham University, Maha Sarakham 44000, Thailand
wongpanya.nu@rmu.ac.th

Abstract. The primary objective of this research was to improve the predictive model to prevent dropouts among university students. There were two secondary research objectives: (1) to study the context and improve the student dropout prevention model and (2) to compare the past university student dropout models. The research population was students in the Business Computer Department at the School of Information and Communication Technology, University of Phayao. A research tool was a model development process using majority voting and data mining techniques. The results showed that the model for predicting dropout prevention among university students was more effective. The model obtained was 83.62% accurate with 3-ensemble majority voting, including Generalized Linear Model (GLMs), Neural Network (NN), and Decision Tree (DT). The F1-Score for the dropped and scheduled graduation class was very high with 99.57% and 81.82%. The model derived from this research improved efficiency and predicted student dropout at the university level better than the previous model. Therefore, in future curriculum improvements, method matter issues that influence the dropout of university students should be considered.

Keywords: Dropout preventing · Educational data mining · Majority voting · Students dropout model · University dropout

1 Introduction

A university is an educational institution that allows students to learn to develop themselves into opportunities and career possibilities in the future. The university is responsible for producing quality graduates with the skills and potential to apply the knowledge gained and develop them appropriately for their prospective careers. In any case, the potential and learning styles of students at universities affect students' learning achievement. Numerous studies have compiled a list of phenomena that affect tertiary students who unexpectedly drop out of the education system by various factors: academic exhaustion, satisfaction with education, willingness to dropout, academic achievement performance, funding, and disabilities [1–4]. A fundamental problem discovered by many studies is that most university students have dropout problems in their first year

© The Author(s), under exclusive license to Springer Nature Switzerland AG 2022
O. Surinta and K. Kam Fung Yuen (Eds.): MIWAI 2022, LNAI 13651, pp. 61–72, 2022.
https://doi.org/10.1007/978-3-031-20992-5_6

of study [1, 2, 5]. Additionally, dropout issues were highlighted, including data scientists and artificial intelligence. The use of educational data mining and machine learning to encounter solutions for student dropouts has become a research area that combines scientific and social science knowledge [2, 6–8]. The dropout problem among students at all educational levels is an academic and social waste that educators and scientists should not pass on.

Researchers in this research, who are responsible for curricula management at the University of Phayao, face the problem of dropouts among many students. Therefore, it is necessary to solve the problem of dropouts among university students. In the past, Pratya Nuankaew [9] has developed models using decision tree classification techniques. He found that the developed model had an accuracy of 87.21%, predicting two aspects of learning achievement. That research also showed weaknesses with the development of only one modeling technique. Subsequently, Nuankaew et al. [10] jointly develop further research to select techniques for developing models that can predict student achievement in more diverse programs. They have added three classification techniques to compare and select the best model with the highest accuracy. They found the Naïve Bayes technique to be the most accurate, with an accuracy of 91.68%, which the Department of Business Computer can use to plan the prevention of dropouts among current students effectively. However, the dropout problem has now been eliminated, but the problem of delayed graduation is increasing among the next generation of students. Therefore, this research aimed to create a predictive model for preventing dropouts and predicting a group of students with a chance of delaying graduation. There are two objectives of the research. The first objective is to study the context and improve the student dropout prevention model at the university level. The second objective is to compare the past university students' dropout models. The research population was students in the Department of Business Computing, School of Information and Communication Technology, the University of Phayao during the academic year 2012–2016. The research tool offers a new and sophisticated approach called majority voting. In addition, the researchers opted for a more diverse prediction technique, including Generalized Linear Model (GLMs), Neural Network (NN), Decision Tree (DT), Naïve Bayes (NB), and k-Nearest Neighbor (k-NN). Finally, the researchers used cross-validation techniques and confusion matrix assessment to assess the model's effectiveness.

Therefore, the researcher is interested in studying to prevent students from dropping out and delaying graduation to formulate a strategic plan for the next generation of educational administration. Researchers firmly believe that this research will significantly impact on improving the quality of education.

2 Materials and Methods

2.1 Population and Sample

The research population was students in the Department of Business Computing, School of Information and Communication Technology, the University of Phayao during the academic year 2012–2016. The data used as a research sample were students who had registered and received academic results in the Bachelor of Business Administration program in Business Computer.

Research samples are summarized and classified by academic year as presented in Table 1.

Table 1. Data collection

Academic year	Total students	Graduated		Dropped out
		Scheduled	Delayed	
2012–2015	99 (28.45%)	32 (9.20%)	26 (7.47%)	41 (11.78%)
2013–2016	92 (26.44%)	28 (8.05%)	24 (6.90%)	40 (11.49%)
2014–2017	57 (16.38%)	24 (6.90%)	12 (3.45%)	21 (6.03%)
2015–2018	46 (13.22%)	33 (9.48%)	6 (1.72%)	7 (2.01%)
2016–2019	54 (15.52%)	31 (8.91%)	17 (4.89%)	6 (1.72%)
Total	348 (100%)	148 (42.53%)	85 (24.43%)	115 (33.05%)

Table 1 presents a summary of data collection for research purposes. It contains 5 data sets of students in the Business Computer Program from the School of Information and Communication Technology at the University of Phayao. The data in Table 1 showed that the overall number of students decreased. There are also three points of interest: the number of graduates as scheduled is only 42.53%, while the number of graduates as delayed is 24.43%. There are as many as 33.05% of students who drop out. Therefore, research is a reason for developing predictive models to prevent students dropouts.

2.2 Data Acquisition Procedure

The data acquisition process consists of five phases. The first phase is a process of studying the feasibility and problems of research. Researchers found that students in the Business Computer Program from the School of Information and Communication Technology at the University of Phayao continued to decline. It also covers the issue of delayed graduation and dropout as the main problem. Researchers were given the policy in the second phase to find solutions that led to the research problem. The research problem is what factors affect the student's academic achievement? In Phase 3, researchers have requested human research ethics, which the University of Phayao has approved (UP-HEC: 2/020/63). In Phase 4, researchers coordinated to request academic achievement data from the University of Phayao, which received 254,456 transactions of student achievement data.

The researchers kept the information confidential and not disclosed according to the regulations of the University of Phayao. In Phase 5, researchers extracted data to prepare an analysis for model development. Researchers classified the data into three groups. The first group was students who graduated as scheduled, the second group was students who graduated as delayed, and the last group was dropped out students.

Furthermore, the researchers found that many students dropped out in the first academic year, as shown in Table 2.

Table 2. Student dropout statistics

Academic year	Total dropped out	Classified by academic year level				
		1st year	2nd year	3rd year	4th year	More 4
2012–2015	41 (35.65%)	23 (20.00%)	12 (10.43%)	3 (2.61%)	1 (0.87%)	2 (1.74%)
2013–2016	40 (34.78%)	21 (18.26%)	10 (8.70%)	5 (4.35%)	1 (0.87%)	3 (2.61%)
2014–2017	21 (18.26%)	13 (11.30%)	7 (6.09%)	1 (0.87%)	0	0
2015–2018	7 (6.09%)	5 (4.35%)	2 (1.74%)	0	0	0
2016–2019	6 (5.22%)	5 (4.35%)	1 (0.87%)	0	0	0
Total	115 (100%)	67 (58.26%)	32 (27.83%)	9 (7.83%)	2 (1.74%)	5 (4.35%)

Table 2 clearly shows that the dropout problem is significant. The students enrolled in 1st year had the highest number of dropouts, with 67 students (58.26%). Students in the 2nd year have the second dropout number, with 32 students (27.83%). For this reason, the researchers limited the scope of the first-year academic achievement data to create a predictive model to prevent students' dropout in the Bachelor of Business Administration program in Business Computer at the School of Information and Communication Technology, the University of Phayao.

2.3 Model Construction Tools

This section aims to design machine learning tools to construct predictive models to prevent students' dropout in the Bachelor of Business Administration program in Business Computer at the School of Information and Communication Technology, the University of Phayao. In the past, Pratya Nuankaew [9] has developed models using decision tree classification techniques. He found that the developed model had an accuracy of 87.21%, predicting two aspects of learning achievement. That research also showed weaknesses with the development of only one modeling technique. Subsequently, Nuankaew et al. [10] jointly developed further research to select techniques for developing models that can predict student achievement in more diverse programs. They have added three classification techniques to compare and select the best model with the highest accuracy. They found the Naïve Bayes technique to be the most accurate, with an accuracy of 91.68%, which the Department of Business Computer can use to plan the prevention of dropouts among current students effectively. However, the dropout problem has now been eliminated, but the problem of delayed graduation is increasing among the next generation of students.

Therefore, this research aimed to create a predictive model for preventing dropouts and predicting a group of students with a chance of delaying graduation. As mentioned above, the predictive model class consists of three domains: scheduled graduation, delayed graduation, and dropout. The researchers used the majority voting technique to select the most efficient models for more outstanding performance. The model development framework is presented in Fig. 1.

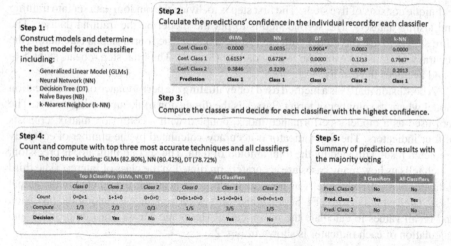

Step 1:
Construct models and determine the best model for each classifier including:

- Generalized Linear Model (GLMs)
- Neural Network (NN)
- Decision Tree (DT)
- Naïve Bayes (NB)
- k-Nearest Neighbor (k-NN)

Step 2:
Calculate the predictions' confidence in the individual record for each classifier

	GLMs	NN	DT	NB	k-NN
Conf. Class 0	0.0000	0.0035	0.9904*	0.0002	0.0000
Conf. Class 1	0.6153*	0.6726*	0.0000	0.1213	0.7987*
Conf. Class 2	0.3846	0.3239	0.0096	0.8784*	0.2013
Prediction	**Class 1**	**Class 1**	**Class 0**	**Class 2**	**Class 1**

Step 3:
Compute the classes and decide for each classifier with the highest confidence.

Step 4:
Count and compute with top three most accurate techniques and all classifiers

- The top three including: GLMs (82.80%), NN (80.42%), DT (78.72%)

	Top 3 Classifiers (GLMs, NN, DT)			All Classifiers		
	Class 0	Class 1	Class 2	Class 0	Class 1	Class 2
Count	0+0+1	1+1+0	0+0+0	0+0+1+0+0	1+1+0+0+1	0+0+0+1+0
Compute	1/3	2/3	0/3	1/5	3/5	1/5
Decision	No	Yes	No	No	Yes	No

Step 5:
Summary of prediction results with the majority voting

	3 Classifiers	All Classifiers
Pred. Class 0	No	No
Pred. Class 1	Yes	Yes
Pred. Class 2	No	No

Fig. 1. The model development framework

There are five steps to improving predictive models to prevent student dropouts in higher education using majority voting and data mining techniques. The first step is constructing models and determining the best model for each classifier. The selected classifiers consisted of five techniques: Generalized Linear Model (GLMs), Neural Network (NN), Decision Tree (DT), Naïve Bayes (NB), and k-Nearest Neighbor (k-NN). The models for each classifier chosen are present in Table 3. The second step is calculating the prediction confidence in each record for the classifier. The calculations in step 2 aim to find the conclusions for each prediction of each technique. The third step is to decide the answer based on the highest confidence value.

The fourth step is the crucial step of the process. This step is divided into two parts and four sub-steps. The first part was to consider the majority vote with the top three most accurate models. The second part uses all the models developed to determine the vote. The four sub-steps of both sections perform the same: counting the vote statistics, calculating the stats divided by the number of classifiers, averaging, and deciding a reasonable class. Step 4 in Fig. 1 describes this process. The fifth step summarizes the majority vote and compares the decision of the two parts in Step 4. As shown in Step 5, an example of a comparison of the two parts is shown, indicating that the votes of both parts give the same class.

2.4 Model Performance Evaluation Tools

The purpose of model performance evaluation is to verify the validity obtained from the model's predictive results compared to the actual data. The techniques decide to assess the effectiveness of the model in this work. It consists of two approaches: the cross-validation technique and the confusion matrix assessment [11].

Principles and testing of cross-validation technique consist of dividing the data into two parts. The first part used to create the model is called the training dataset. The rest used to test the model is called the testing dataset. The workflow of the cross-validation technique consists of five steps: The first step is to divide the random data set into training and testing datasets. The second step is to put the model on the training dataset. The third step is to test the model with the testing dataset. The fourth step is calculating the accuracy of statistics using the testing dataset (Step 3). The final step repeats steps 1 to 4 and averages the results.

A confusion matrix is a method used for evaluating the performance of a classification model where the number of target classes is the dimension of the upcoming matrix. The tool used as a model's performance index, coupled with a confusion matrix, consists of four indicators. The first indicator is accuracy, calculated by the number of correctly predicted results divided by the total amount of data. The second indicator is precision, which tells us how many cases are accurately predicted in the class of interest. The third indicator is recall, which tells us how many cases are accurately predicted in the actual class. The last indicator is F1-Score, which shows performance by taking the precision and recall values to calculate the mean, called Harmonic Mean. The composition and calculation of each indicator is shown in Fig. 2.

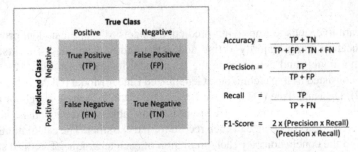

Fig. 2. The elements and calculations in the confusion matrix

This research used cross-validation and confusion matrix techniques in two phases. The first phase evaluates model performance for each classifier in step 2 of the research framework, and the second phase estimates the model's performance using the majority voting technique in step 5. Dividing the data for testing and evaluating in Step 2 and Step 5 consisted of two types of cross-validation: 10-Fold and Leave-one-out cross-validation. The best results of testing and evaluating model performance are shown in Tables 3 and 4, respectively.

3   Research Results

The research results are divided into two parts, with the first part presenting the results of the model development of each classifier. The second part presents the results of model development with majority voting techniques.

3.1 Generated Model Results

Five classification techniques for decision-making are provided in the first step of the research framework. The excellent performance analysis model results with the cross-validation technique and confusion matrix assessment for each predictive classifier are presented in Tables 3 and 4, respectively.

Table 3. Summarizes the results of the five classifiers' performance model analysis

Classifiers	Generalized linear model			Neural Network (NN)		
	Precision	Recall	F1-Score	Precision	Recall	F1-Score
Class dropped	99.13%	99.13%	99.13%	99.12%	98.26%	98.69%
Class scheduled	77.44%	85.81%	81.41%	75.78%	82.43%	78.97%
Class delayed	68.12%	55.29%	61.04%	61.64%	52.94%	56.96%
Accuracy	82.80%			80.42%		
Classifiers	Decision Tree (DT)			Naïve Bayes (NB)		
	Precision	Recall	F1-Score	Precision	Recall	F1-Score
Class dropped	99.13%	99.13%	99.13%	98.21%	95.65%	96.91%
Class scheduled	72.09%	83.78%	77.50%	77.05%	63.51%	69.63%
Class delayed	59.02%	42.35%	49.31%	50.88%	68.24%	58.30%
Accuracy	78.72%			75.29%		
Classifiers	k-Nearest Neighbor (k-NN)					
	Precision		Recall		F1-Score	
Class dropped	90.65%		84.35%		87.39%	
Class scheduled	66.31%		83.78%		74.03%	
Class delayed	42.59%		27.06%		33.09%	
Accuracy	70.09%					

Table 3 summarizes the performance analysis results of the five predictive classifiers, which showed that the classifier with the highest accuracy was the Generalized Linear Model (GLMs), with 82.80% accuracy. The second most accurate predictive classifier is the Neural Network (NN), with 80.42% accuracy. The third most accurate predictive classifier is the Decision Tree (DT), with 78.72% accuracy. The top three models with the highest accuracy were computed for majority voting to create a predictive model that re-tested the original data on the cross-validation technique and confusion matrix assessment. The detailed results of the performance model analysis organized by the classifier are presented in Table 4.

Table 4. The results of the performance model analysis organized by the classifier

Generalized Linear Model (GLMs): Accuracy 82.77%

Predicted\Actual	True dropped	True scheduled	True delayed	Class precision
Pred. dropped	114	0	1	99.13%
Pred. scheduled	0	127	37	77.44%
Pred. delayed	1	21	47	68.12%
Class recall	99.13%	85.81%	55.29%	

Neural Network (NN): Accuracy 80.42%

Predicted\Actual	True dropped	True scheduled	True delayed	Class precision
Pred. dropped	113	0	1	99.12%
Pred. scheduled	0	122	39	75.78%
Pred. delayed	2	26	45	61.64%
Class recall	98.26%	82.43%	52.94%	

Decision Tree (DT): Accuracy 78.72%

Predicted\Actual	True dropped	True scheduled	True delayed	Class precision
Pred. dropped	114	0	1	99.13%
Pred. scheduled	0	124	48	72.09%
Pred. delayed	1	24	36	59.02%
Class recall	99.13%	83.78%	42.35%	

Naïve Bayes (NB): Accuracy 75.29%

Predicted\Actual	True dropped	True scheduled	true delayed	Class precision
pred. dropped	110	0	2	98.21%
Pred. scheduled	3	94	25	77.05%
Pred. delayed	2	54	58	50.88%
Class recall	95.65%	63.51%	68.24%	

k-Nearest Neighbor (k-NN): Accuracy 70.09%

Predicted\Actual	True dropped	True scheduled	True delayed	Class precision
Pred. dropped	97	2	8	90.65%
Pred. scheduled	9	124	54	66.31%
Pred. delayed	9	22	23	42.59%
Class recall	84.35%	83.78%	27.06%	

3.2 Majority Voting Prototype Model

After developing and selecting the model with the five classifiers, this section carried out two subsections: The first subsection is ensemble techniques for creating the majority voting models with the top three and all classifiers. The second subsection evaluates the two models' comparative majority voting model performance.

The first subsection started in the second step of the research framework. The second step was calculating the confidence value of each record's prediction with previously selected techniques classified by class to vote. The third step is considering voting to choose a category from each classifier's highest predicted confidence value. In the fourth step, two parts of the majority voting model exist. The first part was a majority voting with the top three most accurate models, and the second was majority voting with all five modeling techniques.

The results of the confident analysis of each classifier in the second and third step calculations and the consequences of two ensemble majority voting models in the fourth step were released as follows: https://bit.ly/3oGWf4l. To conceal the data and prevent compromise on the rights of the informant, the researchers reworked the student code, which made it irreversible or damaging to the person providing the information.

The operating result of the second subsection is a comparison of two majority voting models. A summary of the majority voting for both models was published as follows: https://bit.ly/3oGWf4l. The researchers then compared the majority voting results with the actual data to calculate the efficiency of the two models. The results are summarized in Tables 5 and 6, respectively.

Table 5. The comparison of two majority voting models

Vote ensemble	3-Ensemble			All classifiers		
	Precision	Recall	F1-Score	Precision	Recall	F1-Score
class dropped	99.14%	100.00%	99.57%	97.46%	100.00%	98.71%
Class scheduled	78.75%	85.14%	81.82%	79.11%	84.46%	81.70%
Class delayed	69.44%	58.82%	63.69%	68.06%	57.65%	62.42%
Accuracy	83.62%			83.04%		

Table 5 compares two models using ensemble techniques to select the best predictive model for preventing students' dropout. The researchers found that the 3-ensemble technique model with three classifiers had the highest accuracy, with an accuracy of 83.62%. The three classification techniques consist of Generalized Linear Model (GLMs), Neural Network (NN), and Decision Tree (DT). The model performance of the 3-ensemble classifiers is presented in Table 6.

Table 6 presents the efficacy evaluation of the model. The researchers found that the model could predict the dropout students with 100% accuracy based on the displayed recall values. In addition, the overall model accuracy was high, with an accuracy of 83.62%. The researchers compared their findings with past research and discussed important issues later.

Table 6. The model performance of the 3-ensemble classifiers

3-Ensemble Classifiers: Accuracy 83.62%				
Predicted\Actual	True dropped	True scheduled	True delayed	Class precision
Pred. dropped	115	0	1	99.14%
Pred. scheduled	0	126	34	78.75%
Pred. delayed	0	22	50	69.44%
Class recall	100.00%	85.14%	58.82%	

4   Research Discussion

In this research, researchers studied and developed a predictive model for preventing student dropout at the university level using majority voting and data mining technique. The most rational model of this research was the preventing prediction model with a 3-ensemble majority voting technique, as shown in Table 5. The machine learning tools used as a component of the majority voting model included Generalized Linear Model (GLMs), Neural Network (NN), and Decision Tree (DT). There are interesting findings from this research. From the development of the model, researchers found that the model could predict the results with a high level of accuracy (83.62%). The weak point of this model was that it signified a moderately delayed class, as shown in the F1-Score, which was 63.69%, as shown in Table 5. However, the model predicted dropped and scheduled classes with high accuracy with the F1-Score of 99.57% and 81.82%, as shown in Table 5. Additionally, the model could predict student dropout with 100% accuracy by analyzing the model's performance with cross-validation techniques and confusion matrix assessment, as shown in the Recall value in Table 6.

This research refutes Nuankaew's research [9, 10] by providing a substantial improvement in the original study. Nuankaew's [9] weakness is that it uses only one prediction technique. Nuankaew's [10] weakness is that it doesn't consider the problem of students' delayed graduation. All the weaknesses have been refined and revised to a more excellent quality that the entire process in this research has been presented.

5   Conclusion

The dropout problem among university students is a loss of educational opportunities leading to a shortage of skilled and knowledgeable workers in the labor market. In this research, the main research objectives were to improve the predictive model for preventing dropouts among university students using majority voting and data mining techniques. There are two objectives of the research. The first objective is to study the context and improve the student dropout prevention model at the university level. The second objective is to compare the past university students' dropout models. The data used in this research were students' academic achievements in the Department of Business Computer at the School of Information and Communication Technology,

University of Phayao, during the academic year 2012–2016. There are a total of 254,456 transactions, which have been extracted from the data of 348 students.

The researchers found that the highest number of dropouts in the first-year university were 67 students, representing 58.26%, as shown in Table 2. Therefore, the researchers developed a predictive model for preventing dropout among university students based on course achievement in the first and second semesters of first-year university studies. The model that has been developed uses a combination of majority voting techniques and data mining techniques. The researchers found that the practical model for this research was using 3-ensemble majority voting techniques with a high level of accuracy, with an accuracy of 83.62%, as shown in Table 5. Furthermore, the efficacy evaluation results of the 3-ensemble majority voting model are presented in Table 6. The researchers found that the improved model performed better than Nuankaew's research [9, 10]. This research addresses the weaknesses of all previous research [9, 10], which uses a wider variety of machine learning techniques and controls to prevent students' delayed graduation in higher education.

Based on this research, the researchers would like to suggest guidelines for using the research results as information to solve the problem of student dropout at the university level as follows: (1) educational institutions should focus on and formulate a plan to solve the problem of long-term dropouts through the cooperation of educational institutions and program administrators. (2) Those involved should put the research results into practice to prevent student dropouts at the university level and manage students to complete their studies on time.

6 Limitation

The limitation of this research is that the researcher takes a long time to collect the data, and this is because the program has a four-year study plan and allows students to spend twice the time in their educational program. It may seem that researchers have used outdated data. In fact, these research findings are used in parallel with the current curriculum, effectively helping to prevent student dropouts.

Acknowledgement. This research project was supported by the Thailand Science Research and Innovation Fund and the University of Phayao (Grant No. FF65-UoE006). The authors would like to thank all of them for their support and collaboration in making this research possible.

Conflicts of Interest. The authors declare no conflict of interest.

References

1. Casanova, J.R., Gomes, C.M.A., Bernardo, A.B., Núñez, J.C., Almeida, L.S.: Dimensionality and reliability of a screening instrument for students at-risk of dropping out from Higher Education. Stud. Educ. Eval. **68**, 100957 (2021). https://doi.org/10.1016/j.stueduc.2020.100957

2. Karimi-Haghighi, M., Castillo, C., Hernández-Leo, D.: A causal inference study on the effects of first year workload on the dropout rate of undergraduates. In: Rodrigo, M.M., Matsuda, N., Cristea, A.I., Dimitrova, V. (eds.) Artificial Intelligence in Education: 23rd International Conference, AIED 2022, Durham, UK, July 27–31, 2022, Proceedings, Part I, pp. 15–27. Springer International Publishing, Cham (2022). https://doi.org/10.1007/978-3-031-11644-5_2

3. Saccaro, A., França, M.T.A.: Stop-out and drop-out: The behavior of the first year withdrawal of students of the Brazilian higher education receiving FIES funding. Int. J. Educ. Dev. **77**, 102221 (2020). https://doi.org/10.1016/j.ijedudev.2020.102221

4. Luo, Y., Zhou, R.Y., Mizunoya, S., Amaro, D.: How various types of disabilities impact children's school attendance and completion – Lessons learned from censuses in eight developing countries. Int. J. Educ. Dev. **77**, 102222 (2020). https://doi.org/10.1016/j.ijedudev.2020.102222

5. Tinto, V.: From theory to action: exploring the institutional conditions for student retention. In: Smart, J.C. (ed.) Higher Education: Handbook of Theory and Research, pp. 51–89. Springer Netherlands, Dordrecht (2010). https://doi.org/10.1007/978-90-481-8598-6_2

6. Burgos, C., Campanario, M.L., de la Peña, D., Lara, J.A., Lizcano, D., Martínez, M.A.: Data mining for modeling students' performance: a tutoring action plan to prevent academic dropout. Comput. Electr. Eng. **66**, 541–556 (2018). https://doi.org/10.1016/j.compeleceng.2017.03.005

7. de Oliveira, C.F., Sobral, S.R., Ferreira, M.J., Moreira, F.: How does learning analytics contribute to prevent students' dropout in higher education: a systematic literature review. Big Data Cogn. Comput. **5**, 64 (2021). https://doi.org/10.3390/bdcc5040064

8. Nuankaew, P., Nuankaew, W., Nasa-ngium, P.: Risk management models for prediction of dropout students in Thailand higher education. Int. J. Innov. Creativity Chang. **15**, 494–517 (2021)

9. Nuankaew, P.: Dropout situation of business computer students, university of Phayao. Int. J. Emerg. Technol. Learn. (iJET) **14**, 115–131 (2019). https://doi.org/10.3991/ijet.v14i19.11177

10. Nuankaew, P., Nuankaew, W., Teeraputon, D., Phanniphong, K., Bussaman, S.: Prediction model of student achievement in business computer disciplines. Int. J. Emerg. Technol. Learn. (iJET). **15**, 160–181 (2020). https://doi.org/10.3991/ijet.v15i20.15273

11. Deng, X., Liu, Q., Deng, Y., Mahadevan, S.: An improved method to construct basic probability assignment based on the confusion matrix for classification problem. Inf. Sci. **340–341**, 250–261 (2016). https://doi.org/10.1016/j.ins.2016.01.033

LCIM: Mining Low Cost High Utility Itemsets

M. Saqib Nawaz[1], Philippe Fournier-Viger[1(✉)], Naji Alhusaini[2],
Yulin He[1,3], Youxi Wu[4], and Debdatta Bhattacharya[5]

[1] Shenzhen University, Shenzhen, China
{msaqibnawaz,philfv}@szu.edu.cn
[2] Chuzhou University, Anhui, China
naji@chzu.edu.cn
[3] Guangdong Laboratory of Artificial Intelligence and Digital Economy (SZ),
Shenzhen, China
yulinhe@gml.ac.cn
[4] Hebei University of Technology, Tianjin, China
[5] Koneru Lakshmaiah Education Foundation, Vaddeswaram, India

Abstract. In data science, a key task is high utility itemset mining (HUIM), that is determining the values that co-occur in data and have a high utility (importance). That task is applied for instance to identify the most profitable sets of products in transactions. A shortcoming of current algorithms is that they focus on the utility of patterns, but ignore their cost (e.g. time, effort, money or other resources that are consumed). Hence, this paper defines the problem of low cost high utility itemset mining. The aim is to find patterns that have a high average utility and a low average-cost. An example application is to find patterns indicating learners' studying patterns in an e-learning platform that result in obtaining high grades (utility) for a relatively small effort (cost). An efficient algorithm named LCIM (Low Cost Itemset Miner) is proposed to solve this problem. To reduce the search space, LCIM uses a novel lower bound on the average cost. Observations from experiments confirm that LCIM find interesting patterns and is efficient.

Keywords: Pattern mining · Itemset · Cost function · Utility function

1 Introduction

In data science, pattern mining is the process of searching for significant and interesting patterns in databases [1]. The focus of early pattern mining studies has been on identifying frequent itemsets using the support (frequency) function. A frequent itemset is a group of values that co-occur many times in data [1,7]. Finding frequent itemsets, which is called Frequent itemset mining (FIM), has many practical uses. As example, FIM can analyze university course selection data to discover those that are frequently selected together. Another example is

O. Surinta and K. Kam Fung Yuen (Eds.): MIWAI 2022, LNAI 13651, pp. 73–85, 2022.
https://doi.org/10.1007/978-3-031-20992-5_7

to identify products that people like to buy together online. However, a drawback of FIM is that frequency is not the only criterion that matters in many situations.

Hence, a generalization of FIM called high utility itemset mining (HUIM) was introduced [2,6]. The objective is to find high utility itemsets (sets of values that are deemed to provide high benefits according to a utility function). For instance, in the context of shopping, utility may represent the profit obtained by selling sets of products. In HUIM, the search space of patterns can be huge. Over the years, efficient algorithms have been proposed for HUIM [8,10–12]. HUIM can reveal interesting patterns in many domains [6]. Nonetheless, the focus is on the utility of patterns and the cost associated with these patterns is ignored.

For domains such as e-learning, utility and cost are two important dimensions that should be jointly considered. For example, the cost may be the study time during learning activities and the utility may be the grades subsequently obtained. Another example is medical data, where the cost may be the time or money spent by a patient for each treatment and the utility may be the result of finally being cured or not. Hence, the *utility* of a pattern can represent benefits generated such as the grades or profit that is yielded by the pattern, while the *cost* can refers to drawbacks of the pattern such as the effort, time or resources consumed to apply this pattern.

Jointly considering utility and cost in pattern mining is desirable but not simple and could be done in many ways. One way is to subtract the cost from the utility and then apply HUIM algorithms. However, this approach is inadequate for applications such as e-learning as utility and cost may be expressed in different units (e.g. hours, grades). Besides, for such applications, it is more meaningful to consider the average utility and the average cost of patterns rather than their sums. For example, it is useless to know that some students took a total of 350 min to do activities and received a total of 400 points at the final exam, but it is meaningful to know that on average they took 1.2 h each with an average grade of 80 points. Hence, this motivates us to separately model the utility and cost, and to consider their average. So far, only one study [4] has integrated the cost in pattern mining. But algorithms from that study are for analyzing event sequences, while this paper focuses on mining itemsets in transactions, which is different and more common in real-life. For example, such data are sets of courses selected by students or treatments taken by hospital patients. Due to different data types, prior algorithms cannot be reused.

This paper makes four contributions: (1) A novel problem called low cost HUIM is formalized to introduce the concept of cost in itemset mining. The aim is to find itemsets that have a high average utility, and a low average cost. (2) An algorithm named LCIM (Low Cost Itemset Miner) is designed for solving this problem efficiently. (3) For search space reduction, LCIM applies a lower bound on the average cost called Average Cost Bound (ACB). (4) Four datasets are used in experiments to evaluate LCIM. Results show that LCIM is not only efficient but also reveal some interesting patterns in e-learning data.

The rest of this paper is organized as follows. Section 2 presents the related work. Section 3 defines the problem of low cost HUIM. Section 4 describes the proposed LCIM algorithm. Section 5 reports the experimental results. Finally, Sect. 6 draws the conclusion.

2   Related Work

FIM [1] takes a *transaction database* as input. Each transaction (record) in the database represents a set of items (symbols). The goal is to find frequent itemsets, where the support of an itemset is its occurrence frequency. All efficient FIM algorithms such as Eclat, FP-Growth and Apriori [7] find the frequent itemsets without exploring all possibilities. For this, they rely on a property of the support function, known as the *anti-monotonicity property*, indicating that no subset of an itemset can have a greater support than the itemset.

HUIM is a generalization of FIM, initially designed to find profitable sets of items in shopping data [2,6]. The input is a *quantitative transaction database* containing additional utility information. In a transaction, each item is associated with a utility value (a positive number) that indicates the importance of that item in the transaction (e.g. profit). The aim of HUIM is to discover the itemsets with a high utility as measured by a utility function [2,6]. The two most popular functions are the total utility [2] (e.g. total profit) and the length-average utility[1] [9] (e.g. the profit of an itemset divided by its number of items). Compared to FIM, HUIM is harder as there is no anti-monotonicity property for most utility functions. Hence, FIM algorithms cannot be directly applied for HUIM. Efficient HUIM algorithms such as MLHUI-Miner [11], UD-Growth [14], ULB-Miner [3], and REX [12]) utilize upper bounds on the utility that are anti-monotonic to reduce the search space. Besides, various strategies are used such as a breadth-first or depth-first search [6], or a horizontal [8] or vertical data format [13]. Until now, no HUIM studies has integrated the concept of cost.

Recently, the concept of cost was studied to find sequential patterns (subsequences) in multiple sequences of events [4]. That study has shown that the cost is an interesting function for some applications. But the aim of analyzing sequences is very different from the focus of this paper on analyzing transactions to find itemsets. Thus, algorithms from that study cannot be reused.

There are major differences between this paper and prior work on HUIM. In the current paper, two functions (utility and cost) are combined to identify itemsets having a low cost and a high utility. This combination is motivated by applications such as e-learning where these two dimensions are important. The data representation is different from HUIM. Rather than associating a utility value to each item, a single utility value is associated to each transaction, such that the utility represents its outcome (e.g. the final grade at an exam) after using items (e.g. studying some lessons). Then, a novel utility function is used to evaluate itemsets called average utility (e.g. average time spent on a lesson), which is different from the length-average utility function from HUIM (e.g. average time spent on lessons divided by the number of lessons) and more meaningful for applications such as e-learning. Besides, a cost value is assigned to each item to indicate its cost (e.g. time spent on each lesson). Due this different definition of utility and the addition of cost, prior HUIM cannot be applied to solve the new problem. A key challenge of this paper is also that there is an aim to maxi-

---

[1] The original name is *average utility* but it is renamed to be more precise.

mize utility while minimizing cost. Thus, not only an upper bound on the utility must be used but also a lower bound on the cost to mine patterns efficiently.

3 Problem Definition

The proposed problem aims to discover itemsets in a *transaction database with cost values*. The data format is defined as follows. Let $I = \{i_1, i_2, \ldots, i_n\}$ be a finite set of items (symbols). A **transaction database** is a set of transactions $D = \{T_1, T_2, \ldots T_m\}$ where each **transaction** $T_j \in D$ is a finite set of items, i.e. $T_j \subseteq I$. Each transaction $T_j \in D$ has a unique identifier j. For each item i in a transaction T, i.e. $i \in T$, a positive number $c(i, T)$ is assigned representing the **cost of the item** i in T. Moreover, a positive number is assigned to each transaction T, denoted as $u(T)$, which is called the **utility of transaction** T.

Table 1, for example, shows an example database containing seven distinct items $I = \{a, b, c, d, e, f, g\}$ and five transactions $T_1, T_2, \ldots T_5$. The first transaction T_1 contains the items a, b, c, d, e, and f, with the cost values $c(a, T_1) = 5$, $c(b, T_1) = 10$, $c(c, T_1) = 1$, $c(d, T_1) = 6$, $c(e, T_1) = 3$, and $c(f, T_1) = 5$. The utility values of the transactions are $u(T_1) = 40$, $u(T_2) = 20$, $u(T_3) = 18$, $u(T_4) = 37$, and $u(T_5) = 21$. Each transaction can represent the lessons (items) taken by some students (transactions) where cost is time and utility is final grades.

Table 1. A small transaction database with cost and utility values

Transaction	Items (*item, cost*)	Utility
T_1	$(a, 5), (b, 10), (c, 1), (d, 6), (e, 3), (f, 5)$	40
T_2	$(b, 8), (c, 3), (d, 6), (e, 3)$	20
T_3	$(a, 5), (c, 1), (d, 2)$	18
T_4	$(a, 10), (c, 6), (e, 6), (g, 5)$	37
T_5	$(b, 4), (c, 2), (e, 3), (g, 2)$	21

An **itemset** X is a set such that $X \subseteq I$. An itemset X having k items is called a k-itemset. Let $g(X) = \{T | X \subseteq T \in D\}$ be the set of transactions where X appears. The **support of an itemset** X in a database D is defined and denoted as $s(X) = |g(X)|$. For example, the itemset $\{b, c\}$ is a 2-itemset. It appears in the transactions $g(\{b, c\}) = \{T_1, T_2, T_5\}$. Thus, $s(\{b, c\}) = 3$.

The **average cost of an itemset** X in a transaction T such that $X \subseteq T$ is defined and denoted as $c(X, T) = \sum_{i \in X} c(i, T)$. The **cost of an itemset** X in a database D is defined and denoted as $c(X) = \sum_{T \in g(X)} c(X, T)$. The **average cost of an itemset** X in a database D is defined and denoted as $ac(X) = c(X) \div s(X)$.

For instance, the cost of itemset $\{b, c\}$ in transaction T_1 is $c(\{b, c\}, T_1) = c(b, T_1) + c(c, T_1) = 10 + 1 = 11$. The average cost of itemset $\{b, c\}$ is $[c(\{b, c\}, T_1) + c(\{b, c\}, T_2) + c(\{b, c\}, T_5)] \div s(\{b, c\}) = [11 + 11 + 6] \div 3 = 28/3$, which can represent the average time to study lesson b and c in an e-learning context.

The **utility of an itemset** X in a database D is defined and denoted as $u(X) = \sum_{T \in g(X)} u(T)$ and represents how positive the outcome of transaction is. The **average utility of an itemset** X in a database D is defined and denoted as $ac(X) = u(X) \div s(X)$.

For example, the utility of itemset $\{b, c\}$ is $u(\{b, c\}) = 40 + 20 + 21 = 81$. Itemset $\{b, c\}$ average utility is $u(\{b, c\}) \div s(\{b, c\}) = 81 \div 3 = 27$. In e-learning, this can indicate that the average grade is 27 for students doing lessons b and c. The proposed problem is defined as follows.

Definition 1 (problem definition). *Let there be some user-specified thresholds minsup > 0, minutil > 0, and maxcost > 0. An itemset X is a **low cost itemset** if and only if $au(X) \geq minutil$, $ac(X) \leq maxcost$ and $s(X) \geq minsup$.*

This definition is meaningful for applications such as e-learning to find sets of lessons that on average lead to high scores with a small study time.

4   The LCIM Algorithm

The proposed LCIM algorithm is presented in this section. Subsection 4.1 first describes the search space pruning properties of LCIM. Subsection 4.2 presents its novel cost-list data structure. Finally, Subsect. 4.3 describes the algorithm.

4.1   Search Space Exploration and Pruning Properties

LCIM explores the itemsets search space by starting from itemsets having one item, and then recursively look for itemsets having more items. To avoid considering an itemset multiple times, larger itemsets are explored by applying a process called *extension*, defined as follows.

Definition 2 (Extension). *It is assumed, without loss of generality, that items in each itemset are sorted using a total order $\succ$, called the **processing order**. Two itemsets X and Y can be joined to obtain a new itemset $Z = X \cup Y$ if all items in X and Y are the same except the last one according to $\succ$. The itemset Z is then said to be an **extension** of X and Y.*

For instance, assume that the processing order is the lexicographical order $(f \succ e \succ d \succ c \succ b \succ a)$. Then, the two itemsets $X = \{a\}$ and $X = \{b\}$ can be joined to obtain an itemset $Z = \{a, b\}$. Similarly, the itemsets $\{a, b\}$ and $\{a, c\}$ can be joined to obtain an itemset $\{a, b, c\}$. However, the itemsets $\{a, b, c\}$ and $\{b, e\}$ cannot be joined because they are not the same except the last item.

By recursively performing extensions, it can be shown that the whole search space of itemsets can be explored. However, to have an efficient algorithm, it is necessary to be able to reduce the search space. To reduce the search space, the Apriori pruning property based on the support is used [1].

Property 1 (Support pruning). For any two itemsets $X \subseteq Y$, $s(X) \geq s(Y)$.

Besides, to reduce the search space using the cost, a lower bound on the cost is introduced (inspired by the ASC lower bound used in sequence mining [4]):

Definition 3 (Lower bound on the cost). *Let there be an itemset X, which appears in the transactions $g(X) = \{T_1', T_2', \ldots, T_N'\}$. The **sequence of cost values** of X is the unique sequence $A(X) = (a_i)_{i=1}^{N}$ where $a_i = c(X, T_i')$. Let $sort(A(X))$ be the unique non decreasing sequence $B = (b_i)_{i=1}^{N}$ satisfying $\forall i \leq K \leq N$ $|\{i \in \mathbb{N} | a_i = a_K\}| = |\{i \in \mathbb{N} | b_i = a_K\}|$. The K **largest cost values** of X is the sequence $A(X)^{(K)} = (c_i)_{i=1}^{K}$ of real numbers satisfying $\forall 1 \leq i \leq K$, $c_i = b_{N-K+i}$. The **average cost bound (ACB)** of X is defined as $acb(X) = \frac{\sum_{c_i \in A(X)^{(minsup)}} c_i}{s(X)}$.*

For instance, let $minsup = 1$ and $X = \{b, c\}$. The sequence of cost values of X is $A(X) = \langle 11, 11, 6 \rangle$. Then, $sort(A(X)) = \langle 6, 11, 11 \rangle$, and $A(X)^{(1)} = \langle 6 \rangle$. The average cost bound of X is $acb(X) = \frac{6}{3} = 2$. If $minsup = 2$, $A(X)^{(2)} = \langle 6, 11 \rangle$, and $acb(X) = \frac{6+11}{3} = \frac{17}{3}$.

Property 2 (lower bound of the ACB on the average cost). For any itemset X, the average cost bound of X is a lower bound on the average cost of X. In other words, $acb(X) \geq ac(X)$.

Proof. By definition, $acb(X) = \frac{\sum_{c_i \in A(X)^{(minsup)}} c_i}{s(X)}$, while the average cost can be expressed as $ac(X) = \frac{\sum_{c_i \in sort(A(X))} c_i}{s(X)}$. It is clear that $A(X)^{(minsup)}$ is a subsequence of $sort(A(X))$. Hence, the numerator of $acb(X)$ is no greater than that of $ac(X)$. Thus, $acb(X) \leq ac(X)$.   □

Property 3 (anti-monotonicity of the ACB). For any two itemsets $X \subseteq Y$, then $acb(X) \leq acb(Y)$.

Proof. We have $acb(X) = \frac{\sum_{c_i \in A(X)^{(minsup)}} c_i}{s(X)}$ and $acb(Y) = \frac{\sum_{c_i \in A(Y)^{(minsup)}} c_i}{s(Y)}$. Since $X \subseteq Y$, it follows that $g(Y) \subseteq g(X)$ and that $s(Y) \leq s(X)$. Hence, the denominator of $acb(Y)$ is greater or equal to that of $acb(X)$. For the numerators, we know that $A(X)^{(minsup)}$ and $A(Y)^{(minsup)}$ both contain $minsup$ cost values but cost values in the latter must be greater than those in the former since Y is a larger itemset. Hence, the numerator of $acb(Y)$ must be larger than that of $acb(X)$. Thus, $acb(X) \leq acb(Y)$.   □

Property 4 (Search space pruning using the ACB). For an itemset X, if $acb(X) > maxcost$, X and its supersets are not low cost itemsets.

Proof. This directly follows from the two previous properties.

4.2   The Cost-List Data Structure

Another key consideration for the design of an efficient algorithm is how to efficiently calculate the utility and cost values of itemsets and also the ACB lower bound for reducing the search space. For this purpose, the designed LCIM algorithm relies on a novel data structure called the *cost-list*.

Definition 4 (cost-list). *The **cost-list** of an itemset X is a tuple $L(X) = (utility, cost, tids, costs)$ that stores information in four fields. The field utility contains $u(X)$. The field cost stores $c(X)$. The field tids stores $g(X)$, while costs stores $A(X)$. In the following, the notation $L(X).field$ refers to the value of the field field in $L(X)$.*

For instance, Table 2 shows the cost-lists of itemset $\{a\}$, $\{b\}$ and $\{a, b\}$.

Table 2. The cost-lists of $\{a\}$, $\{b\}$ and $\{a, b\}$

$L(\{a\}$		$L(\{b\}$		$L(\{a,b\}$	
utility	95	utility	81	utility	40
cost	20	cost	22	cost	15
tids	$\{T_1, T_3, T_4\}$	tids	$\{T_1, T_2, T_5\}$	tids	$\{T_1\}$
costs	$\langle 5, 5, 10 \rangle$	costs	$\langle 10, 8, 4 \rangle$	costs	$\langle 15 \rangle$

The cost-lists of an itemset X is useful as it contains all the required information about it. The cost-list of X allows to directly obtain its support as $s(X) = |L(X).tids|)$, its average utility as $au(X) = L(X).utility/s(X)$, and its average cost as $ac(X) = L(X).utility/s(X)$. Moreover, the ACB lower bound can be calculated by finding the *minsup* smallest values in $L(X).costs$.

By reading the database, the proposed algorithm builds the cost-list of each 1-itemset. Then, the cost-list of any larger itemset is obtained without reading the database, by applying a join operation on cost-lists of some of its subsets, as follows.

Consider two itemsets X and Y that are joined to obtain an extension $Z = X \cup Y$. The cost-list $L(Z)$ is derived directly from the cost-lists $L(X)$ and $L(Y)$ as follows. The field $L(Z).costs$ is obtained by merging the cost values corresponding to the same transactions in $L(X).cost$ and $L(Y).costs$. The field $L(Z).tids = L(X).tids \cap L(Y).tids$. The field $L(Z).cost$ is the sum of values in $L(Z).costs$. The field $L(Z).utility$ is calculated as the sum of utility values for transactions in $L(Z).tids$.

4.3   The Algorithm

LCIM (Algorithm 1) takes as input (1) a transaction database with cost/utility and (2) the *minsup*, *minutil* and *maxcost* thresholds. The database is first scanned by LCIM to calculate the support of each item. This allows determining the set ω of all frequent items (having a support no less than $minsup$). Then, LCIM utilizes this information to establish a processing order $\succ$ on items. Thereafter, LCIM scans the database again to create the cost-lists of all items in ω. This provides the information for calculating the ACB lower bound of each item $i \in \omega$. Each item having a lower bound value that is no greater than $maxcost$ is put in a set γ. Then, the recursive procedure $Search$ is called with γ to search for low cost itemsets. Other items can be ignored as they cannot be part of a low cost itemset based on Property 4.

The $Search$ procedure is shown in Algorithm 2. It takes a input a set of itemsets P and their cost-lists, as well as the $minsup$, $minutil$ and $maxcost$ thresholds. The procedure outputs the set of low cost itemsets in P or itemsets that are extensions of itemsets in P. For each itemset $X \in P$, the procedure first calculates its average utility and average cost from its cost-list $L(X)$. Then, if the average utility of X is no less than $minutil$ and its average cost is no greater than $maxcost$, the itemset X is output as a low cost itemset. Then, the procedure initializes a variable $XExtend$ to store extensions of P that contain one more item than X and may be low cost itemsets. Thereafter, for each itemset Y in P that can be joined with X, the extension $Z = X \cup Y$ is created, as well as its cost-list $L(Z)$ by calling the $Construct$ procedure. The cost-list $L(Z)$ allows to directly obtain the support $s(Z)$ and the ACB lower bound $acb(Z)$ without scanning the database. Then, if $s(Z)$ is no less than $minsup$ and the $acb(Z)$ is no greater than $maxcost$, the itemset Z is added to $XExtend$. This is because Z and its recursive extensions may be low cost itemsets. Afterwards, the search procedure is called with the set $XExtend$ to explore extensions of X recursively. When the loop of all itemsets in P ends, all low cost itemsets that are in P or are extensions of itemsets in P have been output.

Algorithm 1: LCIM

input   : D: a transaction database,
           $minsup, minutil, maxcost$
output : all the low cost itemsets

1 Calculate the support of all items by reading the database;
2 Store the frequent items in a set ω;
3 Etablish the order of support ascending values on ω, and denote it as $\succ$;
4 Create the cost-list of all frequent items in ω;
5 Put each item i from ω in a set γ if $acb(\{i\}) \leq maxcost$ according to $L(\{i\})$;
6 Search $(\gamma, minsup, minutil, maxcost)$;

The $Construct$ procedure is shown in Algorithm 3. The input is the cost-lists $L(X)$ and $L(Y)$ of two itemsets X and Y that can be joined together to form an extension $Z = X \cup Y$. The output is the cost-list $L(Z)$. This procedure first initializes the cost-list of $L(Z)$ such that $L(Z).utility = 0$, $L(Z).tids = \emptyset$ and $L(Z).tids = \emptyset$. Then a loop is performed to check each transaction T_w that is in $L(X).tids$ to see if it also appears in $L(Y).tids$. For each such transaction T_w, it is added to $L(Z).tids$, and then the utility $u(T_w)$ is added to $L(Z).utility$. Then, $L(Z).costs$ is updated by adding the cost of Z in T_w. This cost is calculated by

---

Algorithm 2: *Search*

---

input   : P: some itemsets with their cost-lists,
          $minsup, minutil, maxcost$
output : a set of low cost itemsets

1 **foreach** *itemset* $X \in$ P **do**
2   **if** $au(X) \geq minutil \wedge ac(X) \leq maxcost$ **then** Output X Initialize $XExtend$ as the empty set;
3   **foreach** *itemset* $Y \in$ P *that can be joined with* X **do**
4         $Z \leftarrow X \cup Y$;
5         $L(Z) \leftarrow$ Construct $(L(X), L(Y))$;
6   **if** $s(Z) \geq minsup \wedge acb(Z) \leq maxcost$ **then**
7            $XExtend \leftarrow XExtend \cup \{Z\}$;
8   **end**
9   **end**
10   Search $(XExtend, minsup, minutil, maxcost)$;
11 **end**

---

a procedure called Merge, which does the sum of the cost of X in T_w and the cost of Y in T_w (this information is obtained from $L(X)$ and $L(Y)$). Finally, after the loop is completed, $L(Z).cost$ is calculated as the sum of all values in $L(Z).costs$, and $L(Z)$ is returned.

Algorithm 3: Construct procedure

---

input   : $L(X), L(Y)$: the cost utility list of two itemsets X and Y
output : the cost-list $L(Z)$ of $Z = X \cup Y$

1 Initialize a cost-list $L(Z)$ such that $L(Z).utility = 0$, $L(Z).tids = \emptyset$, and $L(Z).costs = \emptyset$;
2 **foreach** *transaction* $T_w \in L(X).tids$ **do**
3   **if** $\exists T_w \in L(Y).tids$ **then**
4         $L(Z).tids \leftarrow L(Z).tids \cup \{T_w\}$;
5         $L(Z).utility \leftarrow L(Z).utility + u(T_w)$;
6         $L(Z).costs \leftarrow Merge(L(X).costs, L(Y).costs)$;
7   **end**
8 **end**
9 $L(Z).cost = \sum L(Z).costs$;
10 **return** $L(Z)$;

It can be observed that the whole search space of itemsets can be explored by recursively performing extensions, and that only itemsets that are not low cost itemsets are pruned by the pruning properties, which are proven in Sect. 4.1. Hence, LCIM can find all low cost itemsets. The complexity of LCIM is a function of the number of itemsets that LCIM visits in the search space, which depends on how $minsup$, $minutil$ and $maxcost$ are set. In the worst case, there are $2^{|I|}-1$ itemsets. For each visited itemset, a cost-list is created in linear time, which has a size bounded by the database size.

Two Optimizations. We also include two performance optimization: (1) *Matrix Support Pruning* (MSP) consists of precalculating the support of all pairs of items in the initial database scan. Then, two itemsets X and Y are not joined as $X \cup Y$ if their last items have a joint support below $minsup$. (2) Efficient List

Construction (ELC) the construct procedure is stopped as soon as there are not enough transactions left in $L(X).tids$ to attain $L(Z).tids \geq minsup$.

5   Experimental Evaluation

LCIM is implemented in Java. For the experiments, we take the LCIM algorithm without the two optimizations and consider it as a baseline since there is no prior algorithm. The performance of the baseline is compared with LCIM on four benchmark datasets, namely Chess, Mushroom, Accidents and E-Learning. The source code of LCIM and datasets can be downloaded from the SPMF data mining library [5]. Chess has 3,196 transactions, 37 distinct items, and an average transaction length of 75 items. Mushroom contains 8,416 transactions, 119 distinct items, and the average transaction length is 23 items. Accidents contains 340,183 transactions with 468 distinct items, and an average transaction length of 34 items. But only 10% of Accidents was used. E-Learning contains 54 transactions, 11 distinct items, and the average transaction length is 3.8 items. The experiments were conducted on a laptop with an Intel Celeron processor and 16 GB of RAM running 64-bit Windows 10.

Runtime and Pattern Count. In the first experiment, the performance of LCIM was evaluated on four datasets in terms of execution time and number of patterns found. Fig 1 (a, c, e and g) show the execution time and pattern count on Chess, Mushroom, Accidents and E-Learning, respectively, for various $minsup$ values. For the Chess, Mushroom, Accidents and E-Learning datasets, the $maxcost$ ($minutil$) values were set to 100 (100), 50 (50), 100 (100) and 100 (10), respectively. Fig 1 (b, d, f and h) show the execution time and discovered patterns on Chess, Mushroom, Accidents and E-Learning, respectively, for various $maxcost$ and $minutil$ values. For the Chess, Mushroom, Accidents and E-Learning datasets, $minsup$ was set to 0.7%, 0.5%, 0.7% and 0.2%, respectively. It is observed that the baseline and LCIM are fast. The execution time and pattern count for LCIM increased with a decrease in $minsup$ and an increase in $maxcost$ values, which show the effectiveness of pruning properties. For $minutil$, it has a negligible effect on the execution time as it is not used for pruning. Interestingly, the pattern count remained the same for various $minutil$ values. This is why the execution time and pattern count results are omitted for various $minutil$ values on the E-learning dataset. Compared to LCIM, the baseline algorithm takes more time, particularly on the Chess and Mushroom datasets, when $minsup$ is decreased. For $maxcost$ and $minutil$, the baseline algorithm takes the same amount of time. Interestingly, the baseline algorithm is slightly faster, on overall, for experiments of varying $maxcost$ and $minutil$.

Pattern Analysis for e-learning. The Chess, Mushroom and Accidents datasets have synthetic values for cost and utility, while E-learning has real cost and utility values. Hence, to evaluate the quality of patterns found, we look at patterns found in E-learning. It contains sets of online activities done by 54 students during Session 4 of an e-learning environment. Each transaction is the

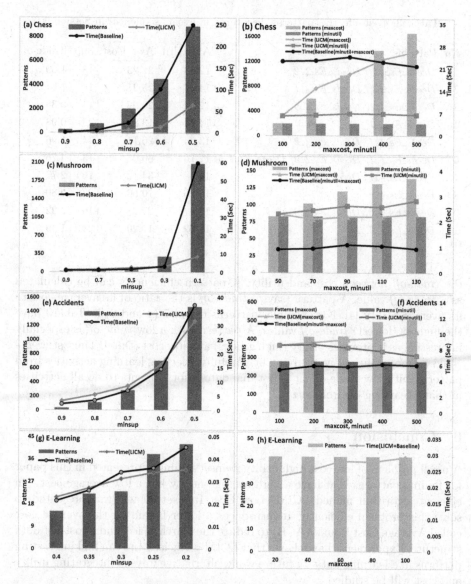

Fig. 1. Runtime of the baseline and LCIM for varying *minsup, maxcost* and *minutil*

list of activities performed by a student. Each activity is associated with a cost for the time spent by the student on the activity and each transaction has a utility value that is the student score in a test at the end of the session. Table 3 lists the patterns obtained in that dataset by setting *minutil, maxcost* and *minsup* to 10, 100 and 0.2% respectively.

A manual analysis of activities confirmed that the patterns are reasonable for learners. But to compare the efficiency of these patterns, we can further check

Table 3. Cost-effective patterns discovered in events sequences in Session 4

No	Patterns	Avg. Util	Avg. Cost	Sup	Trade-off
1	*Deeds_Es_4_3, Deeds_Es_4_2*	12.53	21.23	13	1.69
2	*Deeds_Es_4_4, Deeds_Es_4_1*	14.07	25.21	14	1.81
3	*Deeds_Es_4_4, Deeds_Es_4_5*	12.42	28.92	14	2.38
4	*Deeds_Es_4_1*	14.21	13.82	23	0.98
5	*Deeds_Es_4_1, Deeds_Es_4_2*	13.64	26.71	14	1.96
6	*Deeds_Es_4_1, Deeds_Es_4_2, Deeds_Es_4_5*	12.76	60.0	13	4.76
7	*Deeds_Es_4_1, Deeds_Es_4_5*	12.5	34.12	16	2.77
8	*Deeds_Es_4_2*	13.26	10.60	23	0.80
9	*Deeds_Es_4_2, Deeds_Es_4_5*	12.47	27.68	19	2.22
10	*Deeds_Es_4_5*	11.62	17.20	24	1.49

the *trade-off* between cost and utility. A pattern efficiency's can be calculated as a *trade-off* value. A pattern (say p) *trade-off* is the ratio of its average cost to its average utility [4]. For example, patterns 6 and 7 (4 and 8) in Table 3 have the highest (lowest) *trade-off* values. A pattern with a low *trade-off* is especially interesting as it provides utility (high grades) at a low cost (time). Thus, students could be more efficient at studying by carefully selecting learning activities from patterns with low trade-off (it is not mandatory for students to do all activities in that e-learning environment).

6   Conclusion

A novel problem of low cost high utility itemset mining is presented in this paper for finding patterns that have a high average utility but a low average-cost. An efficient algorithm named LCIM (Low Cost Itemset Miner) was presented to solve this problem efficiently. It introduces a lower bound on the average cost called Average Cost Bound (ACB) to reduce the search space, and a cost-list data structure. Experiments have shown that LCIM is efficient and can find interesting patterns in e-learning data. In future work, alternative ways of integrating utility and cost will be studied.

References

1. Agrawal, R., Srikant, R.: Fast algorithms for mining association rules. In: Proceedings of VLDB, vol. 1215, pp. 487–499 (1994)
2. Chan, R., Yang, Q., Shen, Y.: Mining high utility itemsets. In: Proceedings of ICDM, pp. 19–26 (2003)
3. Duong, Q.-H., Fournier-Viger, P., Ramampiaro, H., Nørvåg, K., Dam, T.-L.: Efficient high utility itemset mining using buffered utility-lists. Appl. Intell. **48**(7), 1859–1877 (2017). https://doi.org/10.1007/s10489-017-1057-2

4. Fournier-Viger, P., Li, J., Lin, J.C., Truong-Chi, T., Kiran, R.U.: Mining cost-effective patterns in event logs. Knowl. Based Syst. **191**, 105241 (2020)
5. Fournier-Viger, P., et al.: The SPMF open-source data mining library version 2. In: Berendt, B., et al. (eds.) ECML PKDD 2016. LNCS (LNAI), vol. 9853, pp. 36–40. Springer, Cham (2016). https://doi.org/10.1007/978-3-319-46131-1_8
6. Fournier-Viger, P., Chun-Wei Lin, J., Truong-Chi, T., Nkambou, R.: A survey of high utility itemset mining. In: Fournier-Viger, P., Lin, J.C.-W., Nkambou, R., Vo, B., Tseng, V.S. (eds.) High-Utility Pattern Mining. SBD, vol. 51, pp. 1–45. Springer, Cham (2019). https://doi.org/10.1007/978-3-030-04921-8_1
7. Fournier-Viger, P., Lin, J.C.W., Vo, B., Chi, T.T., Zhang, J., Le, B.: A survey of itemset mining. WIREs Data Min. Knowl. Discov. **7**(4), e1207 (2017)
8. Fournier-Viger, P., Wu, C.-W., Zida, S., Tseng, V.S.: FHM: faster high-utility itemset mining using estimated utility co-occurrence pruning. In: Andreasen, T., Christiansen, H., Cubero, J.-C., Raś, Z.W. (eds.) ISMIS 2014. LNCS (LNAI), vol. 8502, pp. 83–92. Springer, Cham (2014). https://doi.org/10.1007/978-3-319-08326-1_9
9. Kim, H., et al.: Efficient list based mining of high average utility patterns with maximum average pruning strategies. Inf. Sci. **543**, 85–105 (2021)
10. Nawaz, M.S., Fournier-Viger, P., Yun, U., Wu, Y., Song, W.: Mining high utility itemsets with hill climbing and simulated annealing. ACM Trans. Manag. Inf. Syst. **13**(1), 1–22 (2022)
11. Peng, A.Y., Koh, Y.S., Riddle, P.: mHUIMiner: a fast high utility itemset mining algorithm for sparse datasets. In: Kim, J., Shim, K., Cao, L., Lee, J.-G., Lin, X., Moon, Y.-S. (eds.) PAKDD 2017. LNCS (LNAI), vol. 10235, pp. 196–207. Springer, Cham (2017). https://doi.org/10.1007/978-3-319-57529-2_16
12. Qu, J., Fournier-Viger, P., Liu, M., Hang, B., Wang, F.: Mining high utility itemsets using extended chain structure and utility machine. Knowl. Based Syst. **208**, 106457 (2020)
13. Qu, J.-F., Liu, M., Fournier-Viger, P.: Efficient algorithms for high utility itemset mining without candidate generation. In: Fournier-Viger, P., Lin, J.C.-W., Nkambou, R., Vo, B., Tseng, V.S. (eds.) High-Utility Pattern Mining. SBD, vol. 51, pp. 131–160. Springer, Cham (2019). https://doi.org/10.1007/978-3-030-04921-8_5
14. Verma, A., Dawar, S., Kumar, R., Navathe, S., Goyal, V.: High-utility and diverse itemset mining. Appl. Intell. **51**(7), 4649–4663 (2021). https://doi.org/10.1007/s10489-020-02063-x

MaxFEM: Mining Maximal Frequent Episodes in Complex Event Sequences

Philippe Fournier-Viger[1], M. Saqib Nawaz[1]([✉]), Yulin He[1,2],
Youxi Wu[3], Farid Nouioua[4], and Unil Yun[5]

[1] Shenzhen University, Shenzhen, China
{philfv,msaqibnawaz}@szu.edu.cn
[2] Guangdong Laboratory of Artificial Intelligence and Digital Economy (SZ),
Shenzhen, China
yulinhe@gml.ac.cn
[3] Hebei University of Technology, Tianjin, China
[4] University of Bordj Bou Arreridj, El Anceur, Algeria
yunei@sejong.ac.kr
[5] Department of Computer Engineering, Sejong University, Seoul, Republic of Korea

Abstract. For the analysis of discrete sequences, frequent episode mining (FEM) is a key technique. The goal is to enumerate all subsequences of symbols or events that are appearing at least some minimum number of times. In the last decades, several efficient episode mining algorithms were designed. Nonetheless, a major issue is that they often yield a huge number of frequent episodes, which is inconvenient for users. As a solution, this paper presents an efficient algorithm called MaxFEM (Maximal Frequent Episode Miner) to identify only the maximal frequent episodes of a complex sequence. A major benefit is to reduce the set of frequent episodes presented to the user. MaxFEM includes many strategies to improve its performance. The evaluation of MaxFEM on real datasets confirms that it has excellent performance.

Keywords: Discrete sequence · Frequent episodes · Maximal episodes

1 Introduction

Over the last decades, various algorithms have been designed for analyzing data of different types such as transactions, sequences, graphs and trees. Among those data types, more and more attention is given to discrete sequences. A *discrete sequence* is a list of events or symbols. It can encode varied data such as sequences of moves in a Chess game, sequences of clicks on a website, sequences of alarms generated by a system [13], sequences of nucleotides in a virus genome [14], and sequences of words in a novel [5].

To uncover interesting patterns in data, a large body of research has focused on designing algorithms to extract frequent subsequences in discrete sequences. These studies can be generally categorized as addressing one of two tasks: *sequential pattern mining* (SPM) [5,15] and *frequent episode mining* (FEM) [13]. The

O. Surinta and K. Kam Fung Yuen (Eds.): MIWAI 2022, LNAI 13651, pp. 86–98, 2022.
https://doi.org/10.1007/978-3-031-20992-5_8

objective of the former task is finding patterns in several discrete sequences, while that of the latter is identifying patterns in a very long sequence. Algorithms for these problems are quite different and both have practical uses. The focus of this paper is on FEM.

The three inputs to FEM are (1) a discrete sequence, (2) a window size $maxWindow$ and (3) a minimum support ($minsup$) threshold. FEM outputs all the frequent episodes, that is the subsequences that appears no less than $minsup$ times in the input sequence. Finding frequent episodes is useful but very difficult computationally, especially for long sequences, low $minsup$ values and large $maxWindow$ values. For this reason, several efficient algorithms have been proposed. The first two algorithms are MINEPI and WINEPI [13]. WINEPI can identify serial episodes (where events are all sequentially ordered), parallel episodes (where all events are unordered) and composite episodes (where events are partially ordered). To find frequent episodes, WINEPI employs a breadth-first search and utilizes a sliding-window model. WINEPI computes the occurrence frequency (also called support) of an episode as the number of windows that contains an occurrence of the episode. As noted by Iwanuma et al. [9], a drawback of that definition is that a same occurrence may be counted multiple times. To avoid this problem, MINEPI was designed. It is a breadth-first search algorithm that only counts the minimal occurrences of each episode [13]. Thereafter, another occurrence counting function was proposed called the *head frequency*, which is used by several recent FEM algorithms such as EMMA, MINEPI+ [8], and TKE [7] as it is more suitable for prediction [8]. EMMA and TKE rely on a depth-first search in combination with a memory anchor structure to speed up the search, and were shown to outperform several earlier algorithms such as MINEPI [13] and MINEPI+ [8] by a large margin. In FEM, new algorithms and extensions are published regularly such as for discovering extended episode types such as high utility episodes [6,12] and online episodes [2].

Though frequent episodes can reveal useful information, a major issue is that current FEM algorithms can generate huge result sets, sometimes containing millions of frequent episodes, and that these episodes are often very similar to each other. For instance, when analyzing the data of a customer in a store, a frequent episode may indicate that the person bought milk, then bread, and then some oranges. But all the subsequences of this pattern would generally be also frequent such as the episode of buying milk followed by bread, the episode of buying bread followed by oranges, or the episode of buying milk followed by oranges. This is a major problem because all these patterns can be viewed as redundant as they are included in the first episode, and combing through large sets of episodes can be very time-consuming for users.

In recent years, some researchers have attempted to propose a solution to this problem by designing algorithms to discover concise representations of frequent episodes such as closed episodes [1,11] and maximal episodes [3]. The aim is to find a subset of all episodes that summarize them. But the majority of these algorithms are only able to analyze *simple sequences* (without simultaneous events) [1,3,11]. This greatly simplifies the problem of mining episodes but makes these algorithms unusable for analyzing many real life event sequences such as customer transactions (as customers may buy multiple products at the same time). Thus, it is important to address the general problem of mining concise representations of episodes in complex sequences (with simultaneous events).

To address this need, this paper presents a new algorithm called MaxFEM (Maximal Frequent Episode Miner) to mine maximal frequent episodes in complex event sequences. A maximal frequent episode is a frequent episode that is not included in larger frequent episodes. The key benefit of mining maximal episodes is that the number of frequent episodes presented to the user can be greatly reduced, as it will be shown in the experimental evaluation. To our best knowledge, MaxFEM is the first algorithm to discover maximal episodes in complex sequences. To efficiently discover the maximal frequent episodes, MaxFEM includes three strategies to improve its performance, named Efficient Filtering of Non-maximal episodes (EFE), Skip Extension checking (SEC), and Temporal pruning (TP). An evaluation of MaxFEM's performance on public datasets confirms that it has excellent performance.

The next sections have the following content. Section 2 describes the problem of FEM and the novel problem of maximal FEM. Then, Sect. 3 presents the MaxFEM algorithm. Section 4 reports results for the performance evaluation. Lastly, Sect. 5 concludes the paper with several directions for future work.

2   Problem Definition

This section provides a definition of the problem of FEM, discusses its properties, and then describes the proposed problem of maximal FEM.

The input data in FEM is a discrete sequence [8,13]. Assume that there is a finite set $E = \{i_1, i_2, \ldots, i_m\}$ of *events* (also called items or symbols). A subset $X \subseteq E$ is said to be *an event set*. A *discrete sequence*, also called a *complex event sequence*, is defined as a finite ordered list $S = \langle (SE_{t_1}, t_1), (SE_{t_2}, t_2), \ldots, (SE_{t_n}, t_n) \rangle$ of pairs of the form (SE_{t_i}, t_i) where $SE_{t_i} \in E$ is an event set and t_i is an integer representing a time-stamp. A sequence is ordered by time, that is for any integers $1 \leq i < j \leq n$, the relationship $t_i < t_j$ holds. An event set SE_{t_i} of a sequence contains events that are assumed to have occurred at the same time, and for this reason it is called a *simultaneous event set*. In the case, where a complex event sequence contains event sets each only having one event, it is said to be a *simple event sequence*. It is to be noted that a same event can appear multiple times in a sequence (in different event sets). Besides, although the definition of sequence includes time-stamps, it can also be used to model sequences that do not have time-stamps such as sequence of words by assigning contiguous integers as time-stamps (e.g. $1, 2, 3, 4, 5$).

To illustrate these definitions, a complex event sequence is illustrated in Fig. 1, which has eight event sets and time-stamps from 1 to 11. A formal representation of that sequence is $S = \langle (\{a, c\}, 1), (\{a\}, 2), (\{a, b\}, 3), (\{a\}, 6), (\{a, b\}, 7), (\{c\}, 8), (\{b\}, 9), (\{d\}, 11) \rangle$. That sequence S will be utilized through the paper as example. The interpretation of S is that events a and c occurred at time 1, were followed by event a at time 2, and then by a and b at time 3. Then, the event a was observed at time 6, the events a and b at time 7, the event c at time 8, the event b at time 9, and lastly event d at time 11. As shown in this example, time-stamps are not required to be contiguous. This type of sequences can store various information such as a list of events from a complex system, network data [10], cloud data [1], malicious attacks [16], and stock data [12].

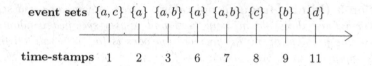

Fig. 1. A complex event sequences with eight event sets

In *FEM*, the goal is to uncover all frequent episodes in a complex event sequence. A frequent episode is an episode that has a large support (appear several times in the sequence). There are three types of episodes [13]. A *composite episode* α is a list of simultaneous event sets. A composite episode α having p event sets is represented as $\alpha = \langle X_1, X_2, \ldots, X_p \rangle$, where $X_i \subseteq E$, and X_i is said to appear before X_j for any integers $1 \leq i < j \leq p$. The *size* of α is defined as $size(\alpha) = \bigcup_{i \in [1,p]} |X_i|$. A *parallel episode* is a composite episode that contains a single event set. A *serial episode* is a composite episode where no event set has more than one event. Several FEM mining algorithms are only able to handle the special case of serial episodes, while others can find all composite episodes [8,13].

To find frequent episodes, the concept of support is crucial. Multiple functions have been proposed to compute the support (count occurrences of an episode in a sequence), which have different advantages and limitations. In this study, the *head frequency* support function [9] is used, which has been used in several recent algorithms such as MINEPI+ [8], EMMA [8] and TKE [7]. The concept of occurrence is first presented and then the head support function.

Definition 1 (Occurrence). *An* occurrence *of an episode* $\alpha = \langle X_1, X_2, \ldots, X_p \rangle$ *in a complex event sequence* $S = \langle (SE_{t_1}, t_1), (SE_{t_2}, t_2), \ldots, (SE_{t_n}, t_n) \rangle$ *is a time interval* $[t_s, t_e]$ *that satisfies* $X_1 \subseteq SE_{z_1}$, $X_2 \subseteq SE_{z_2}$, $\ldots$, $X_p \subseteq SE_{z_w}$ *for some integers* $t_s = z_1 < z_2 < \ldots < z_w = t_e$. *In an occurrence* $[t_s, t_e]$, t_s *is said to be the start point, while* t_e *is the end point. The length of an occurrence* $[t_s, t_e]$ *is defined as* $t_s - t_e$. *The notation* $occSet(\alpha)$ *represents the set of all occurrences of* α *that have a length that is smaller than some maximum length* wlen *set by the user.*

As example, if $wlen = 3$, the composite episode $\alpha = \langle \{a\}, \{a, b\} \rangle$ has an occurrence set with three occurrences, i.e. $occSet(\alpha) = \{[t_1, t_3], [t_2, t_3], [t_6, t_7]\}$.

Definition 2 (Head support). *Let* S *and* α *represent a composite sequence and an episode, respectively. The support of* α *in* S *is given by* $sp(\alpha) =$

$|\{t_s | [t_s, t_e] \in occSet(\alpha)\}|$, *that is how many start points in the occurrence set of α [8].*

Continuing the previous example, the support of $\alpha = \langle \{a\}, \{a, b\} \rangle$ is $sp(\alpha) = 3$ because there are three different start points in $occSet(\alpha)$, namely t_1, t_2, and t_6.

The problem of mining frequent episodes is then defined as:

Definition 3 (Mining frequent episodes). *Given, a complex event sequence S, a user-defined threshold $minsup > 0$ and a user-specified window length $wlen > 0$, the problem of mining frequent episodes is to enumerate all frequent episodes appearing in S. An episode α is frequent if $sp(\alpha) \geq minsup$ [8].*

For instance, for $minsup = 2$ and $wlen = 3$, there are seven frequent episodes in the sequence depicted in Fig. 1. Those are $\langle \{a\} \rangle$, $\langle \{b\} \rangle$, $\langle \{c\} \rangle$ $\langle \{a\}, \{b\} \rangle$, $\langle \{a, b\} \rangle$, $\langle \{a\}, \{a\} \rangle$, and $\langle \{a\}, \{a, b\} \rangle$. The support of these episodes are respectively 5, 3, 2, 2, 2, 3, and 2.

For the frequent episode mining problem, several algorithms were proposed. These algorithms can find the frequent episodes without considering all possible episodes. They use a powerful search space pruning property of the support, called the downward closure property, which indicates that an episode support cannot be greater than that of its prefix episodes [8]. Formally, this means that the relationship $sp(\alpha) \leq sp(\beta)$ holds for any episode $\beta = \langle X_1, X_2, \ldots, X_i \rangle$ and episode $\alpha = \langle X_1, X_2, \ldots, X_p \rangle$ where $i < p$.

A major problem with current algorithms for FEM is that too many frequent episodes may be discovered. To address this issue, we propose to discover only the maximal frequent episodes. Following is the definition of this problem.

Definition 4 (Mining maximal frequent episodes in a complex event sequence). *Given, a complex event sequence S, a user-defined threshold $minsup > 0$ and a user-specified window length $wlen > 0$, the problem of mining maximal frequent episodes is to enumerate all frequent episodes that are not strictly included in another frequent episode [8]. An episode $\alpha = \langle Y_1, Y_2, \ldots, Y_i \rangle$ is strictly included in an episode $\beta = \langle X_1, X_2, \ldots, X_p \rangle$ if and only if $Y_1 \subseteq X_{k_1}$, $Y_2 \subseteq X_{k_2} \ldots Y_i \subseteq X_{k_i}$ for some integers $1 \leq k_1 < k_2 < \ldots < k_i \leq p$. This relation is denoted as $\alpha \sqsubseteq \beta$.*

For instance, in the same example, there are only two maximal frequent episodes that are $\langle \{c\} \rangle$ and $\langle \{a\}, \{a, b\} \rangle$. Thus, five non-maximal frequent episodes are omitted, which can be viewed as redundant, as they are strictly included in the maximal episodes.

To solve the problem of mining maximal frequent episodes, a naive approach is to first discover all frequent episodes using a traditional algorithm such as EMMA [8] or TKE [7], and then to perform a post-processing step to compare frequent episodes to filter episodes that are non-maximal. This approach would work. However, it is inefficient because it requires keeping in memory all frequent episodes, and there can be a huge number. Results will be presented in Sect. 4

indicating that the number of maximal episodes can be much smaller than that of frequent episodes in practice. Hence, it is desirable to design an algorithm that does not require maintaining all frequent episodes in memory. The next section presents the MaxFEM algorithm.

3   The MaxFEM Algorithm

MaxFEM is the first algorithm to mine maximal frequent episodes in a complex event sequence (the general case). Also, differently from prior work [3], MaxFEM relies on the head frequency to count the support of episodes [7,8]. For exploring the search space of frequent episodes, MaxFEM performs a depth-first search using the basic search procedure of EMMA [8]. This procedure was selected as basis for MaxFEM because it is efficient for exploring the search space of frequent episodes with the head frequency. The procedure consists of first discovering frequent single events, then to combine these events to find frequent parallel episodes, and finally, to join the frequent parallel episodes to obtain frequent composite episodes. However, this procedure is not designed for identifying the maximal frequent episodes.

To find only the maximal frequent episodes and avoid the naive solution of filtering non-maximal episodes by post-processing, MaxFEM adopts the following approach. MaxFEM is equipped with a data structure called W for storing at any moment the current maximal frequent episodes. Then, MaxFEM starts searching for episodes. When MaxFEM finds a new frequent composite episode X, MaxFEM compares X with the episodes already in W. If X is strictly included in an episode already in W, then X is ignored as it is not maximal. In the other case where X is maximal, any episode in W that is strictly included in X is removed from W. When the algorithm terminates, this ensure obtaining the maximal frequent episodes. The next paragraphs present each step of the MaxFEM algorithm. Then, three additional optimizations are introduced to obtain a more efficient algorithm.

MaxFEM's input is (1) S: a complex event sequence, and (2) the *minsup* and *wlen* parameters. MaxFEM's output is the maximal frequent episodes. The pseudocode is shown in Algorithm 1. The key steps are the following:

Step 1. Finding the Frequent Events. MaxFEM reads S (the input sequence) to computes each single event support, that is $sp(e)$ for each $e \in E$. This allows determining the set $Z \leftarrow \{e|e \in E \land sp(e) \geq minsup\}$ of frequent events.

For example, consider the input sequence $S = \langle(\{a,c\}, 1), (\{a\}, 2), (\{a,b\}, 3), (\{a\}, 6), (\{a,b\}, 7), (\{c\}, 8), (\{b\}, 9), (\{d\}, 11)\rangle$ depicted in Fig. 1, $minsup = 2$ and $wlen = 3$. The frequent events are a, b and c, since they have a support of 5, 3 and 2, respectively, which is no less than *minsup*. The event d is infrequent because it has a support of $1 < minsup$. Thereafter, infrequent events ($e \notin Z$) will be ignored as they cannot appear in frequent episodes.

Algorithm 1: MaxFEM

---

    input : S: a complex event sequence, *wlen*: the window length, *minsup*: the
                 required minimum support,
    output: all episodes that are maximal and frequent

1 Count the support $sp(e)$ of each event e by scanning the sequence S;
2 Let Z denotes the frequent events (other events are not needed from now on);
3 Initialize and fill the location lists of frequent events based on the input
   sequence;
4 Initialize the set of parallel episodes as $ParE \leftarrow Z$;
5 **foreach** *frequent episode $ep \in ParE$ and frequent event $e \in Z$* **do**
6 | $ex \leftarrow extendParallelAndCreateLocationList(ep, e)$;
7 | Insert ex into $ParE$ if it is frequent according to its location list;
8 **end**
9 Initialize a set of potential maximal episodes as $W \leftarrow ParE$;
10 Using the episodes in $ParE$, transform the input sequence into a sequence S';
11 **foreach** *frequent composite episode $ep \in W$ and frequent event $e \in ParE$* **do**
12 | $ex \leftarrow extendSerialAndCreateBoundList(ep, e)$;
13 | **if** *ex is frequent according to its bound list and ex has no superset in W*
       | **then**
14 | | Insert ex in the set W;
15 | | Remove all subsets of ex that are in W;
16 | **end**
17 **end**
18 Return W;

Step 2. Build the Location-Lists of Frequent Events. Next, the sequence S is read another time to generate a vertical structure, named *location list* [8], for each frequent event. A formal definition of this structure is given:

Definition 5 (Location list). *Let there be an input sequence $S = \langle (SE_{t_1}, t_1),$ $(SE_{t_2}, t_2), \ldots, (SE_{t_n}, t_n) \rangle$. Furthermore, assume that events from each event set in S are sorted by a total order $\prec$ on events. Note that the total order can be any order, for example the alphabetical order ($a \prec b \prec \ldots \prec y \prec z$). If e (that represents an event) is included in the i-th event set SE_{t_i} of the input sequence, then e is said to appear at position $\sum_{w=1,\ldots,i-1} |SE_{t_w}| + |\{y|y \in SE_{t_i} \land y \prec e\}|$. With respect to S, the* location list *of e is the list of its time-stamps and is written as $locList(e)$. An interesting property is that e's support can be computed as the cardinality of its location list, which means $sp(e) = |locList(e)|$.*

Continuing the running example, the location lists of frequent events a, b and c are $locList(a) = \{1, 2, 3, 6, 7\}$, $locList(b) = \{3, 7, 9\}$ and $locList(c) = \{1, 8\}$, respectively.

Step 3. Finding the Frequent Parallel Episodes. In the third step, frequent episodes are recursively extended to find all frequent parallel episodes, as in EMMA [8]. A set to store frequent parallel episodes, called $ParE$, is created and initialized as $ParE = Z$. Then, MaxFEM tries extending each episode ep

in $ParE$ that is frequent by adding to it each frequent event $e \in Z$ such that $e \notin ep \land \forall f \in ep, f \prec e$ to obtain a larger parallel episode $ex = ep \cup \{e\}$. The resulting episode ex is said to be a *parallel extension* of ep with event e. To determine the support of ex, its location list is built by intersecting the location lists of e and ep. That is the location list of ex is created as $locList(ex) = locList(e) \cap locList(ep)$. If the support $|locList(ex)|$ is equal or greater than $minsup$, ex is added to $ParE$ (with its location list) because it is a frequent parallel episode. After recursively performing parallel extensions of episodes in $ParE$, this latter contains all frequent parallel episodes. For instance, the episode $\langle\{a\}\rangle$ can be extended with the frequent event c, to obtain the parallel episode $\langle\{a, c\}\rangle$. The location list of that episode is $loclist(\langle\{a, c\}\rangle) = loclist(\langle\{a\}\rangle) \cap loclist(\langle\{c\}\rangle) = \{1, 2, 3, 6, 7\} \cap \{1, 8\} = \{1\}$. Hence, the support of $\langle\{a, c\}\rangle$ is $sp(\langle\{a, c\}\rangle) = |loclist(\langle\{a, c\}\rangle)| = 1$ and this parallel extension is infrequent. After repeating this process to generate all parallel extensions, it is found that parallel frequent episodes are: $\langle\{a\}\rangle$, $\langle\{b\}\rangle$, $\langle\{c\}\rangle$, and $\langle\{a, b\}\rangle$. Their support values are 5, 3, 2, 2, respectively.

Step 4. Using Parallel Episodes to re-encode the Sequence. Next, a unique identifier is assigned to each parallel frequent episode by MaxFEM. It then transforms S into a *re-encoded sequence* S'. This is done by substituting events from S by episodes from $ParE$. For the running example, MaxFEM assigns #1, #2, #3 and #4 as identifiers for the episodes $\langle\{a\}\rangle$, $\langle\{b\}\rangle$, $\langle\{c\}\rangle$, and $\langle\{a, b\}\rangle$. Then, S is transformed into: $S' = \langle(\{\#1\#3\}, 1), (\{\#1\}, 2), (\{\#1, \#2, \#4\}, 3), (\{\#1\}, 6), (\{\#1, \#2, \#4\}, 7), (\{\#3\}, 8), (\{\#2\}, 9)\rangle$.

Step 5. Finding the Maximal Frequent Composite Episodes. Thereafter, MaxFEM searches for frequent maximal composite episodes using the re-encoded sequence S'. A data structure W is first initialized to store the maximal frequent composite episodes. All parallel frequent episodes are added to W, as they are currently considered to be maximal. Then, MaxFEM attempts to build larger frequent composite episodes by recursively performing serial extensions of episodes in W. A serial extension is the combination of an episode $ep = \langle SE_1, SE_2, \ldots, SE_x\rangle \in W$ with a parallel episode $pe \in ParE$ to obtain a larger composite episode $extendSerial(ep, pe) = \langle SE_1, SE_2, \ldots, SE_x, pe\rangle$.

For each serial extension $extendSerial(ep, pe)$, MaxFEM creates its *bound list* structure, defined as:

Definition 6 (Bound list). *Let there be a re-encoded sequence $S' = \langle(SE_{t_1}, t_1), (SE_{t_2}, t_2), \ldots, (SE_{t_n}, t_n)\rangle$. The bound list of a parallel episode pe is defined as $boundList(pe) = \{[t, t] | pe \subseteq SE_t \in S'\}$. The bound list of the serial extension of a composite episode ep with pe, is defined as: $boundList(extendSerial(ep, pe)) = \{[u, w] | [u, v] \in boundList(ep) \land [w, w] \in boundList(pe) \land w - u < wlen \land v < w\}$. The bound list of a composite episode ep allows deriving its support as $sp(ep) = |\{t_s | [ts, te] \in boundList(ep)\}|$.*

MaxFEM combines each episode in W with each parallel episode appearing in a same window $wlen$ in S' to create serial extensions. If an extension $extendSerial(ep, pe)$ is frequent and not strictly included in an episode already in W, then (1) it is added to W and (2) each episode $ee \in W$ that is strictly included in $extendSerial(ep, pe)$ is removed from W because it is not maximal. This process ensures maintaining the current maximal frequent composite episodes in W at any moment. When no more serial extensions can be done, W contains all maximal frequent episodes and W is returned to the user.

As example, consider the serial extension of $\langle\{a\}\rangle$ with $\langle\{a\}\rangle$, which results in $f = \langle\{a\}, \{a\}\rangle$. The bound list of f is $boundList(f) = \{[t_1, t_2], [t_2, t_3], [t_6, t_7]\}$. Hence, $sp(f) = |\{t_1, t_2, t_6\}| = 3$. Since this serial extension is frequent, it is added to W and $\langle\{a\}\rangle$ is removed from W. This process is repeated for other serial extensions. In the end, the set of maximal frequent episodes W is: $\langle\{c\}, \{a\}\rangle$, $\langle\{a\}, \{c\}\rangle$ and $\langle\{a\}, \{a, c\}\rangle$, with a support of 2, 2, and 3 respectively (the end result).

Completeness. It can be seen that MaxFEM is a complete algorithm as it relies on the search procedure of EMMA to explore the search space of frequent episodes, and MaxFEM only eliminates non-maximal episodes during the final step where composite episodes are generated (Step 4).

It can be tempting to also eliminate non-maximal episodes during the earlier step of generating parallel episodes (Step 3). But if this would be done, the algorithm would become incomplete. This is demonstrated by an example. If the parallel episode $\langle\{a\}\rangle$ is eliminated early in Step 3 because it is strictly included in the parallel episode $\langle\{a, c\}\rangle$, then the maximal episode $\langle\{a\}, \{a, c\}\rangle$ will not be generated in Step 4 and thus it would be missed in the final result.

Optimizations. MaxFEM applies three strategies to improve performance.

Strategy 1. Efficient Filtering of Non-maximal episodes (EFE). This strategy consists of using an appropriate data structure to implement W and to optimize the two operations that are done using it: (1) searching for episodes strictly included in an episode e (sub-episode checking) and (2) searching for episodes in which e is strictly included (super-episode checking). Because these checks are relatively costly, two ideas are used to reduce the number of checks.

First, W is implemented as a list of heaps $W = \{W_1, W_2, ...W_n\}$ where n is the size of the longest frequent episode discovered until now. In W, the heap W_x ($1 \leq x \leq n$) stores the maximal episodes found until now of size x. Then, to do super-episode (sub-episode) checking for an episode ep having w events, MaxFEM only compares ep with episodes in $W_{w+1}, W_{w+2}...W_n$ ($W_1, W_2...W_{w-1}$). This is because an episode can only be strictly included (strictly include) an episode if it has a larger (smaller) size.

Second, each event from the input sequence is encoded as a distinct integer. Then, a hash value $hash(ep)$ is calculated for each episode ep as the sum of its events. For instance, if the events a, b, c are encoded as 1, 2, and 3, the hash value of the episode $\langle\{a\}, \{a, c\}\rangle$ is $1 + 1 + 3 = 5$ Based on these hash values, episodes stored in each heap of W are sorted by decreasing hash values. This allows optimizing super-episode checking as follows. For a heap W_x and an episode α, if $hash(\alpha) > hash(\beta)$ for any episode $\beta \in W_x$, then it is unnecessary to check if $\alpha \sqsubset \beta$ for β and all episodes after β in W_x. Similarly, for a heap

W_x and an episode α, if $hash(\beta) > hash(\alpha)$ for any episode $\beta \in W_x$, then it is unnecessary to check $\beta \sqsubseteq \alpha$ as well as all episodes after β in W_x when W_x is traversed in reverse order.

Strategy 2. Skip Extension Checking (SEC). This strategy is based on the depth-first exploration of composite episodes. If a frequent episode ep is extended by serial extension to form another frequent episode, then it is unnecessary to do super-pattern and sub-pattern checking for ep as ep cannot be maximal. Thus, ep is only considered to be added to W if it has no frequent serial extensions.

Strategy 3. Temporal Pruning (TP). The third optimization aims at reducing the cost of creating bound lists. Creating the bound list of an extension $extendSerial(ep, pe)$ requires to compares elements in the bound lists of ep and pe one by one. If at any point the number of remaining elements is not enough to satisfy $minsup$, the construction of the bound-list is stopped.

4   Experimental Evaluation

A performance evaluation has been carried out to investigate MaxFEM's performance. The runtime of MaxFEM was compared with the EMMA [8] algorithm. EMMA is selected as baseline as MaxFEM relies on the search procedure of EMMA, and they both use the head frequency measure for counting episode occurrences, and they mine composite episodes for the general case of a complex sequence. Also, EMMA is also faster than some recent algorithms such as TKE [7]. All algorithms have been implemented in Java and the experiments were run on a laptop with Windows 11 and a Intel Core i7-8565U CPU @ 1.80 GHz and 16 GB of RAM. The memory usage of algorithms was captured using the Java API. Datasets and source code of the algorithms are available in the SPMF library (www.philippe-fournier-viger.com/spmf) [4].

Several datasets have been used and gave similar results but due to space limitations results for only two datasets are shown, called *Kosarak* and *Retail*, which are popular benchmark datasets for pattern mining and represent different data types. *Kosarak* is click-stream dataset from a Hungarian news portal containing 990,000 event sets, 41,270 distinct event types and an average event set size of 8.1 items. *Retail* is transaction data from a Belgian retail store containing 88,162 event sets, 16,470 distinct event types and an average event set size of 10.3 items. Table 1 presents the main characteristics of the datasets.

Table 1. Main characteristics of the two datasets

Dataset	Avg. Sequ. Len.	#Events	#Sequences	Density(%)
Kosarak	8.1	41,270	990,000	0.02
Retail	10.3	16,470	88,162	0.06

On each dataset, EMMA and MaxFEM were run with $wlen \in \{5, 10, 15\}$ while $minsup$ was decreased until a clear performance trend was observed or algorithms would fail to terminate due to a 300 s time limit set for experiments. Results shown in Fig. 2 compares the runtime and number of patterns found by each algorithm. It is observed that MaxFEM is always about 10% to 40% faster than EMMA. This is due to the three novel optimizations since EMMA and MaxFEM uses the same basic search procedure.

It is also observed that the number of maximal episodes is much smaller than all frequent episodes. For example, on Kosarak for $minsup = 20,000$ and $wlen = 5$, MaxFEM finds 694 maximal episodes, while EMMA finds 2,583 frequent episodes. Thus, it can be concluded that the performance of MaxFEM is acceptable and maximal episodes provide a compact summary of all frequent episodes. Results (not shown) on other tested datasets are similar.

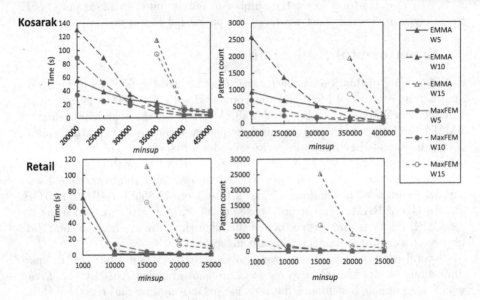

Fig. 2. Comparison of runtime and pattern count

5   Conclusion

This paper has proposed a novel algorithm named MaxFEM for discovering maximal episodes for the general case of a complex event sequence, and using the head frequency function. MaxFEM includes three strategies to improve its performance, named Efficient Filtering of Non-maximal episodes (EFE), Skip Extension checking (SEC), and Temporal pruning (TP). An experimental evaluation on real datasets has shown that maximal episodes provides a compact summary of all frequent episodes and that MaxFEM has a significant speed advantage over the EMMA algorithm. In future work, an interesting plan is to extend MaxFEM for other frequency functions and sequences types and to design a parallel and distributed version.

The source code of MaxFEM is available in the SPMF library [4], as well as a version of MaxFEM for mining all frequent episodes called AFEM (All Frequent Episode Miner). AFEM has the same output as EMMA but benefits from the optimizations of MaxFEM to improve efficiency.

References

1. Amiri, M., Mohammad-Khanli, L., Mirandola, R.: An online learning model based on episode mining for workload prediction in cloud. Futur. Gener. Comput. Syst. **87**, 83–101 (2018)
2. Ao, X., Luo, P., Li, C., Zhuang, F., He, Q.: Online frequent episode mining. In: Proceedings of the 31st IEEE International Conference on Data Engineering, pp. 891–902 (2015)
3. Ao, X., Shi, H., Wang, J., Zuo, L., Li, H., He, Q.: Large-scale frequent episode mining from complex event sequences with hierarchies. ACM Trans. Intell. Syst. Technol. **10**(4), 1–26 (2019)
4. Fournier-Viger, P., et al.: The SPMF open-source data mining library version 2. In: Berendt, B., et al. (eds.) ECML PKDD 2016. LNCS (LNAI), vol. 9853, pp. 36–40. Springer, Cham (2016). https://doi.org/10.1007/978-3-319-46131-1_8
5. Fournier-Viger, P., Lin, J.C.W., Kirah, U.R., Koh, Y.S.: A survey of sequential pattern mining. Data Sci. Pattern Recogn. **1**(1), 54–77 (2017)
6. Fournier-Viger, P., Yang, P., Lin, J.C.-W., Yun, U.: HUE-Span: fast high utility episode mining. In: Li, J., Wang, S., Qin, S., Li, X., Wang, S. (eds.) ADMA 2019. LNCS (LNAI), vol. 11888, pp. 169–184. Springer, Cham (2019). https://doi.org/10.1007/978-3-030-35231-8_12
7. Fournier-Viger, P., Yang, Y., Yang, P., Lin, J.C.-W., Yun, U.: TKE: mining top-k frequent episodes. In: Fujita, H., Fournier-Viger, P., Ali, M., Sasaki, J. (eds.) IEA/AIE 2020. LNCS (LNAI), vol. 12144, pp. 832–845. Springer, Cham (2020). https://doi.org/10.1007/978-3-030-55789-8_71
8. Huang, K., Chang, C.: Efficient mining of frequent episodes from complex sequences. Inf. Syst. **33**(1), 96–114 (2008)
9. Iwanuma, K., Takano, Y., Nabeshima, H.: On anti-monotone frequency measures for extracting sequential patterns from a single very-long data sequence. In: Proceedings of the IEEE Conference on Cybernetics and Intelligent Systems, vol. 1, pp. 213–217 (2004)
10. Li, L., Li, X., Lu, Z., Lloret, J., Song, H.: Sequential behavior pattern discovery with frequent episode mining and wireless sensor network. IEEE Commun. Mag. **55**(6), 205–211 (2017)
11. Liao, G., Yang, X., Xie, S., Yu, P.S., Wan, C.: Mining weighted frequent closed episodes over multiple sequences. Tehnički vjesnik **25**(2), 510–518 (2018)
12. Lin, Y., Huang, C., Tseng, V.S.: A novel methodology for stock investment using high utility episode mining and genetic algorithm. Appl. Soft Comput. **59**, 303–315 (2017)
13. Mannila, H., Toivonen, H., Verkamo, A.I.: Discovering frequent episodes in sequences. In: Proceedings of the 1st International Conference on Knowledge Discovery and Data Mining (1995)

14. Nawaz, M.S., Fournier-Viger, P., Shojaee, A., Fujita, H.: Using artificial intelligence techniques for COVID-19 genome analysis. Appl. Intell. **51**(5), 3086–3103 (2021). https://doi.org/10.1007/s10489-021-02193-w

15. Nawaz, M.S., Sun, M., Fournier-Viger, P.: Proof guidance in PVS with sequential pattern mining. In: Hojjat, H., Massink, M. (eds.) FSEN 2019. LNCS, vol. 11761, pp. 45–60. Springer, Cham (2019). https://doi.org/10.1007/978-3-030-31517-7_4

16. Su, M.Y.: Applying episode mining and pruning to identify malicious online attacks. Comput. Electr. Eng. **59**, 180–188 (2017)

Method for Image-Based Preliminary Assessment of Car Park for the Disabled and the Elderly Using Convolutional Neural Networks and Transfer Learning

Panawit Hanpinitsak[1,2]($\boxtimes$), Pitiphum Posawang[2,3], Sumate Phankaweerat[2], and Wasan Pattara-atikom[2]

[1] Department of Computer Engineering, Khon Kaen University, Khon Kaen 40002, Thailand
panaha@kku.ac.th

[2] Intelligent Transportation Systems Laboratory, National Electronics and Computer Technology, National Science and Technology Development Agency, Pathumthani 12120, Thailand

[3] Department of Computer Science, Vongchavalitkul University, Nakhon Ratchasima 30000, Thailand

Abstract. It is critical to assess the standards of disabled facilities in order to ensure the comfort and safety of disabled individuals who use them. In this study, deep convolutional neural networks (CNNs) with multi-label classification capability are employed for a preliminary evaluation of the car park for the disabled and the elderly in accordance with ministerial regulations, reducing the burden of on-site inspection by specialists. Using a transfer learning technique, the weights of an Inception-V3, Xception, and EfficientNet-B2 architectures previously trained on the ImageNet dataset were updated with the disabled car park image dataset. We used 4,812 training images and 355 test images to train, evaluate, and compare the model. The results revealed that the EfficientNet-B2 model yielded the best performance for 5 out of 6 classes, with the F1-score between 79.8% and 95.6%. In contrast, the remaining one class was best predicted by the Xception model, where the F1-score was 83.33%. This implies that it is possible to apply CNNs to aid in the evaluation of handicap facilities.

Keywords: Deep convolutional neural networks · Transfer learning · Multi-label classification · Disabled facilities assessment

1 Introduction

The World Health Organization (WHO) estimates that today roughly 15% of the world's population is disabled, or over 1 billion people, and this number is constantly rising [12]. As a result, organizations and public places should provide

O. Surinta and K. Kam Fung Yuen (Eds.): MIWAI 2022, LNAI 13651, pp. 99–110, 2022.
https://doi.org/10.1007/978-3-031-20992-5_9

facilities for people with disabilities and the elderly (hereinafter referred to as disabled facilities) that meet the standards so that the disabled and elderly people can travel to various places in comfort and safety.

For this purpose, several nations' governmental institutions have imposed disability laws and regulations, which include prescribing the characteristics of disabled facilities as recommendations for organizations to follow [11]. However, due to a lack of understanding about these laws, there are still many places where facilities do not or only partially fulfill the regulations. This makes travelling difficult and occasionally unsafe for handicapped people.

Thus, specialists must examine the standards of those facilities in order for the owners of these establishments to be aware of the problem and, as a result, improve the facilities. Disabled facilities examination may includes going to the actual place, checking whether these facilities contain the characteristics of interest defined by the regulations (such as checking whether the toilet closet and basin have handrails, or parking lot has the disabled sign), and filling out the detailed dimensions for each type of facility and each location through checklists, such as [2]. Because some places, such as hotels, shopping malls, and shopping centers, are huge and multi-story, these processes may take a long time and burdensome as there are a variety of amenities to consider.

To address the aforementioned issue, this paper studies the method for preliminary assessment of disabled facilities from their photos using convolutional neural networks (CNNs) with multi-label classification [29, 35] capability, where the CNN model evaluates whether the input facility images includes the characteristics of interests. After that, the evaluation results are used to decide whether the disabled facilities passed the initial screening and experts should be notified for a more thorough examination, or failed the initial screening and the building owners should be asked to get the facilities repaired. As a preliminary study, we performed this method on the disabled car park dataset. The characteristics of interests are determined based on Thailand's ministerial regulation [5–7]. To reduce the number of required training data, we fine-tuned Inception V3 [31], Xception [19], and EfficientNet-B2 [32] models previously trained on ImageNet [27] using the transfer learning technique [33]. Experimental results illustrate that the performance of the EfficientNet-B2 model was mostly superior to the other two models, with the F1-score in the range of 79.8%–95.6%.

2 Related Work

2.1 Manual Assessment of the Disabled Facilities

Traditionally, assessing the disabled facilities has been conducted via on-site inspection from experts, such as architects. The inspection is carried out in accordance with laws and regulations prescribing the characteristics of disabled facilities such as Americans with Disabilities Act (ADA) [25] of the United States, and Equality Act [8] of the United Kingdom. Since we would like to use this method to assess facilities in Thailand, we based the assessment on three Thailand's ministerial regulations, which are

1. Ministerial Regulations Prescribing Facilities in Buildings for the Disabled or Handicapped and the Elderly, B.E. 2548 (2005) [5],
2. Ministerial Regulations Prescribing the Characteristics or Provision of Equipment, Facilities or Services in Buildings, Places or Other Public Services for the Disabled to Access and Utilize, B.E. 2555 (2012) [7], and
3. Ministerial Regulations Prescribing Facilities in Buildings for the Disabled or Handicapped and the Elderly (No. 2), B.E. 2564 (2021) [6].

It is obvious that this method is the most precise. It is, however, expensive and time consuming. As a result, computer vision-based systems that are automatic or semi-automatic should be viable low-cost options.

2.2 Computer Vision Techniques for Assessing Disabled Facilities or Accessibility

Based on the authors' thorough literature review, almost all of the computer vision works addressing disabled facilities or public accessibility are about determining the accessibility of crosswalks and sidewalks. For instance, Hara and his colleagues [22–24] applied deformable part models (DPM) [20] to recognize curb ramps from Google Street View (GSV) [16] images. Few works [13,17,18] applied CNN to detect curb ramps and/or crosswalks from GSV images and/or other map databases. After that, [14] extended these works to detect eight micro-scale features including streetlight, walk signals, and bike symbols. In contrast, [30] utilized CNN to find street regions where curb ramps should be present but are missing. In [15], zebra crossing was detected from Google maps' satellite images exploiting zebra-localizer algorithm. [21,34] used Residual neural network to assess the usability of sidewalks.

To the best knowledge of the authors', computer vision has not previously been applied to detect the characteristics of interest of disabled facilities belonging to organizations such as disabled car park, yet in the open literature.

3 Research Methods

3.1 Data Collection and Labeling

We collected and augmented a total of 4,812 training images, and collected 355 test images of disabled car park. The photos were gathered from three sources: 1) images on the internet, 2) photos taken by the authors in the provinces of Nakhon Ratchasima, Pathumthani, and Khon Kaen, and 3) the database of crowd-sourced images across Thailand [1]. Table 1 shows the characteristics of interest and corresponding class division. The disabled car park consist of three characteristics of interest, each of which is divided into positive and negative classes. The positive class indicates that the component is present in the image, whereas the negative class indicates that it is not. The characteristics of interests to be used for automatic detection are selected in accordance with the three Thailand's ministerial regulations previously mentioned in Sect. 2.1.

All of the images were manually labeled. There are three labeling cases: First, if the image contains the characteristics of interest, positive label of 1 is assigned to its positive class, and negative label of 0 is assigned to its negative class. Second, if the image does not possess the characteristics of interest, the positive class is set to 0 and the negative class is set to 1. Third, if it is unclear if the image includes the characteristics of interest, 0 is assigned to both the positive and negative classes. Figure 1 depicts the example images and their corresponding positive labels, while Table 2 provides the number and proportion of images with positive labels assigned to them, as well as total number of images. Because each image may be associated with several labels, the sum of the number of images in each class does not equal the total number of images.

Table 1. Characteristics of interest and corresponding class division of car park

Facility	Characteristics of interest	Class division
Car park	Disabled symbol on the floor	Positive: with disabled symbol on the floor
		Negative: without disabled symbol on the floor
	Floor color	Positive: floor color is blue
		Negative: floor color is not blue
	Empty space beside the car park	Positive: with empty space beside car park
		Negative: without empty space beside car park

Table 2. Number and proportion of positively labeled images for each class

Facility	Class names	No. positively labeled images	
		Training dataset	Test dataset
Car park	With disabled symbol on the floor	3175 (66.0%)	260 (73.2%)
	Without disabled symbol on the floor	1565 (32.5%)	93 (26.2%)
	Floor color is blue	2373 (49.3%)	178 (50.1%)
	Floor color is not blue	2427 (50.4%)	176 (49.6%)
	With empty space beside car park	2548 (53.0%)	180 (50.7%)
	Without empty space beside car park	2264 (47.0%)	173 (48.7%)
	Total number of images	4,812 (100%)	355 (100%)

3.2 Preliminary Assessment Method

The method for preliminary assessment of facilities has three main steps. First, the transfer learning technique is used to train the pre-trained classification model. Second, the re-trained model is utilized to detect the characteristics of interest. Finally, the detection results are used to evaluate the facilities.

With disabled symbol on the floor
Floor color is blue
With empty space beside car park

With disabled symbol on the floor
Floor color is not blue
Without empty space beside car park

Without disabled symbol on the floor
Floor color is not blue
Without empty space beside car park

With disabled symbol on the floor
Floor color is blue
Without empty space beside car park

Without disabled symbol on the floor
Floor color is blue
Without empty space beside car park

With disabled symbol on the floor
Floor color is not blue
With empty space beside car park

Fig. 1. Example car park images and corresponding positive labels.

Training the Convolutional Neural Network Using Transfer Learning Concept. For training the model, we fine-tune Inception V3 [31], Xception [19], and EfficientNetB2 [32] models previously trained on ImageNet [27] so that high accuracy could be achieved even with a small number of training data. Although there are few other pre-trained models with better accuracy [4], these three models are chosen in this preliminary study as the number of parameters and inference time were not too high. As shown in Fig. 2, transfer learning is done by removing the last layer of the pre-trained model, and replacing with dropout and dense layers with the number of nodes matching to the number of classes to be predicted. Then, the sigmoid activation function is applied to the output layer. Sigmoid activation function was chosen instead of softmax since it allows the network to predict multiple classes at once [29]. Finally, the binary cross entropy (BCE) loss function was employed to update the weights, which is given by

$$L = -\frac{1}{n} \sum_{i=1}^{n} \left[y^{(i)} \log(\hat{y}^{(i)}) + (1 - y^{(i)}) \log(1 - \hat{y}^{(i)}) \right] \tag{1}$$

where n depicts the number of training samples for each training batch, $y^{(i)}$ and $\hat{y}^{(i)}$ are the ground-truth label vector and predicted score vector, respectively, of the i-th sample.

As for the training details, the model were trained using Keras [3] and Tensorflow [9]. The model validation was also performed at the end of each epoch using the test images. Table 3 shows the hyper-parameters used for training the CNN model. All the images are resized to 299×299 (Inception-V3, Xception)

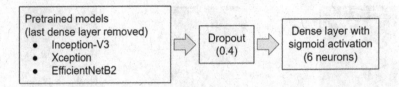

Fig. 2. Transfer learning with inception V3, Xception, and EfficientNetB2 model.

or 260×260 (EfficientNet-B2) and are grouped with a batch size of 64. Adam optimizer [26] was used for the optimization, and the dropout rate before the last layer was set to 0.4. The training has two stages [10]. First, meaningful features from the new dataset were extracted by unfreezing only the output layer of the network and training the model with the learning rate of 0.0001 for 10 iterations. Second, fine-tune the weights by unfreezing the last few layers of the network, and training the model with learning rate of 0.00001 for another 10 iterations, or until the validation loss starts to increase or remains stable. We chose 10 as the number of epoch as we experimentally found out that with this hyper-parameters setup the network roughly converges after only few epochs.

Table 3. Hyper-parameters used for training the CNN model

Hyper-parameters	Value
Image size	299×299 (Inception-V3, Xception), 260×260 (EfficientNetB2)
Batch size	64
Dropout rate	0.4
Optimization algorithm	Adam
Number of epoch	10
Learning rate	Feature extraction step: 0.0001
	Fine-tuning step: 0.00001
Unfrozen layers	Feature extraction step: Output layer
	Fine-tuning step: From 280-th layer (Inception-V3), From 120-th layer (Xception), From 235-th layer (EfficientNetB2)

Characteristics of Interest Detection and Preliminary Assessment of Facilities. After the multi-label CNN models described in the previous subsection are trained, they are used to detect the characteristics of interest by classifying the input image into multiple classes with confidence scores, and assessing them based on those values. Figure 3 depicts the process of assessing disabled facilities. The confidence scores of each of the characteristics of interest were output by the trained CNN model. The maximum between confidence scores of positive class and negative class is then calculated for each of the characteristics of interest and compared to a pre-determined threshold. It is estimated that the image includes the characteristics of interest if the positive class's confidence score is larger than both the negative class's confidence score and the threshold. In contrast, if the negative class's confidence score is higher than both the positive class's confidence score and the threshold, the image is predicted as not possessing the characteristics of interest. Once all characteristics of interest are predicted, the overall standards of the facility could be assessed. One may then arbitrarily establish the condition for sending the notification to professionals for a more detailed assessment or to the owners for repair depending on these detection results once the system has been launched for actual use.

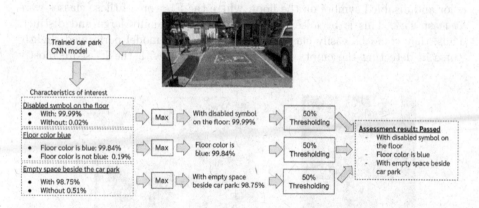

Fig. 3. Process of assessing car park.

3.3 Evaluating the Performance of the Method

This research uses three measures to analyze the method's performance: precision, recall, and F1-Score.

Precision is computed from the ratio between the number of images correctly predicted as being the positive class (true positive) and the total number images that is predicted as belonging to the positive class.

$$Precision = \frac{TP}{(TP + FP)} \tag{2}$$

Recall is calculated from the number of images in the true positive category divided by the number images that actually belongs to positive class.

$$Recall = \frac{TP}{(TP + FN)} \tag{3}$$

Finally, F1 score is the mean of precision and recall, which is computed by

$$F1 = 2 \cdot \frac{Precision \times Recall}{Precision + Recall} \tag{4}$$

Precision, recall, and F1 score are computed from the assessment results using the threshold of 50% as shown in Fig. 3.

4   Results and Discussion

Figure 4 show examples of classification results from the test dataset using Inception-V3 model. Correct labels are depicted in green, whereas the incorrect ones are depicted in red. Table 4 depicts the precision, recall, and F1 score of each class and model. All three models performed well on detecting the floor color and disabled symbol on the floor, where the F1-score of those classes were at least 85%. This is because these attributes are usually large and distinct. Thus, they could be easily classified. In contrast, the model performed slightly worse in detecting the empty space beside car park with the F1-score mostly

With disabled symbol on the floor: 99.48%
Floor color is blue: 99.66%
With empty space beside car park: 90.24%

With disabled symbol on the floor: 99.99%
Floor color is not blue: 97.07%
With empty space beside car park: 99.91%

Without disabled symbol on the floor: 74.66%
Floor color is not blue: 95.48%
Without empty space beside car park: 82.94%

Without disabled symbol on the floor: 94.65%
Floor color is not blue: 99.98%
Without empty space beside car park: 99.05%

Fig. 4. Examples of classification results from the test dataset using Inception-V3 model. (Color figure online)

Table 4. Precision, recall, and F1-score of each class

Model	Class	Precision	Recall	F1-score
Xception	With disabled symbol on the floor	93.87%	94.23%	94.05%
	Without disabled symbol on the floor	**90.48%**	81.72%	85.88%
	Floor color is blue	85.93%	96.07%	90.72%
	Floor color is not blue	96.08%	83.52%	89.36%
	With empty space beside car park	**80.73%**	**86.11%**	**83.33%**
	Without empty space beside car park	**84.87%**	74.57%	79.38%
Inception-V3	With disabled symbol on the floor	93.87%	94.23%	94.05%
	Without disabled symbol on the floor	90.36%	80.64%	85.22%
	Floor color is blue	**89.67%**	92.70%	91.16%
	Floor color is not blue	92.77%	**87.50%**	90.06%
	With empty space beside car park	78.57%	79.44%	79.01%
	Without empty space beside car park	81.37%	75.72%	78.44%
EfficientNet-B2	With disabled symbol on the floor	**95.40%**	**95.77%**	**95.59%**
	Without disabled symbol on the floor	89.13%	**88.17%**	**88.65%**
	Floor color is blue	89.53%	96.07%	92.68%
	Floor color is not blue	**96.25%**	87.50%	91.67%
	With empty space beside car park	80.54%	82.78%	81.64%
	Without empty space beside car park	82.21%	**77.46%**	**79.76%**

fell slightly below 80%. One possible explanation is because empty spaces come in different sizes and forms, and some are painted with faded-color as shown in Fig. 4, making it difficult for the model to learn and predict.

When comparing the performances among three models, in the case of ImageNet, the EfficientNet-B2 yielded the best top-1 accuracy at 80.1%, followed by Xception and Inception-V3 models at 79.0% and 77.9%, respectively [4]. Similar trends could be observed after fine-tuning the models with disabled car park dataset, where the Inception-V3 model was inferior to the other two models. However, it still yielded the best precision for the "floor color is blue" class at 89.7%. Moreover, five out of six classes were best predicted with the EfficientNet-B2 model, with the F1-score from 79.76% to 95.59%. In contrast, the Xception model showed best accuracy in predicting the empty space beside car park with the F1-score of 83.33%. This implies that although EfficientNet-B2 have a better accuracy overall, other inferior models may be good at predicting some certain features, which was consistent with the study in [36]. Thus, ensemble learning [28] might be a good approach to increase the performance. Furthermore, since the results were mostly consistent with those of ImageNet, it might be possible to improve the performance by using larger variants of EfficientNet.

5   Conclusion and Future Work

This paper studied the method for preliminary assessment of the disabled car park by detecting the characteristics of interest using CNNs and transfer learning. We fine-tuned three models previously trained on ImageNet. Then the these models were used for detecting the characteristics of interests and preliminary assessment. Experimental results showed that the floor color and presence of disabled symbol could be predicted well. Furthermore, EfficientNet-B2 model had the best accuracy, followed by the Xception model and Inception-V3 model, which were consistent with the ImageNet classification results. In the future work, we will investigate the performance with larger EfficientNet architectures, as well as evaluate the method on other types of disabled facilities. We may also investigate whether ensemble learning could improve the accuracy.

References

1. https://ud.traffy.in.th/
2. Institute for Human Centered Design, ada checklist for existing facilities (2016). https://www.adachecklist.org/doc/fullchecklist/ada-checklist.pdf
3. Keras. https://keras.io/
4. Keras applications. https://keras.io/api/applications/
5. Ministry of interior, ministerial regulations prescribing facilities in buildings for the disabled or handicapped and the elderly, b.e. 2548 (in thai). https://download.asa.or.th/03media/04law/cba/mr/mr48-58e-upd(02).pdf
6. Ministry of interior, ministerial regulations prescribing facilities in buildings for the disabled or handicapped and the elderly (no. 2), b.e. 2564 (in thai). http://www.ratchakitcha.soc.go.th/DATA/PDF/2564/A/016/T_0019.PDF
7. Ministry of interior, ministerial regulations prescribing the characteristics or provision of equipment, facilities or services in buildings, places or other public services for the disabled to access and utilize, b.e. 2555 (in thai). https://www.doe.go.th/prd/assets/upload/files/BKK_th/d2d8c77204d9b6d2853cd9cd9240c23f.pdf
8. Parliament of the United Kingdom, equality act (2010). https://www.legislation.gov.uk/ukpga/2010/15/contents
9. Tensorflow. https://www.tensorflow.org/
10. Transfer learning and fine-tuning. https://www.tensorflow.org/tutorials/images/transfer_learning/
11. United Nations, disability laws and acts by country/area. https://www.un.org/development/desa/disabilities/disability-laws-and-acts-by-country-area.html
12. World Health Organization, 10 facts on disability. https://www.who.int/news-room/facts-in-pictures/detail/disabilities
13. Abbott, A., Deshowitz, A., Murray, D., Larson, E.C.: Walknet: a deep learning approach to improving sidewalk quality and accessibility. SMU Data Sci. Rev. 1(1), 7 (2018)
14. Adams, M.A., Phillips, C.B., Patel, A., Middel, A.: Training computers to see the built environment related to physical activity: detection of micro-scale walkability features using computer vision (2022)

15. Ahmetovic, D., Manduchi, R., Coughlan, J.M., Mascetti, S.: Zebra crossing spotter: automatic population of spatial databases for increased safety of blind travelers. In: Proceedings of the 17th International ACM SIGACCESS Conference on Computers & Accessibility, pp. 251–258 (2015)

16. Anguelov, D., et al.: Google street view: capturing the world at street level. Computer **43**(6), 32–38 (2010)

17. Berriel, R.F., Rossi, F.S., de Souza, A.F., Oliveira-Santos, T.: Automatic large-scale data acquisition via crowdsourcing for crosswalk classification: a deep learning approach. Comput. Graph. **68**, 32–42 (2017)

18. Blanc, N., et al.: Building a crowdsourcing based disabled pedestrian level of service routing application using computer vision and machine learning. In: 2019 16th IEEE Annual Consumer Communications & Networking Conference (CCNC), pp. 1–5. IEEE (2019)

19. Chollet, F.: Xception: Deep learning with depthwise separable convolutions. In: Proceedings of the IEEE Conference on Computer Vision and Pattern Recognition, pp. 1251–1258 (2017)

20. Felzenszwalb, P., McAllester, D., Ramanan, D.: A discriminatively trained, multi-scale, deformable part model. In: 2008 IEEE Conference on Computer Vision and Pattern Recognition, pp. 1–8. IEEE (2008)

21. Froehlich, J.: Combining crowdsourcing and machine learning to collect sidewalk accessibility data at scale. Technical report (2021)

22. Hara, K., Froehlich, J.E.: Characterizing and visualizing physical world accessibility at scale using crowdsourcing, computer vision, and machine learning. ACM SIGACCESS Accessibility Comput. **113**, 13–21 (2015)

23. Hara, K., Le, V., Sun, J., Jacobs, D., Froehlich, J.: Exploring early solutions for automatically identifying inaccessible sidewalks in the physical world using google street view. Human Comput. Interact. Consortium (2013)

24. Hara, K., Sun, J., Moore, R., Jacobs, D., Froehlich, J.: Tohme: detecting curb ramps in google street view using crowdsourcing, computer vision, and machine learning. In: Proceedings of the 27th Annual ACM Symposium on User Interface Software and Technology, pp. 189–204 (2014)

25. Kent, J.: ADA in Details: Interpreting the 2010 Americans with Disabilities Act Standards for Accessible Design. John Wiley & Sons, Hoboken (2017)

26. Kingma, D.P., Ba, J.: Adam: a method for stochastic optimization. arXiv preprint. arXiv:1412.6980 (2014)

27. Krizhevsky, A., Sutskever, I., Hinton, G.E.: Imagenet classification with deep convolutional neural networks. In: Advances in Neural Information Processing Systems, vol. 25 (2012)

28. Sagi, O., Rokach, L.: Ensemble learning: a survey. Wiley Interdisc. Rev. Data Min. Knowl. Discovery **8**(4), e1249 (2018)

29. Stivaktakis, R., Tsagkatakis, G., Tsakalides, P.: Deep learning for multilabel land cover scene categorization using data augmentation. IEEE Geosci. Remote Sens. Lett. **16**(7), 1031–1035 (2019). https://doi.org/10.1109/LGRS.2019.2893306

30. Sun, J., Jacobs, D.W.: Seeing what is not there: learning context to determine where objects are missing. In: Proceedings of the IEEE Conference on Computer Vision and Pattern Recognition, pp. 5716–5724 (2017)

31. Szegedy, C., Vanhoucke, V., Ioffe, S., Shlens, J., Wojna, Z.: Rethinking the inception architecture for computer vision. In: Proceedings of the IEEE Conference on Computer Vision and Pattern Recognition (CVPR) (2016)

32. Tan, M., Le, Q.: Efficientnet: rethinking model scaling for convolutional neural networks. In: International Conference on Machine Learning, pp. 6105–6114. PMLR (2019)

33. Torrey, L., Shavlik, J.: Transfer learning. In: Handbook of Research on Machine Learning Applications and Trends: Algorithms, Methods, and Techniques, pp. 242–264. IGI global (2010)

34. Weld, G., Jang, E., Li, A., Zeng, A., Heimerl, K., Froehlich, J.E.: Deep learning for automatically detecting sidewalk accessibility problems using streetscape imagery. In: The 21st International ACM SIGACCESS Conference on Computers and Accessibility, pp. 196–209 (2019)

35. Wu, J., et al.: Multi-label active learning algorithms for image classification: overview and future promise. ACM Comput. Surv. (CSUR) 53(2), 1–35 (2020)

36. Xue, D., et al.: An application of transfer learning and ensemble learning techniques for cervical histopathology image classification. IEEE Access 8, 104603–104618 (2020)

Multi-resolution CNN for Lower Limb Movement Recognition Based on Wearable Sensors

Narit Hnoohom[1] ⓘD, Pitchaya Chotivatunyu[1] ⓘD, Sakorn Mekruksavanich[2] ⓘD,
and Anuchit Jitpattanakul[3] (✉) ⓘD

[1] Image, Information and Intelligence Laboratory, Department of Computer Engineering,
Faculty of Engineering, Mahidol University, Nakorn Pathom, Thailand
narit.hno@mahidol.ac.th, pitchaya.cht@student.mahidol.ac.th
[2] Department of Computer Engineering, School of Information and Communication
Technology, University of Phayao, Phayao, Thailand
sakorn.me@up.ac.th
[3] Intelligent and Nonlinear Dynamic Innovations Research Center, Department of Mathematics,
Faculty of Applied Science, King Mongkut's University of Technology North Bangkok,
Bangkok, Thailand
anuchit.j@sci.kmutnb.ac.th

Abstract. Human activity recognition (HAR) remains a difficult challenge in human-computer interaction (HCI). The Internet of Healthcare Things (IoHT) and other technologies are expected to be used primarily in conjunction with HAR to support healthcare and elder care. In HAR research, lower limb movement recognition is a challenging research topic that can be applied to the daily care of the elderly, fragile, and disabled. Due to recent advances in deep learning, high-level autonomous feature extraction has become feasible, which is used to increase HAR efficiency. Deep learning approaches have also been used for sensor-based HAR in various domains. This study presents a novel method that uses convolutional neural networks (CNNs) with different kernel dimensions, referred to as multi-resolution CNNs, to detect high-level features at various resolutions. A publicly available benchmark dataset called HARTH was used to evaluate the recognition performance to collect acceleration data of the lower limb movements of 22 participants. The experimental results show that the proposed approach improves the F1 score and achieves a higher score of 94.76%.

Keywords: Human activity recognition · Deep learning · Wearable sensor · Accelerometer · Multi-Resolution CNN

1 Introduction

Human motion analysis is a topic that receives much attention in robotics and medicine. Research on ambulatory activities is being conducted in rehabilitation science to improve the quality of life and context awareness in designing human-machine interfaces. For example, in [1], an intelligent system for elderly and disabled people is proposed where

O. Surinta and K. Kam Fung Yuen (Eds.): MIWAI 2022, LNAI 13651, pp. 111–119, 2022.
https://doi.org/10.1007/978-3-031-20992-5_10

the user can communicate with a robot via gesture recognition and recognition of every-day activities. These technologies help monitor the health status of patients and older people. In [2], a multi-sensor system is proposed to allow continuous rehabilitation monitoring. Diagnosing diseases such as multiple sclerosis, Parkinson's disease, and stroke [3] has been performed using human gait analysis.

Moreover, human gait has been utilized to develop indoor pedestrian navigation systems that can lead users to a specific area or track their daily activity level [4]. Multimodal systems have been designed for gait analysis for biometric applications [5]. Upper and lower limb motion analyses are also helpful for the development of prosthetic limbs for amputees [6].

Recognizing lower limb movements is essential for the daily care of the elderly, the weak, and the disabled. It is widely accepted that approaches for identifying lower limb movement can be divided into three types [7]: computer vision-based, ambient device-based, and wearable sensor-based. Computer vision-based types can monitor activities by analyzing video footage captured by cameras with multiple viewpoints placed at the desired location [8]. The implementation of computer vision-based technology is restricted by the space required to install the sensors [9]. The ambient device-based type provides for installing ambient sensors to measure the frequency of vibrations caused by regular activities for motion detection [10].

Nevertheless, activity monitoring can be severely affected by various environmental conditions. Aside from that, privacy concerns may arise with this approach [11]. The wearable sensor-based type uses multiple compact, wireless, and low-cost wearable sensor devices to record lower limb activity information [12]. The wearable sensor is suitable for outdoor use and compatible with the physical environment, and is primarily used for lower limb motion detection [13].

This work was motivated by the desire to develop and propose a method for recognizing lower limb movement that is highly accurate and capable of extracting useful information from inertial signals. To assess the multi-dimensional information included within the inertial signal, the multi-resolution convolutional neural network (M-CNN) was introduced to pull out high-level features and efficiently identify lower limb movements. The proposed model's performance in recognition is assessed with the help of training and testing data taken from a reference dataset known as HARTH, which is open to the public. Finally, the evaluated metrics are compared with three basic deep learning (DL) models.

The following structure can be seen throughout the remainder of this article's content: Sect. 2 presents recent related work on DL approaches for lower limb movement. Section 3 describes in detail the multi-resolution CNN model utilized in this study. Section 4 demonstrates our experimental results using a publicly available benchmark dataset. This section also contrasts the outcomes of the proposed model with those of the fundamental DL models. Section 5 concludes this work and identifies areas for potential future research.

2   Related Works

2.1   Types of Sensor Modalities

Even though many HAR techniques can be generalized to all sensor modalities, most are specialized and have a limited scope. Modalities can be divided into three categories: body-worn sensors, ambient sensors, and object sensors.

One of the most common HAR modalities is the use of body-worn sensors. Examples of body-worn sensors include gyroscopes, magnetometers, and accelerometers. These devices can collect information about human activity by analyzing angular velocity and acceleration variations. Several studies on DL for lower limb movements have used body-worn sensors; nevertheless, most studies have concentrated on the data gathered from accelerometers. Gyroscopes and magnetometers are commonly used in conjunction with accelerometers to detect lower limb movements [14]. Ambient sensors are often embedded in a user's smart environment and consist of sound sensors, pressure sensors, temperature sensors, and radar. They are commonly used in data collection to study people's interactions and environment. The movement of objects can be measured with various object sensors, while ambient sensors can detect changes in the surrounding environment. Several research papers have investigated ambient sensors for HAR in ADL and hand movements [15]. Some experiments have used accelerometers or sensors in combination with ambient sensors to optimize the HAR accuracy. This shows that adopting hybrid sensors that collect different data sets from other sources can considerably boost research in HAR and encourage applications such as commercial smart home systems [16].

2.2   Deep Learning Approaches

The challenges associated with feature extraction in conventional machine learning (ML) can potentially be solved by DL [17]. Figure 1 demonstrates how DL can improve HAR performance using different network configurations. The features are extracted, and the models are trained simultaneously in DL. The network can learn the features automatically instead of manually hand-crafted as in conventional ML approaches.

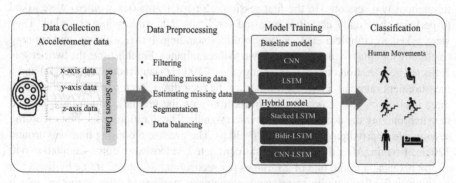

Fig. 1. DL-based-HAR pipeline.

3 The Sensor-Based HAR Framework

The sensor-based HAR framework consists of four main processes: (1) data acquisition, (2) data pre-processing, (3) data generation, and (4) training models and classification, as shown in Fig. 2.

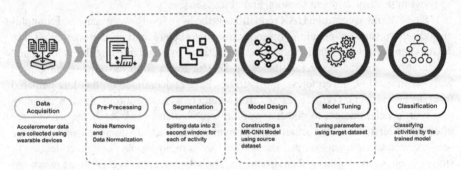

Fig. 2. The framework for HAR developed using sensors was used in this work.

3.1 HARTH Dataset

The human Activity Recognition Trondheim dataset, also known as HARTH, is available as a public dataset [18]. Twenty-two participants were recorded for 90 to 120 min during their regular working hours using two triaxial accelerometers attached to the lower back and thighs and a camera attached to the chest. Experts annotated the data independently using the camera's video signal. They labeled twelve activities. For the HARTH dataset, two triaxial Activity AX3 accelerometers [19] were used to collect data. The AX3 is a compact sensor that weighs only 11 g. Configurable parameters include sampling rate (between 12.5 and 3,200 Hz), measurement range ($\pm 2/4/8/16$ g), and resolution (which can be up to 13 bits).

A total of twelve different types of physical activities were recorded for the dataset throughout two sessions. In the first session, 15 participants (six women) were asked to perform their daily activities as usual for 1.5 to 2 h while being recorded. They were asked to complete each activity: sitting, standing, lying, walking, and running (including jogging) for a minimum of two to three minutes. For this time, the two sensors collected acceleration data at a sampling rate of 100 Hz (later reduced to 50 Hz) and a measurement range of ± 8 g. At the start of the recordings, each participant conducted three heel drops (i.e., dropped their heels firmly on the ground), which later assisted in synchronizing the acceleration and video signals. The duration of the first recording session was approximately 1,804 min ($\approx$30 h). The average recording time was around 120 ± 21.6 min. After the recording was completed, videos were down-sampled to 640 $\times$ 360 pixels at a frame rate of 25 frames per second and annotated frame by frame. In addition to the five activities presented, participants performed other activities, which we labeled as follows: climbing Stairs (up), climbing Stairs (down), shuffling (standing with leg movement), cycling (standing), cycling (sitting), transportation (sitting) (e.g., in a car), and transportation (standing) (e.g., in a bus). This resulted in a total of twelve different designations.

3.2 Data Pre-processing

Raw sensor data were processed in the data preprocessing as follows: Removal of noise and normalization of the data. In this work, an average smoothing filter was applied to gyroscope and accelerometer sensors in all three dimensions to remove noise from the signals. Then, the sensor data is normalized, which helps to solve the model learning problem by bringing all data values into a similar range. As a result, the gradient descents can converge faster. Next, the normalized data were segmented using a sliding window with a fixed width of two seconds and a percentage overlap of 50%.

3.3 The Proposed Multi-resolution CNN Model

The multi-resolution technology CNN stands for a convolutional neural network with advanced features. It consists of filters with different kernel sizes, and these filters must be used in each layer to extract relevant information from the convolutional layers successfully. Nafea et al. [16] demonstrated encouraging HAR results with multi-resolution modules based on the inception modules provided by Szegedy et al. [20]. This inspired us to investigate them in more detail. Multiple kernel sizes are used, and the results of these kernel sizes are combined, as opposed to the standard CNN practice of using only a single kernel size in a single layer. The result is that a single layer is used to extract features from various scales. Figure 3 shows the proposed multi-resolution CNN.

3.4 Performance Measurement Criteria

Four standard evaluation metrics, e.g., accuracy, recall, and F1-score, are calculated using 5-fold cross-validation to evaluate the effectiveness of the suggested DL model. The mathematical formulas for the four metrics are given below:

$$Accuracy = \frac{TP + TN}{TP + TN + FP + FN} \tag{1}$$

$$Precision = \frac{TP}{TP + FP} \tag{2}$$

$$Recall = \frac{TP}{TP + FN} \tag{3}$$

$$F1 - score = 2 \times \frac{Precision \times Recall}{Precision + Recall} \tag{4}$$

These four metrics were used to quantify the effectiveness of HAR. The recognition was a true positive (TP) for the class under consideration and a true negative for all other classes (TN). Misclassified sensor data may result in a false positive (FP) recognition for the class under consideration. Sensor data that should belong to another class may be misclassified, resulting in a false negative (FP) recognition of that class.

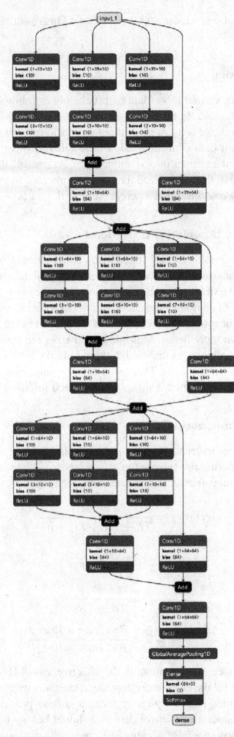

Fig. 3. A detailed description of the proposed multi-resolution CNN.

4   Experiments and Results

We have described the experimental setup and provided the experimental results to evaluate three basic DL models (CNN, LSTM, and CNN-LSTM), including the proposed multi-resolution CNN.

4.1   Experiments

All experiments were conducted on the Google Colab Pro with a Tesla V100. NumPy (NumPy 1.18.5) was used to work with matrices, Pandas (Pandas 1.0.5) was used to work with CSV files, and Scikit-Learn was used to evenly divide examples by class for the training, testing, and validation datasets. The Python programming (Python 3.6.9) and other libraries (Keras 2.3.1 and TensorFlow 2.2.0) were used to perform the experiments.

4.2   Experimental Results

The performance of DL models for recognizing data from wearable sensors is shown in Table 1. According to the experimental results, the proposed MR-CNN model had the highest performance, measured by an F1-score of 94.76%.

Table 1. Performance metrics of DL models using sensor.

Model	Performance		
	Accuracy	Loss	F1-score
CNN	95.98521% ($\pm$0.06931%)	0.54300 ($\pm$0.02758%)	88.31424% ($\pm$0.82847%)
LSTM	97.19258% ($\pm$0.22752%)	0.14847 ($\pm$0.02141%)	94.03455% ($\pm$0.58847%)
CNN-LSTM	97.45165% ($\pm$0.13398%)	0.15704 ($\pm$0.01128%)	93.99878% ($\pm$0.20887%)
MR-CNN	97.59014% ($\pm$0.19828%)	0.13416 ($\pm$0.02137%)	94.76309% ($\pm$0.55325%)

We considered classification results obtained from the MR-CNN as shown in Table 2. Regarding the activities of sitting in the HARTH dataset, the MR-CNN model achieved an F1-score of 1.00, as these activities do not involve movement. In contrast, F1-score values greater than 0.95 identify walking and running activities in the dataset.

Table 2. Performance metrics of DL models using sensor data of lower limb movement.

Activity	Performance			
	CNN	LSTM	CNN-LSTM	MR-CNN
Walking	0.94	0.95	0.95	0.95
Running	0.99	0.99	0.98	0.99
Ascending	0.59	0.89	0.87	0.80
Descending	0.71	0.89	0.84	0.89
Standing	0.92	0.94	0.95	0.94
Sitting	1.00	1.00	1.00	1.00
Lying	0.99	0.98	0.99	0.99
Cycling (sit)	0.96	0.98	0.98	0.98
Cycling (stand)	0.71	0.81	0.83	0.84
Average	0.87	0.94	0.93	0.94

5   Conclusions

This research proposed a new architecture using multiple convolutional layers with different kernel dimensions to achieve feature recognition with different resolutions. The proposed multi-resolution convolutional neural network (MR-CNN) model outperformed previous work in a public HARTH dataset that does not contain hand-crafted features. A comparison of the confusion matrices shows that the MR-CNN model achieved the highest performance of 94.76% in activity differentiation.

In our future work, we intend to use various types of DL networks, including ResNeXt, InceptionTime, Temporal Transformer, etc., in heterogeneous human activity recognition. Moreover, data augmentation is an exciting technique for model improvement in imbalanced datasets. This technique can be used for this problem.

Acknowledgments. The authors gratefully acknowledge the financial support provided by the Thammasat University Research fund under the TSRI, Contract No. TUFF19/2564 and TUFF24/2565, for the project of "AI Ready City Networking in RUN", based on the RUN Digital Cluster collaboration scheme. This research project was supported by the Thailand Science Research and Innovation fund, the University of Phayao (Grant No. FF65-RIM041), and supported by National Science, Research and Innovation (NSRF), and King Mongkut's University of Technology North Bangkok, Contract No. KMUTNB-FF-66-07.

References

1. Zhu, C., Sheng, W.: Wearable sensor-based hand gesture and daily activity recognition for robot-assisted living. IEEE Transactions on Systems, Man, and Cybernetics – Part A: Systems and Humans **41**(3), 569–657 (2011)

2. González-Villanueva, L., Cagnoni, S., Ascari, L.: Design of a wearable sensing system for human motion monitoring in physical rehabilitation. Sensors **13**(6), 7735–7755 (2013). https://doi.org/10.3390/s130607735

3. Muro-de-la-Herran, A., Garcia-Zapirain, B., Mendez-Zorrilla, A.: Gait analysis methods: an overview of wearable and non-wearable systems, highlighting clinical applications. Sensors **14**(2), 3362–3394 (2014). https://doi.org/10.3390/s140203362

4. Fourati, H.: heterogeneous data fusion algorithm for pedestrian navigation via foot-mounted inertial measurement unit and complementary filter. IEEE Trans. Instrum. Meas. **64**(1), 221–229 (2015)

5. Muaaz, M., Nickel, C.: Influence of different walking speeds and surfaces on accelerometer-based biometric gait recognition. In: 2012 35th International Conference on Telecommunications and Signal Processing (TSP), pp. 508–512. IEEE, Prague, Czech Republic (2012)

6. Gijsberts, A., Caputo, B.: Exploiting accelerometers to improve movement classification for prosthetics. In: 2013 IEEE 13th International Conference on Rehabilitation Robotics (ICORR), pp. 1–5. IEEE, Seattle, WA, USA (2013)

7. Mubashir, M., Shao, L., Seed, L.: A survey on fall detection: principles and approaches. Neurocomputing **100**, 144–152 (2013)

8. Casilari, E., Lora-Rivera, R., García-Lagos, F.: A study on the application of convolutional neural networks to fall detection evaluated with multiple public datasets. Sensors **20**(5), 1466 (2020). https://doi.org/10.3390/s20051466

9. Alves, J., Silva, J., Grifo, E., Resende, C., Sousa, I.: Wearable Embedded Intelligence for Detection of Falls Independently of on-Body Location. Sensors **19**(11), 2426 (2019). https://doi.org/10.3390/s19112426

10. Shah, S.A., Fioranelli, F.: RF sensing technologies for assisted daily living in healthcare: a comprehensive review. IEEE Aerosp. Electron. Syst. Mag. **34**(11), 26–44 (2019)

11. Shahzad, A., Kim, K.: FallDroid: an automated smart-phone-based fall detection system using multiple kernel learning. IEEE Trans. Industr. Inf. **15**(1), 35–44 (2018)

12. Yang, Y.K., et al.: Performance comparison of gesture recognition system based on different classifiers. IEEE Trans. Cogn. Dev. Syst. **13**(1), 141–150 (2021)

13. Xi, X., Tang, M., Miran, S.M., Luo, Z.: Evaluation of feature extraction and recognition for activity monitoring and fall detection based on wearable sEMG sensors. Sensors **17**(6), 1229 (2017). https://doi.org/10.3390/s17061229

14. Hussain, T., Maqbool, H.F., Iqbal, N., Mukhtaj Khan, N.A., Salman, A.A., Sanij, D.: Computational model for the recognition of lower limb movement using wearable gyroscope sensor. Int. J. Sens. Netw. **30**(1), 35 (2019). https://doi.org/10.1504/IJSNET.2019.099230

15. Wang, Y., Cang, S., Yu, H.: A survey on wearable sensor modality centred human activity recognition in health care. Expert Syst. Appl. **137**, 167–190 (2019)

16. Nafea, O., Abdul, W., Muhammad, G., Alsulaiman, M.: Sensor-based human activity recognition with spatio-temporal deep learning. Sensors **21**(6), 2141 (2021). https://doi.org/10.3390/s21062141

17. Baldominos, A., Cervantes, A., Saez, Y., Isasi, P.: A comparison of machine learning and deep learning techniques for activity recognition using mobile devices. Sensors **19**(3), 521 (2019). https://doi.org/10.3390/s19030521

18. Logacjov, A., Bach, K., Kongsvold, A., Bårdstu, H.B., Mork, P.J.: HARTH: a human activity recognition dataset for machine learning. Sensors 2021, **21**, 7853 (2021)

19. Axivity Homepage. https://axivity.com/lncs. Last Accessed 8 May 2022

20. Szegedy, C., et al.: Going deeper with convolutions. In: 2015 IEEE Conference on Computer Vision and Pattern Recognition (CVPR), pp. 1–9 (2015)

News Feed: A Multiagent-Based Push Notification System

Chattrakul Sombattheera(✉)

Multiagent, Intelligent and Simulation Laboratory (MISL),
Department of Information Technology, Faculty of Informatics,
Mahasarakham University, Kantharawichai 44150, Thailand
chattrakul.s@msul.ac.th

Abstract. This document explains a very innovative multiagent-based information system driving personalized data to millions of farmers in Thailand. There are three main agents working in the system. The collective agent collects initial data from large databases and farmers. The analytic agent receives initial data and analyzes it for related keywords and sends them back to the collective agent. The key words are used to search for related external source of data that are useful and appropriately fit to individual needs and interests of farmers. The disperse agent then distributes the data to farmers, categorized into seven layers. Farmers benefit from these sets of information in many ways, including how to plant, grow, maintain and fertile until harvest. Even before planting, the system helps farmers to decide which crops they should choose. After harvesting, the system helps finding appropriate market for their crops.

Keywords: Personalized data · Intelligent agent · Multiagent agent · Push notification

1 Introduction

In this ever changing world, the amount of data has been overwhelming and rapidly increased in the past few decades. The more data we have, the more difficult to collect, store, manage and utilize them. The newly emerged challenge is to select among the vastly abandon amount of data the least but most appropriate in the need of users of an information system. Personalized data is a concept to wisely select such information and present to the user.

The Department of Agriculture Extension of Thailand (DOAE) has very large databases and would like to utilize them to Thai farmers. Over several decades DOAE have been collecting data about farming in Thailand over various issues, including the farmers, farms, crops, harvest, costs and incomes. There are several systems using these databases for different purposes. However, it is yet to streamline the existing data into useful information to farmers. More

Supported by the Department of Agriculture Extension of Thailand.

importantly, the information should be personalized to fit with individual, and possibly unique, need for each farmers. In addition to DOAE's databases, useful data from outside sources should also be collected and fed to interested farmers, individually. Such sources include various pages from Facebook, web pages and external database systems.

This work is driven by the passion of applying advanced research techniques in multiagent systems to real world usage, personalizing DOAE data to fit with individual needs of farmers. Having personalized data, farmers can make better decision then achieve higher yields and net profit. With regards to this passion, DOAE has developed a Personalized Data system, which will select and forward to farmers useful information that they really need. The system is composed of multiple subsystems, equipped with artificial intelligence technologies, accessible from various platforms. Among these system, the Suggestion Subsystem is meant to be very useful to farmers. This system deploy intelligent agents to collect the need of users, analyze for comprehensive need, then feed the appropriate data to the farmers. This system is among, if not, the first application(s) in Thailand that is equipped with such advanced techniques. The system is being used in Thailand, starting from certain areas and to be promoted and extended to farmers across the country. This article is focused on the News Feed, a feature of the system that delivering useful information of interests to farmers.

The paper is structured as following. We review related works in both push notification and agriculture domain. We discuss about the architecture, internal and external data sources of the system. We then present the multiagent system used for feeding news to farmers. This is followed by experimental results. Lastly, we conclude the paper.

2   Review

Delivering useful information to users is widely known as *push notification* [8]. In our context, we are to notify farmers with analyzed information of their interests. Artificial intelligence (AI)has been widely adopted as a smart tool to analyze complex problems in real world applications in recent years. An AI system that works on its own and reacts accordingly to the ever changing environment is defined by Russell et al. [6] as an intelligent agent. In complex systems, intelligent agents work together to accomplish the task of the system. Such systems are known as multiagent systems [7] (MAS). We found that there are not many multiagent systems be used for push notification, particularly, in agriculture domain. Given the complex and unique architecture, we need a simple but robust, yet, flexible, system to deliver information to farmers. Below, we shall review related works in both push notification and using AI in agriculture.

Guthula et al. [1] model a specific troubled agricultural sub-system in India as a Multi-Agent System and use it as a tool to analyze the impact of policies. Some policy options are examine to get an understanding of changes that may happen once such policies are implemented. The recommendations are delivered to only policy makers. Zaryouli et al. [2] develop an analytic system to provide to farmers reports about crop growth decisions by increasing yields and profitability of production for the farmer, to establish a predictive analysis on the impact of climatic change on red fruits. Perez-ponz et al. [3] propose a multiagent system to help business make decisions in the purchase of sustainable agricultural products. The system helps choose a supplier for agricultural future market price forecast. Chevalier et al. [4] investigates the use of a multi agent system for combining quadrotor and tracked robots in watering crops. The system is able to maintain the formation of the ground vehicles and provide a good tracking of the ground vehicles by the quadrotor. Gonzalez et al. [5] use Intelligent multi-agent system for water reduction in automotive irrigation processes. The use of these intelligent technologies in rural areas provides a considerable saving of resources and improves the efficiency and effectiveness of agricultural production systems. Although these work use multiagent systems in agriculture, they differ significantly from our work.

Push Notification is about delivering requested and demanded information to recipients automatically and efficiently. In the following we shall explore related works. Okoshi et al. [9] use adaptive notification to break bottleneck of limited resources of users in Japan. They found that the click rate increases by 60%. Baruah et al. [10] evaluate a utility-based framework (gain vs pain) of push notification systems using Pareto optimality. It is found that the framework accommodate more user models and can work with information-seeking modalities. Wohllebe et al. [8] develop hypotheses on the effect of title, button and image on user interaction with push notifications. It is found that the use of a title seems to have a positive effect on interaction rates. Wheatley et al. [11] explore news organizations' use of alerts, considering whether they attempt to integrate with existing mobile-user behavior patterns or seek to be a disruptive element, garnering attention when audiences are not typically using devices. It is found that news organizations use the mobile channel for attracting and maintaining users' attention, with varying interpretations of temporal customizability. Kodali et al. [12] proposes a solution to monitor weather parameters, push them to cloud and notify their deviations to farmers. Saokaew et al. [13] prototype a portable, small, smart, and off-grid photovoltaic system to provide an alternative electrical supply for a smart agricultural greenhouse. It is found that using internet of things with an MPPT charger controller enhances the prototype of smart farming as an alternative and green electrical resource. Ali et al. [18] deploy A multi-agent coordination and control system to control multiple interacting agricultural vehicles involved in the crop harvesting process. It is found that multi-agent system allows concurrent planning and execution of the process, aiming to increase efficiency of the vehicles and improve cooperation between them.

Kim et al. [14] study the development of basic UX design element for Push Message in mobile commerce service by visual expression. It is found that users are divided into a four-dimensional structure and is able to change according to product, location and customer. Fraser et al. [15] use a number of benchmarks to evaluate process of push notification. They also propose models for users and adapted personalization. Bunch et al. [16] monitor complex chemical processes and flexibly using multiagent paradigm to notify the off-nominal conditions to key plant personnel in chemical industry. A Multi-perspective Analysis of Social Context and Personal Factors in Office Settings for the Design of an Effective Mobile Notification System. Seyma et al. [17] investigate the effects of social context, personal and mobile phone usage using multi-level model. They found that mobile application usage is associated to the responsiveness and work engagement/challenge levels of knowledge workers. They found that it takes 45 min to switch between applications and 5 min to response. Although there are various applications of push notification, none of them is similar to our work that collects data from internal and external sources, analyze the data and deliver to farmers.

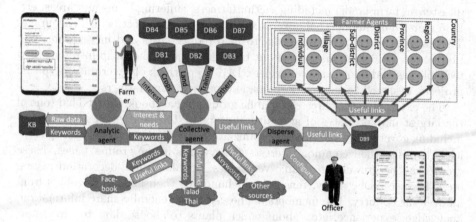

Fig. 1. The overview architecture of the system.

3   Architecture, Internal and External Data Sources

Figure 1 depicts the architecture of this system. The system is composed of internal and external data sources, and four types of agents, residing in application servers and a mobile application. The system is used by farmers and DOAE officers. Millions of farmers in Thailand are categorized, according to their ability to access the information in the system, into seven layers, namely, individual, village, sub-district, district, province, region and country. Officers are be categorized into 4 levels, according to their roles and responsibilities, namely, district, province, region and country. Normally, officers in district level can configure accessibility for farmers in district, sub-district, village and individual levels. Below we shall discuss in details about data sources, auxiliary data sources, DOAE officers and farmers.

Internal data sources are seven major databases, including Farmer Registration (DB1), Digitized Farm Land (DB2), Current Crop (DB3), Disaster Victims(DB4), Large Farm (DB5), Efficiency Enhancement Centre (DB6) and Participating Farmer (DB7). DB1 is the largest one, composed of records of approximately 20 millions farmers in Thailand. The important data stored are details about farmers and their family members, farm lands, and crops. Altogether, millions of pieces of land comprising 24.16 millions hectares ($238769 \, km^2$) of agricultural farms. Major crops include rice, dry crops, fruits, vegetables and others. For each season, the data about lands, owners and crops are updated. DB2 is a very large set of complex information to help visualize lands in DB1. In addition, the data also suggest other useful data, such as water sources, both natural and artificial, elevation, etc. DB3 keeps track of current situation with respect to target plants within each season. DB4 maintains data about natural disaster on farm lands, including victim farmers, suffering farms and areas, etc. DB5 stores data about Thai government's large farm project, which encourages Thai farmers to cooperate in order to help reduce costs and increase negotiation power. DB6 contains data about training projects that help introduce new technologies and knowledge to farmers. DB7 keeps track of government's special projects, designed to support farmers, and participating farmers.

The external data sources are public groups in Facebook, Talad Thai (one of the largest market places of agricultural crops in Thailand), and other sources including government and private organizations. In Facebook, public groups typically specifies their common interests as keywords in the groups' pages. These groups can be growers of organic vegetables, popular fruits, decoration plants, etc. There could be a few, tens or even hundreds thousands of members from all over the country. The members of these groups generally share information, knowledge, experience, etc., about which plants to choose, how to grow, how to take care, where to sell, etc., among themselves. Unfortunately, the access is limited only to members of the groups. It is inconvenient or unlikely for farmers to spend a lot of time to manually scan groups in Facebook for what is interesting for them. Since Thai government wants Thai farmers to try to optimally change crops for better prices, DOAE wants this system to help find interesting crops for farmers. Farmers specify their interests in this system through their mobile phones. The system scans related groups in Facebook and push notification back to farmers. Another source is Talad Thai, one of the largest market places in Thailand. Located just in the north of Bangkok, Talad Thai is a very large centre, where hundreds of tons of crops are collected from and distributed to locations all over the country. Based on this physical characteristic, Talad Thai also maintains a large crop pricing database, which is used as an outside data sources for the Personalized Data project. In the future, data from outside sources, such as weather forecast, irrigation data, can also be supplied to the system via application program interface (API) call between sources and this system.

Data from both internal and external sources are collected by collective agent based on requests of interests posted by farmers, and orders of demand posted by officers from all over the country. Farmers insert their interest in the system and wait for the analyzed information. DOAE personnel can also demand for analyzed data and forward the information to farmers later on. DOAE has nearly nine-hundreds offices located in all districts over Thailand. They simply use their desktop computer to submit the demanded information, which they can forward to farmers located in their respective locations.

In the next section, we shall discuss about our multiagent system.

4   Informative Multiagent-Based Personalized Data System

The main body of this system is a multiagent system, resides in server applications and mobile application. These agents are collective agent, analytic agent, disperse agent, and farmer agents. Instead of using other multiagent system, we did our best to follow the principle of multiagent systems. and make it as light and pragmatic, with regard to modern technologies (such as React Native), as possible. It turns out that we created this multiagent system from scratch. We shall discuss in details about these agents below.

4.1   Components of Agents

There are four types of agents in this system: collective agent, analytic agent, dispense and farmer agents. The first three agents, referred to as server agents, are a set of software residing on server systems in DOAE. Farmer agents are a small piece of software residing on farmers mobile phone.

Server agents are generally composed of Java classes, server shell script and SQL scripts. Both farmers and DOAE personnel interact with the system by specifying their interest via web-based or mobile applications. The interest will be stored in database. Server agents can be configured to work periodically or instantly. For the former, a set of shell scripts will be executed as cron jobs to control back end processes of server agents. Java classes are work horses for server agents. They are responsible for retrieving data from both internal and external sources, compute as needed, coordinate with external libraries for analytical computing, prepare data for visualization, etc.

4.2   Collective Agent

This is the most important part of the system. The first part is to retrieve data from 7 databases, including crops, land, training, etc. These data represent what individual farmers do and are interested. Collective agent then analyze for direct keywords. The output is then sent over to analytic agent for detailed keywords. The detailed keywords are then sent back to collective agent, which use them to search for related issue available on Facebook, Talad Thai, or other sources. It is composed of a number of Java classes, React native files, and shell scripts distributed on various platforms working together as a single unit.

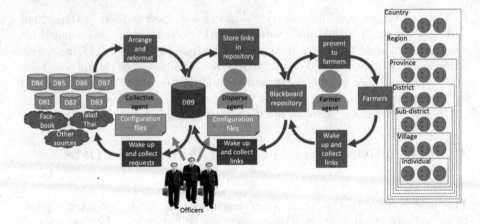

Fig. 2. Delivering data to farmers via collective, disperse and farmer agents.

4.3 Analytic Agent

Analytic agent uses primary keywords from collective agent then further analyzes using its knowledge base for detailed keywords. At this first phase, one of the knowledge bases that can be used is OAM (Ontology Application Management), an ontology library developed particularly for Thai. Other tools can definitely be used. The architecture is designed to be scalable so that new technologies or more advanced algorithms can installed and work seamlessly with existing component in the future. The detailed keywords are then sent back to collective agent.

4.4 Dispense Agent

Disperse agent collects useful links for individual farmers from collective agent. The agent consults with configured data inserted by officer and sent over to DB9 (the database of the Personalized Data system). Note that the configuration is designed so that target farmers will always receive the information they are interested or intended.

4.5 Farmer Agent

This agent is a module resides on a mobile application, used by agent. The application is developed by React Native and is usable on both Android and iPhone, the two most popular smart phone platforms in Thailand. Farmers can configure how often the agent should accessed database and collect in information individually available to farmers. This is due to the fact that accessing database costs farmers some amount of money according to their package contracted to mobile phone service providers.

4.6   Scalable Design

The system is designed as a scalable framework for further extension and enhancement in the future. Better technology can be placed in the system as a module for each agent. For example, analytic agent may be equipped with more efficient ontology for generating related key words.

4.7   Algorithm for Collecting Data

The architecture used in this system is designed to serve with real hierarchical structure of DOAE personnel in Thailand. The architecture allows for an officer at any level, from the top level down to the bottom, of the hierarchy to distribute messages through the structure to farmers. This can be complex and time consuming for distributing messages in many cases. To help avoid delays in delivering messages, the algorithms involved in all processes must be very simple. The most-likely time-consuming process is collecting data from outside sources. We present this algorithm below.

Algorithm 1. Collecting Data Algorithm

while *true* do
  read *configuration*
  prepare *connection*
  read *source$_i$ist* of n sources
  for $i = 1$ to n do
    connect to*source$_i$*
    send *request* to *source$_i$*
    set *data* ← *null*
    while *data* == *null* do
      =*data* ← *request$_r$esult*
    end while
    store *data* to DB_9
  end for
  sleep *sleep$_t$ime*
end while

The algorithm begins with reading configuration files to collect directive data for executing its tasks. The list of external sources is collected. The algorithm then goes through each of the data source *source$_i$*. The *source$_i$* is connected and the *request* is sent. The algorithm awaits for the returned *data* which is stored DB_9. The algorithm then goes to sleep as per specified in the configuration file. The other agents perform their tasks similarly to collective agents.

5   Results

Since this system is to collect useful and interested data from various sources and deliver the data to farmers through multiple layers of agents, it is important that in the worst case scenario the system performs reasonably well. With regards to this, there can be two bottleneck that hinder the performance of the system: i) collecting data from databases and outside sources by collective agent, and ii) distributing data from the blackboard to farmers at all levels. Since the architecture allows agents to sleep, wake up, and execute their tasks as per suggested in the configuration files, we therefore take into account only the time the agents take to execute the tasks after waking up and before going to sleep. Since the architecture is composed of layers of agents and farmers, and agents go to sleep after executing their tasks, the delays can simply take place when i)agents go to sleep, ii) agents collect data from external sources, iii) agents distribute data through layers. For the first case, we set up the sleep time as minimal as required. The more often the agents wake up, the higher power the system consume. For the second and the third cases, we need to carry out experiments to show what delays can happen.

5.1 Collecting Delay Time

Taking in to account the large number for farmers, there could be a lot of request posted to the system. We assume a farmer posts a request to the system. One way to cope with this is to scale the number of collective agents up. We would like to examine what will happen if we scale the number of agents up. Here, we simulate scaling number of agents from 1 to 10. The delays can mainly take place while i) connecting with the source because of the network, ii collecting data from the external sources (which might have their own database and network system), and iii transmitting data back to our system.

When scaling up, we keep the accumulated delay time for collecting and depositing data of all agents. As shown in Fig. 3, the delay time increases when the number of farmers increases. In general, the average delay time of different agents for all number of farmers are about the same, although we do not present the data here because of limited space. In general, having more agents should be able to help perform tasks faster. However, this may not result in decreasing delay time because increasing the number of agents consumes more resources and may take more time to execute and complete their tasks.

5.2 Distributing Delay Time

To examine the performance of distributing messages to farmers, we set up a similar scenario. We assume there are 1 distribute agent for 1,000 to 10,000 farmers over 1 to 7 layers. Note that the message from a higher level will be collected by its adjacent lower level agents. We consider that the sleep time form all agents are minimal and are interested in over all delay times for distributing messages from higher levels to the lowest levels.

When scaling up, we keep the accumulated delay time for collecting and depositing data of all agents. As shown in Fig. 4, the trend of the delay times are generally consistent when the number of agents increase. Here, we present the accumulated time of all cases for sake of detailed data. Although the detailed

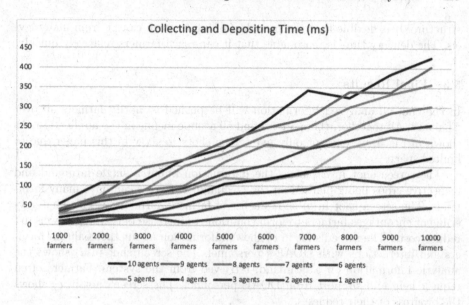

Fig. 3. Delay time for collecting data.

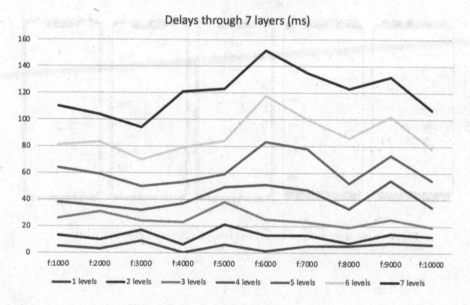

Fig. 4. Delay time for distributing data.

times of 5, 6 and 7 levels looks a little decreasing, the average data do not change significantly.

As we have already discussed in previous sections, the system is quite unique, with regards to DOAE's hierarchical structure. The designed architecture provides many advantages. It allows for delivering information through complex structure. It is flexible that the providers of information can be from many levels. The delivery time is reasonable that it can reach farmers relatively quickly.

5.3 Final Results

In the end, all analyzed information will be pushed to notify farmers all over Thailand. All together, there are around 50 atomic menus in the application. As shown in Fig. 5, we excerpt only five screen shots to show in this paper due to limited space.

The screen shot in a) shows the information about a single farmland and respective crops being planted on the farmland. A farmer can have many farmlands. The screen shot in b) shows a list of farmer's farmlands. The Thai government encourages farmers to form coalitions to increase bargaining power and reduce costs. The screen shot in c) shows information about the coalition farmers and interactions with DOAE's personnel. The screen shot in d) shows the analytic information on a farmland, retrieved from the system. Farmers often request help and support from DOAE personnel. The screen shot in e) shows the progress of their requests.

Fig. 5. Five screen shots excerpted from farmer's mobile application.

6 Conclusion

This paper presents the architecture and important details about the A Multiagent-based Informative Personalized Data System developed and deployed in the Department of Agriculture Extension of Thailand. The system uses internal data sources and receive data from farmers about their interests and necessary data for their crops. There are four types of agents used, collective agent for retrieving data from both internal and external sources, analytic agent for generating related key words, dispense agent, with coordination with officers, for configuring the distribution of data, and farmer agent on mobile phone. In general, the system performs consistently well when the number of farmers increases. The system works well and serving Thai farmers for their well-being.

Acknowledgements. We would like to thank the Department of Agricultural Extension for support on this work.

References

1. Guthula, S., Simon, S., Karnick, H.: Analysis of Agricultural Policy Recommendations using Multi-Agent Systems. Computing Research Repository (CoRR), vol. 1, no. 1, pp. 1–13 (2020)
2. Zaryouli, M., Fathi, M.T., Ezziyyani, M.: Data collection based on multi-agent modeling for intelligent and precision farming in lokoss region morocco. In: 2020 1st International Conference on Innovative Research in Applied Science, Engineering and Technology (IRASET), pp. 1–6 (2020)
3. Pérez-Pons, M.E., Alonso, R.S., García, O., Marreiros, G., Corchado, J.M.: Deep Q-learning and preference based multi-agent system for sustainable agricultural market. Sensor **21**(16), 1–16 (2021)
4. Chevalier, A., Copot, C., De Keyser, R., Hernandez, A., Ionescu, C.: A multi agent system for precision agriculture. In: Buşoniu, L., Tamás, L. (eds.) Handling Uncertainty and Networked Structure in Robot Control. SSDC, vol. 42, pp. 361–386. Springer, Cham (2015). https://doi.org/10.1007/978-3-319-26327-4_15
5. González-Briones, A., Mezquita, Y., Castellanos-Garzón, J.A., Prieto, J., Corchado, J.M.: Intelligent multi-agent system for water reduction in automotive irrigation processes. Procedia Comput. Sci. **151**, 971–976 (2019)
6. Russell, S.J., Norvig, P.: Artificial Intelligence: A Modern Approach. 2nd Edition. Pearson Education (2003)
7. Wooldridge, M.: An Introduction to Multiagent System. John Wiley & Sons Inc., Hoboken (2009)
8. Wohllebe, A., Hübner, D., Radtke, U., Podruzsik, A.: Mobile apps in retail: effect of push notification frequency on app user behavior. Innov. Mark. **17**(05), 102–111 (2021)
9. Okoshi, T., Tsubouchi, K., Tokuda, H.: Real-world product deployment of adaptive push notification scheduling on smartphones. In: Proceedings of the 25th ACM SIGKDD International Conference on Knowledge Discovery & Data Mining 2019. Association for Computing Machinery, New York, NY, USA, pp. 2792–2800 (2019)
10. Baruah, G., Lin, J.: The pareto frontier of utility models as a framework for evaluating push notification systems. In: Proceedings of the ACM SIGIR International Conference on Theory of Information Retrieval, pp. 253–256. Association for Computing Machinery, New York, NY, USA (2017)
11. Wheatley, D., Ferrer-Conill, R.: The temporal nature of mobile push notification alerts: a study of European news outlets' dissemination patterns. Digit. Journalism Routledge **9**(6), 694–714 (2021)
12. Kodali, R.K., Rajanarayanan, S.C., Boppana, L.: IoT based weather monitoring and notification system for greenhouses. In: Proceedings of the 11th International Conference on Advanced Computing (ICoAC), pp. 342–345 (2019)

13. Saokaew, A., Chieochan, O., Boonchieng, E.: A smart photovoltaic system with Internet of Thing: a case study of the smart agricultural greenhouse. In: Proceedings of the 10th International Conference on Knowledge and Smart Technology (KST). pp. 225–230 (2018)

14. Kim, S., Kwon, H.: Study on formalization of push notification UX design: focus on mobile commerce service based on smart offering. In: Proceedings of HCI Korea. Hanbit Media Inc., Seoul, Korea, pp. 323–330 (2015)

15. Fraser, K., Yousuf, B., Conlan, O.: Generation and evaluation of personalised push-notifications. In: Adjunct Publication of the 27th Conference on User Modeling, Adaptation and Personalization. Association for Computing Machinery, New York, NY, USA, pp. 223–224 (2019)

16. Bunch, L.: Software agents for process monitoring and notification. In: Proceedings of the 2004 ACM Symposium on Applied Computing. Association for Computing Machinery, New York, NY, USA, pp. 94–100 (2004)

17. Cavdar, S.K., Taskaya-Temizel, T., Musolesi, M., Tino, P.: A multi-perspective analysis of social context and personal factors in office settings for the design of an effective mobile notification system. In: Proceedings of the ACM Interactive Mobile Wearable Ubiquitous Technologies, March 2020. Association for Computing Machinery, New York, NY, USA, vol. 4, no. 1 (2020)

18. Ali, O., Saint Germain, B., Van Belle, J., Valckenaers, P., Van Brussel, H., Van Noten, J.: Multi-agent coordination and control system for multi-vehicle agricultural operations. In: Proceedings of the 9th International Conference on Autonomous Agents and Multiagent Systems, vol. 1, pp. 1621–1622. International Foundation for Autonomous Agents and Multiagent Systems. Richland, SC, USA (2010)

Optimizing the Social Force Model Using New Hybrid WOABAT-IFDO in Crowd Evacuation in Panic Situation

Hamizan Sharbini[2(✉)], Roselina Sallehuddin[1], and Habibollah Haron[1]

[1] School of Computing, Universiti Teknologi Malaysia, 81310 Johor, Malaysia
[2] Faculty of Computer Science and Information Technology, Universiti Malaysia Sarawak,
94300 Sarawak, Malaysia
shamizan@unimas.my

Abstract. This paper addresses the need for improvement in the Social Force Model (SFM) crowd evacuation model in the context of egress studies and current emergency research. As the current classical evacuation model, the Social Force Model lacks decision-making ability for finding the best directions towards an exit. Crowd searching for route choices in crowd evacuation simulations for panic situations remains inaccurate and unrealistic. There is a need for SFM to be incorporated with an intelligent approach in a simulation environment by adding in behaviour of following the position indicator to guide agents towards the exit to ensure minimal evacuation time. Congestion in pedestrian crowds is a critical issue for evacuation management, due to a lack of or lower presence of obstacles. Thus, this research proposes optimization using the one of the latest nature inspired algorithm namely WOABAT-IFDO (Whale-Bat and Improved Fitness-Dependent Optimization) in the SFM interaction component. Optimization takes place by randomly allocating the best position of guide indicator as an aid to the for better evacuation time and exploring the dynamics of obstacle-non obstacle scenarios that can disperse clogging behavior with different set of agent's number for better evacuation time and comparing it with single SFM simulation. Finally, validation is conducted based on the proposed crowd evacuation simulation time, which is further based on standard evacuation guidelines and statistical analysis methods.

Keywords: Hybrid WOABAT-IFDO and SFM · Nature-inspired optimization · Crowd evacuation simulation · Crowd model validation

1 Introduction

The unexpected occurrence of an emergency in an occupied building may lead to a crowd evacuation in a panic situation. Data regarding time evacuation are difficult to obtain, especially when involving real humans. Thus, there is a need for simulation and modeling as an approach to simulate and analyze crowd evacuation models for fast and efficient evacuations [1]. Computer-based simulations have become vital to analyze and

O. Surinta and K. Kam Fung Yuen (Eds.): MIWAI 2022, LNAI 13651, pp. 133–145, 2022.
https://doi.org/10.1007/978-3-031-20992-5_12

measure the process of evacuation and to evaluate its efficiency [2]. There are numerous techniques that can aid in simulating and optimizing current crowd behavior models. The latest development issues in crowd models, such as the Social Force Model, are still a niche area of research, while optimization based on nature is also widely being used as an aid to produce better simulation outcomes. Inaccuracy in agent searching behaviour can affect agent decision-making while finding an exit. Furthermore, there is a need for SFM improvement with an intelligent approach to allow the agents to follow the signage (sign indicator) to ensure minimal evacuation time [3].

Another important issue regarding the efficiency of evacuation time involves the use of obstacles [1] to help agents evacuate faster, as opposed to the theory of anti-arching phenomenon in the exit way. The focus on nature-inspired algorithms has led to numerous insights into several applications. The need for hybrid is essential for enhancing the evacuation process in current simulation model. The major contributions of this paper are as follows: (i) to optimize the position indicator using hybrid WOABAT-IFDO algorithm as an aid to guide agents towards the exit for minimum evacuation time; (ii) to simulate the evacuation process via the new optimized path planning movement (WOABAT-IFDO and SFM); and (iii) to validate evacuation time based on literature and standard real world evacuation times.

Validation attempts evacuation time analysis based on the following null hypotheses:- a) H01: Total of evacuation time from the proposed hybrid (WOABAT_IFDO + SFM) simulation model is less than SFM; b) H02: Total of evacuation time from the proposed hybrid (WOABAT_IFDO + SFM) simulation model is not the same as standard/certified total of evacuation time; and c) H03: The presence of an obstacle (one or more than one obstacles) in this proposed model of evacuation simulation would not significantly affect in minimizing the total of evacuation time. This paper is organized as follows. Section 2 explains related works pertaining to SFM and nature inspired algorithms (swarm intelligence), including the latest optimization algorithms, namely the original Fitness Dependent Optimization (FDO) and Independent Fitness Dependent Optimization (IFDO) algorithm. Section 3 describes the proposed hybrid WOABAT-IFDO for SFM, while Sect. 4 describes the simulation experiments setting and obstacle condition with output visualization to indicate the effectiveness of the proposed optimization in SFM. Finally, the conclusion and future work is explain in Sect. 5.

2   Related Works

Research into crowd simulation, and especially crowd evacuation, remains a hotspot. Research trends have shown significant growth. The interaction between agents during evacuation situation is crucial in contributing better agent movement by optimizing the layout of facilities of buildings [4]. The most renowned crowd model is the Social Force Model. It is said to be the simplest crowd model which can describe crowd movement under microscopic model. The model was introduced by [5] and the equation is as shown in Eq. (1) where m_i denotes as pedestrian mass, t denotes time, denotes time, $\vec{v}_i$ is the speed, τ_i shows the pedestrian acceleration time, v_i^0 is desired velocity and $\vec{e}_i$ is the desired destination or direction.

$$m_i \underbrace{\frac{d\vec{v}(t)}{dt}}_{Accelaration} = \underbrace{\frac{m_i}{\tau_i}(v_i^0 \overrightarrow{e_i}(t) - \vec{v}_i(t))}_{Driving\ Force} + \underbrace{\sum_{j(\neq i)} \vec{F}_{ij}^{ww}(t)}_{Interactions} + \underbrace{\vec{F}_i^b(t)}_{Borders,\ Fire}$$

$$+ \underbrace{\sum_k \vec{F}_{ik}^{att}(t)}_{Attractions} + \underbrace{\overrightarrow{\xi}_i(t)}_{Fluctuations} \qquad (1)$$

However, one of the most important issues is realism [5], as SFM lacks considering the decision-making processes that can further enhance efficiency during evacuation. The nature of SFM itself is moving by force, or being attracted by other agent's forces; thus, overall, the movement seems to follow the forces of others towards the goal. This emerging behaviour of following the forces can be seen in panic situation. Other issues, such as clogging exit ways, may need more scenarios described via obstacle interaction [6]. The SFM also has issues such as a constant gap of one agent leaving from a group while waiting to be evacuated (seeking another option) [7]. Hence, a path might be unknown to an agent. The use of signage during the evacuation may seem appropriate, but there is a need for further experimentation on how to best allocate the guide indicator (signage) concerning the facility layout to properly guide the agents to the exit point. The main criteria of the position of signage would be on a wall or on the ground. For this research, the main position would be the ground position, as it has less risks fir security and allows more interaction among agents during evacuation process [8]. Another recent work by [9] described there is a need to simulate crowd evacuation that includes signage scenario in panic situation. One of the latest optimization algorithms introduced by [10] is suitable to be used for evacuation purposes. The optimization algorithm is best hybridized with the latest optimization algorithms, namely Whale Optimization [11] and Bat algorithm (WOA-BAT algorithm) [12], as coined by [13] with a recent optimization algorithm.

T good thing about WOABAT hybridization algorithm is it produces better results with minimal iterations incurred. Therefore, the process of searching towards the defined solution will be faster. Nonetheless, the WOABAT algorithm is suggested to aid in crowd evacuation simulation for certain improvement strategies. Another most recent optimization algorithm, namely the Improvement of Fitness Dependent Optimization (IFDO) [14], which is based on Fitness Dependent Algorithm [15], is said to be more efficient in selecting parameters, agent's alignment, and cohesion. It is also good in updating the artificial scout bees (agent), thus making the algorithm to perform better in terms of exploration to find an optimal solution. Another reason for improvement is the definition of weight function (wf) in each iteration of each agent once the solution has been found, making the algorithm able to avoid the unnecessary exploitation process. Nevertheless, the IFDO also can converge to global optimality faster due to its ability to cover reasonable search space. The new movement in IFDO [14] is additional an element of alignment and cohesion, which is expressed as follows:

$$X\_(i, t + 1) = X\_(i, t) + Pace + (alignment * 1/cohesion) \qquad (2)$$

However, there is a limitation that needs to be dealt with IFDO, as the performance is depends on several search agents. In the work of [14], they demonstrated that the crowd only involved quite a small number of agents (>5 agents). The algorithm has a limitation in dealing with accuracy in searching process, such as locating the exit way when the number of simulation agents is increased to more than 5 agents.

3 The Hybrid of WOABAT-IFDO and SFM Optimization Design Framework

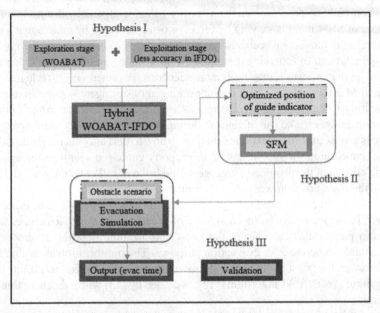

Fig. 1. The design framework for hybrid WOBAT-IFDO optimization in SFM

This section discusses the WOABAT-IFDO hybrid optimization is integrated into SFM (Interaction) module. Figure 1 shows the design framework for the proposed hybrid WOABAT-IFDO optimization in SFM. Originally, the hybrid WOABAT-IFDO has been proposed in our previous work and the details of the benchmark analysis result for the optimization algorithm for comparison of performance of IFDO, FDO, WOA-BAT and PSO to new IFDO_WOABAT in 10 dimensions [16]. From the analysis, it shows WOABAT-IFDO gives the minimum results(fastest) in terms of reaching towards solution. This integration for optimization in SFM interaction component will remark as the novelty of the proposed design framework to lead to a better selection of exit by the particles (agent) in the crowd. The details of parameters in interaction component derived from Eq. (1) is shown in Eq. (3) where the sum of component interactions can be categorized as psychological, physical interactions and interaction between people.

$$\vec{F}_{ij}^{ww}(t) = \underbrace{\vec{F}_{ij}^{psy}(t)}_{\substack{Psychological \\ Repulsion}} + \underbrace{\vec{F}_{ij}^{ph}(t)}_{\substack{Physical \\ Interactions}} + \underbrace{\vec{F}_{ij}^{att}(t)}_{\substack{Interaction \\ between \\ People}} \quad (3)$$

From Eq. (3), the parameter will be selected and combined with the proposed hybrid optimization technique to get the estimated results for simulation evacuation time. The parameters may contain various numbers of obstacles or placements to attain the outcome in different perspectives. Work from other researchers have also modified the component consist of interaction, as in Eq. (3), for they need to be extended to include parameters for group avoidance in the component. This is due to the limitations of psychological repulsion, such as avoiding and following behavior in the current component, to reproduce the agents in a group while moving in same direction towards the same goal. The extended SFM in this component adds on turning and attractive force among group members; thus, pedestrians in the same group can gather and form a spatial structure that is conducive to walking and improve communication among agents [17].

Algorithm 1 shows the proposed WOABAT-IFDO in SFM algorithm. The integration from the new hybrid into the SFM interaction component will ensure the designation of a random guide indicator as an aid for the agent selecting the near optimal or shortest path towards the exit. This can reduce the effects of the agent from moving away from the group during evacuation process. The input data thus includes n number on agents, exits and obstacles. Performance is measured by the results of the simulation evacuation time and decision-making process (accuracy), that also will be repeated and compared with one simulation to another to get minimal time.

Algorithm 1. The proposed WOABAT-IFDO in SFM algorithm.

Input: n total number of agents, n number of obstacles, n number of exits
Output: n total agent evacuated by time t

Step 1: Initialize the number agent n, iteration (MaxGen), and the related parameters.
Step 2: Evaluate the fitness weight based on agent and position update
Step 3: Update the individuals' positions based on WOABAT-IFDO computation
Step 4: Use WOABAT-IFDO to optimize the placement of best indicator position as a guide in SFM interaction component and guide towards exit
Step 5: Return to Step 2 for iteration has been achieved, otherwise, exit the iterations and output the result.

The simulation was developed using MATLAB R2020b under Windows 10 operating system. The parameter in SFM for the simulation is walking speed(adult) = 1.47m/s, radius size (agent) = 0.2, $C\_obs = 1$, $\tau = 0.5s$, while the setting simulation evacuation scene includes hall area = 49.7m x 57.2m, exit(Xe) = 1, exit width = 9m, obstacle $(Xn) = 1$–15, and particles (a) = range from 50–500 agents. Whilst for the hybrid optimization (WOABAT-IFDO) parameter is scout-bee-number = 10, weight_factor = 1, max_gen = 3000, $fmin = 0$, fmax = 2, lb = min(Area) is populated area, $b\_WOA =$

0.001, and number of indicators = 2. The walking speed is based on general adult speed and the radius size are referenced from the published work in literature [18–20], whilst the simulation experiment is using 500 agents is based on the work of [21]. Figure 2 shows the simulation output and the map area used in the simulation is based on the Borneo Convention Centre Kuching (BCCK) main hall area [22].

3.1 Evacuation Time Validation

The validation for the evacuation time is as follows: First null hypothesis, H_{01}: Total of evacuation time from the proposed hybrid (WOABAT_IFDO + SFM) simulation model is less than SFM and is tested using one tailed T-test & Man-Whitney test. Second null hypothesis, H_{02}: Total of evacuation time from the proposed hybrid (WOABAT_IFDO + SFM) simulation model is not the same as standard/certified total of evacuation time, and is tested using using Mann-Whitney Test. Finally, the third null hypothesis H_{03}: The presence of an obstacle (one or more than one obstacles) in this proposed model of evacuation simulation would not significantly affect minimizing the total of evacuation time and is tested using ANOVA Test with Post Hoc. This validation standards are based on available literature and previous research work (Fire Rescue Service Department) [23–26]. The elements to be compared is such as algorithm effectiveness (running time) via evacuation time and the accuracy of predicting the position of optimal exit path and avoiding obstacles.

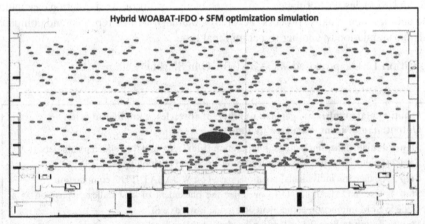

Fig. 2. Example of the evacuation scenario based on 200–500 agents with 15 obstacles. The simulation is repeatedly run with other different scenario such as no obstacle condition and with 2,6 and 15 obstacle(s) with red particle denotes the agents, blue denotes the obstacles, the circle green is automated guide indicator position and horizontal green area denotes the exit (Color figure online).

4 Result of Evacuation Time Hybrid WOABAT-IFDO in SFM vs Single SFM

Table 1 shows that the time taken for SFM that optimized using WOABAT_IFDO algorithm is lower than that of only single SFM simulation time in almost all situations. Optimization randomly uses the possible position of guidance indicator as signage during evacuation simulations. Figure 3 shows the results of hybrid WOABAT-IFDO in SFM compared to single SFM. The dotted line from the resulting graph is the baseline which is the single SFM running to be compared with SFM using WOABAT_IFDO optimization algorithm.

Table 1. The mean evacuation time for SFM +IFDO_WOABAT vs single SFM

Agent No	SFM+IFDO_WOABAT			SFM only	SFM+IFDO_WOABAT			SFM only
	No obstacle (s)	Position of G.I(1)	Position of G.I(2)	No obstacle (s)	1 obstacle (s)	Position of G.I(1)	Position of G.I(2)	1 obstacle (s)
50	149	42,47	45,60	170	151	38,51	35,60	160
100	173	32,59	41,60	181	154	18,44	34,61	167
200	200	40,55	45,64	233	190	34,55	35,61	195
300	250	34,72	44,61	268	203	50,43	33,59	243
400	267	22,46	43,59	271	245	22,52	37,58	251
500	281	15,43	42,58	285	257	15,43	34,58	262

Agent No	SFM+IFDO_WOABAT			SFM only	SFM+IFDO_WOABAT			SFM only
	2 obstacles (s)	Position of G.I(1)	Position of G.I(2)	2 obstacles (s)	6 obstacles (s)	Position of G.I(1)	Position of G.I(2)	6 obstacles (s)
50	132	18,60	40,62	148	189	20,60	36,65	190
100	156	19,60	40,65	174	215	18,63	35,65	230
200	178	18,59	42,59	203	225	23,58	36,56	261
300	210	20,60	43,60	245	242	22,60	33,63	270
400	235	19,62	39,60	261	256	20,57	38,58	283
500	242	18,58	40,61	272	260	21,58	37,60	298

Agent No	SFM+IFDO_WOABAT			SFM only
	15 obstacles (s)	Position of G.I(1)	Position of G.I(2)	15 obstacles (s)
50	175	23,61	38,58	180
100	201	18,58	38,57	221
200	229	22,60	35,60	260
300	243	23,60	40,59	263
400	251	22, 60	37,61	280
500	273	24,61	39,62	293

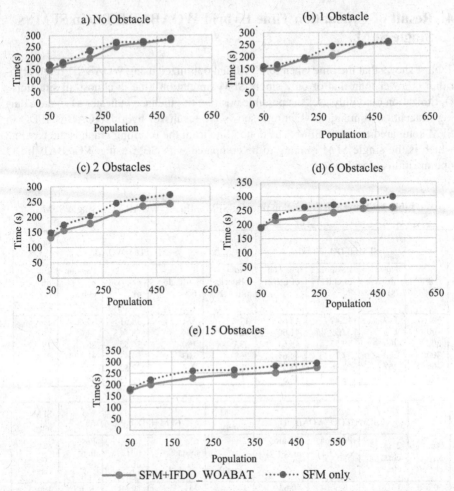

Fig. 3. (a)–(e) shows the graph analysis for the evacuation time for SFM with WOABAT-IFDO optimization compared to single SFM.

4.1   Analysis of the Hypothesis for Evacuation Time Validation

Null Hypothesis 1: H_{01}: Total of evacuation time from the proposed hybrid (WOA-BAT_IFDO + SFM) simulation model is not less than SFM.

Table 2. The t-test performed for first null hypothesis.

Levene's test for equality of variances		t	df	t-Test for equality of means				95%-Confidence interval of the difference	
F	Sig			Significance		Mean diff	Std. error difference	Lower	Upper
				One-sided p	Two-Sided p				
3.023	0.083	−5.29	598	< .001	< .001	−19.21333	3.62955	−26.34154	−12.08512

Based on [21] and [22], the statistical one-tailed T-test and Mann-Whitney U-Test are used to analyze the mean time of evacuation time, and for mean evacuation simulation time using single SFM and mean simulation evacuation time from the proposed hybrid WOABAT-IFDO in SFM. From the analysis, the first null hypothesis is rejected. At alpha level 0.05, the test indicated that the mean time for SFM (M = 233.7967, SD = 45.65988) was significantly higher than the proposed WOABAT_IFDO (M = 214.5833, SD = 43.2118). The Man-Whitney test also indicated that there were significant differences between all the mean evacuation times.

Null hypothesis 2: H_{02}: Total of evacuation time from the proposed hybrid (WOA-BAT_IFDO + SFM) simulation model is not the same as standard/certified total of evacuation time. According to standard evacuation procedure, the total evacuation time ideally is 3 min [19], with a TET of 20 min [20] and less than 6 min for up to 1000 people from public hall [21]. According to the simulation results of WOABAT_IFDO + SFM, the average total evacuation time is 4.35 min (261s). Based on Table 3 and Table 4, the second null hypothesis is rejected. At alpha level 0.05, the test indicated significance, thus reflecting the standard or certified evacuation time.

Table 3. The mean ranks for optimized SFM and single SFM.

Optimization SFM and SFM only	N	Mean rank	Sum of ranks
Hybrid + SFM(s)	300	261.93	78577.50
SFM only (s)	300	339.08	101722.50

Table 4. Hypothesis test summaries

Null hypothesis	Test	Sig. a,b	Decision
The distribution of Second(s) is the same across categories of Optimization SFM and SFM only	Independent Samples Mann- Whitney U Test	< .001	Reject the null hypothesis

a. This significance level is 0.05

Null Hypothesis 3: H_{03}: The presence of an obstacle (one or more than one obstacles) in this proposed model of evacuation simulation would not significantly affect in minimizing the total of evacuation time. The mean differences in various obstacle scenarios are presented in Table 5, whilst Table 6 presents the significant values and mean values based on ANOVA test.

Table 5. The ANOVA test for mean square and significant value

Seconds(s)	Sum of squares	df	Mean square	F	Sig
(a) The ANOVA test for mean square and significant value					
Between groups	153773.357	4	38443.339	21.115	< .001
Within groups	1083272.983	595	1820.627		
Total	1237046.340	599			

For the third hypothesis, based on the ANOVA test, the mean differs significantly, $F(4,595) = 21.115$, $p < 0.001$, n2 = 0.124(eta-squared). n2 = 0.124 shows that there is a large effect. However, for the post hoc test, the mean differences of no obstacle compared with 1–6 obstacles are significant at the chosen alpha = 0.05. Thus, the third hypothesis is rejected. However, in 15 obstacles scenario, the mean difference is not significant compared with non-obstacle. This may indicate that there is a need to further investigate on ideal obstacle's placement.

Table 6. Mean different in various obstacle scenarios

(I) Scenario with different set of obstacles	(J) Scenario with different set of obstacles	Mean difference (I-J)	Std. error	Sig	95% Confidence interval	
					Lower bound	Upper bound
(b) Mean different in various obstacle scenarios						
No obstacle	1 obstacle	20.72500*	5.50852	.002	5.6528	35.7972
	2 obstacles	22.59167*	5.50852	<.001	7.5195	37.6639
	6 obstacles	−15.90000*	5.50852	.033	−30.9722	−.8278
	15 obstacles	−11.74167	5.50852	.208	−26.8139	3.3305
1 obstacle	No obstacle	−20.72500*	5.50852	.002	−35.7972	−5.6528
	2 obstacles	1.86667	5.50852	.997	−13.2055	16.9389
	6 obstacles	−36.62500*	5.50852	<.001	−51.6972	−21.5528
	15 obstacles	−32.46667*	5.50852	<.001	−47.5389	−17.3945
2 obstacles	No obstacle	−22.59167*	5.50852	<.001	−37.6639	−7.5195
	1 obstacle	−1.86667	5.50852	.997	−16.9389	13.2055
	6 obstacles	−38.49167*	5.50852	<.001	−53.5639	−23.4195
	15 obstacles	−34.33333*	5.50852	<.001	−49.4055	−19.2611
6 obstacles	No obstacle	15.90000*	5.50852	.033	.8278	30.9722
	1 obstacle	36.62500*	5.50852	<.001	21.5528	51.6972
	2 obstacles	38.49167*	5.50852	<.001	23.4195	53.5639
	15 obstacles	4.15833	5.50852	.943	−10.9139	19.2305
15 obstacles	No obstacle	11.74167	5.50852	.208	−3.3305	26.8139
	1 obstacle	32.46667*	5.50852	<.001	17.3945	47.5389
	2 obstacles	34.33333*	5.50852	<.001	19.2611	49.4055

5 Conclusions

In this paper, the new hybrid WOABAT-IFDO algorithm in the SFM model has been proposed to optimize the guide indicator position in a crowd evacuation situation. The results show that the integration of hybrid nature inspired optimization in the crowd model give less time in evacuation simulation compared to single social force model. The validation is therefore crucial to a standard evacuation time. In future, there will be a need to study more about various obstacles and shape conditions that may influence evacuation time.

References

1. Li, L., Liu, H., Han, Y.: Optimal design of obstacles in emergency evacuation using an arch formation based fitness function. In: Computer Supported Cooperative Work and Social Computing Communications in Computer and Information Science, pp. 129–145. https://doi.org/10.1007/978-981-13-3044-5_10 (2018)
2. Tan, L., Hu, M.Y., Lin, H.: Agent-based simulation of building evacuation: combining human behavior with predictable spatial accessibility in a fire emergency. Inform. Sci. **295**, 53–66 (2015)
3. Cao, N., Zhao, L., Chen, M., Luo, R.: Fuzzy social force model for pedestrian evacuation under view-limited condition. Math. Probl. Eng. **2020**, 1–16 (2020). https://doi.org/10.1155/2020/2879802
4. Zhou, M., Dong, H., Ioannou, P.A., Zhao, Y., Wang, F.: Guided crowd evacuation: approaches and challenges. IEEE/CAA J. Automatica Sinica **6**(5), 1081–1094 (2019)
5. Helbing, D., Farkas, I., Vicsek, T.: Simulating dynamical features of escape panic. Nature **407**, 487–490 (2000)
6. Liu, H., Chen, H., Hong, R., Liu, H., You, W.: Mapping knowledge structure and research trends of emergency evacuation studies. Saf. Sci. **121**, 348–361 (2020)
7. Liao, C., Zhu, K., Guo, H., Tang, J.: Simulation research on safe flow rate of bidirectional crowds using bayesian-nash equilibrium. Complexity **2019**, 1–15 (2019)
8. Wang, L., Shen, S.: A pedestrian dynamics model based on heuristics considering contact force information and static friction. Transportmetrica B: Transp. Dyn. **7**(1), 1117–1129 (2019). https://doi.org/10.1080/21680566.2019.1568926
9. Minghua, L., Chengyong, X., Yan, X., Li, M., Yu, W.: Dynamic sign guidance optimization for crowd evacuation considering flow equilibrium. J. Adv. Transport. **2022**, 2555350 (2022). https://doi.org/10.1155/2022/2555350
10. Yuan, Z., Jia, H., Zhang, L., Bian, L.: A social force evacuation model considering the effect of emergency signs. Simulation **9**, 723–737 (2017). https://doi.org/10.1177/0037549717741350
11. Fausto, F., Reyna-Orta, A., Cuevas, E., Andrade, Á.G., Perez-Cisneros, M.: From ants to whales: metaheuristics for all tastes. Artif. Intell. Rev. **53**(1), 753–810 (2019). https://doi.org/10.1007/s10462-018-09676-2
12. Mirjalili, S., Lewis, A.: The whale optimization algorithm. Adv. Eng. Softw. **95**, 51–67 (2016)
13. Mohammed, H., Umar, S., Rashid, T.: A systematic and meta-analysis survey of whale optimization algorithm. Comput. Intell. Neurosci. **2019**, 1–25 (2019). https://doi.org/10.1155/2019/8718571
14. Muhammed, D.A., Saeed, S.A.M., Rashid, T.A.: Improved fitness-dependent optimizer algorithm. Access IEEE **8**, 19074–19088 (2020)
15. Abdullah, J.M., Rashid, T.A.: Fitness dependent optimizer: inspired by the bee swarming reproductive process. Neural Evol. Comput. IEEE Access **7**, 43473–43486 (2019). https://doi.org/10.1109/ACCESS2907012
16. Sharbini, H., Sallehuddin, R., Haron, H.: The hybrid of WOABAT-IFDO optimization algorithm and its application in crowd evacuation simulation. In: The 9th International Conference on Computational Science and Technology 2022 (forthcoming)
17. Huang, L., et al.: Social force model-based group behavior simulation in virtual geographic environments. ISPRS Int. J. Geo-Inform. **7**(2), 79 (2018). https://doi.org/10.3390/ijgi7020079.J
18. Li, M., Zhao, Y., He, L., Chen, W., Xu, X.: The parameter calibration and optimization of social force model for the real-Life 2013 Ya'an earthquake evacuation in China. Saf. Sci. **79**, 243–253 (2015). https://doi.org/10.1016/j.ssci.2015.06.018

19. Seah, et al.: Agent-Based Modelling and Simulation. Singapore Management University Report (2018)
20. Wang, S., Liu, H., Gao, K., Zhang, J.: A multi-species artificial bee colony algorithm and its application for crowd simulation. IEEE Access **7**, 2549–2558 (2019). https://doi.org/10.1109/ACCESS.2018.2886629
21. Hussain, N., Cheah, W.: Modelling of crowd evacuation with communication strategy using social force model. J. Optim. Ind. Eng. **15**(1), 233–241 (2022)
22. BCCK Homepage. https://www.bcck.com.my/public/files/BCCKEmergencyProcedures2nde dnCompatibilityMode.pdf. Accessed 25 Oct 2022
23. Fire Service Features of Buildings and Fire Protection Systems Occupational Safety and Health Administration U.S. Department of Labor OSHA 3256-07N (2006). https://www.osha.gov/sites/default/files/publications/OSHA3256.pdf
24. Degala: Minimizing the emergency evacuation time of a building component. Master Thesis, The University of Akron (2017)
25. Weerasekara, N.N.: Modeling and simulation of evacuation plan for hancock stadium. Theses and Dissertations. https://ir.library.illinoisstate.edu/etd/389 (2015)
26. Deng, X,: An aircraft evacuation simulation baseline using DES for passenger path planning. Dissertations and Theses. https://commons.erau.edu/edt/207 (2016)

Recognizing Driver Activities Using Deep Learning Approaches Based on Smartphone Sensors

Sakorn Mekruksavanich[1]([✉]), Ponnipa Jantawong[1], Narit Hnoohom[2], and Anuchit Jitpattanakul[3]

[1] Department of Computer Engineering, School of Information and Communication Technology, University of Phayao, Mueang Phayao, Phayao, Thailand
`sakorn.me@up.ac.th`
[2] Image, Information and Intelligence Laboratory, Department of Computer Engineering, Faculty of Engineering, Mahidol University, Nakhon Pathom, Thailand
`narit.hno@mahidol.ac.th`
[3] Intelligent and Nonlinear Dynamic Innovations Research Center, Department of Mathematics, Faculty of Applied Science, King Mongkut's University of Technology North Bangkok, Bangkok, Thailand
`anuchit.j@sci.kmutnb.ac.th`

Abstract. Human motion detection based on smartphone sensors has gained popularity for identifying everyday activities and enhancing situational awareness in pervasive and ubiquitous computing research. Modern machine learning and deep learning classifiers have been demonstrated on benchmark datasets to interpret people's behaviors, including driving activities. While driving, driver behavior recognition may assist in activating accident detection. In this paper, we investigate driving behavior detection using deep learning techniques and smartphone sensors. We proposed the DriveNeXt classifier, which employs convolutional layers to extract spatial information and multi-branch aggregation transformation. This research evaluated the proposed model using a publicly available benchmark dataset that captures four activities: a driver entering/exiting and sitting/standing out of a vehicle. Classifier performance was evaluated using two common HAR indicators (accuracy and F1-score). The recommended DriveNeXt outperforms previous baseline deep learning models with the most fantastic accuracy of 96.95% and the highest F1-score of 96.82%, as shown by many investigations.

Keywords: Human activity recognition · Deep learning · Smartphone sensors · Driver activities

1 Introduction

The domain of human activity recognition (HAR) in artificial intelligence has seen significant growth in recent years. Current HAR study findings have inspired

O. Surinta and K. Kam Fung Yuen (Eds.): MIWAI 2022, LNAI 13651, pp. 146–155, 2022.
https://doi.org/10.1007/978-3-031-20992-5_13

several applications in medical and related domains, including athletic measuring performance, rehabilitation tracking, and lousy habit identification. Based on the collection of activity data, the development of innovative wearable technology has advanced the progression of HAR research owing to the offering of various and increased activity data. Smartphones and smartwatches are two wearable gadgets that feature sensors such as accelerometers, gyroscopes, and magnetometers that individuals use throughout the globe in their everyday lives.

In the preceding ten years, the HAR research has led to the development of machine learning and deep learning techniques [9]. Nonetheless, machine learning is constrained by the need for individual specialists to extract distinguishing characteristics from raw sensor data. Using convolutional operators as the initial step of recognition models has enabled automatic feature extraction inside deep learning methodologies.

Convolutional neural networks (CNN) and long short-term memory (LSTM) neural networks were determined for the HAR deep learning approaches based on a review of the relevant literature. Several accomplished models have motivated the development of unique architectures for studying computer vision and natural language processing [13], including InceptionTime, Temporal Transformer, and ResNet. Based on these models, unfortunately, recognition performance has been restricted due to a lack of knowledge of the class hierarchy of human activities.

Activity recognition algorithms based on CNNs often use activity labels encoded as one-hot vectors. Because the one-hot encoding considers each class separate from one another, most activity identification models are trained, disregarding the links between activities. Nonetheless, hierarchical linkages between actual actions exist based on sensor data similarity [15]. For instance, when considering four stationary classes, such as walking, ascending, and descending stairs, the three other categories might be regarded as abstract and non-stationary.

Many fields, such as healthcare, sports, tactical awareness, fall detection, and accident identification employ a broad range of HAR solutions [5,10,11]. In order to track vehicle movement for the purpose of accident prevention, current smartphone-based applications and research rely on GPS transceivers [16]. A vehicle is in motion if its GPS coordinates reveal a considerable shift. Nevertheless, these GPS-based systems cannot detect slight displacements, preventing the incident detection approach from activating if GPS coordinates do not move beyond a specific threshold. Therefore, a driver must be spotted as soon as they enter a vehicle, without the car going a significant distance. Multiple benefits might result from this kind of early detection, including the launch of an autonomous or innovative agent-based accident warning system and increased situational awareness [4]. An intelligent agent is a self-aware entity that acts upon its surroundings by observing it using sensors and then actuating it. For instance, a smartphone application uses built-in sensors to detect human behavior or any significant event.

We use deep learning neural networks and smartphone sensor data to solve the abovementioned issues to recognize driver behavior. We unveiled the

DriveNeXt deep learning model, inspired by the ResNeXt image classification framework. To validate the effectiveness of the presented model, we utilized a publicly standard dataset consisting of smartphone sensor data for various driving actions. This paper's essential contribution can be defined as follows: 1) To introduce a unique deep learning classifier based on multi-branch aggregation transformation, 2) To determine the optimal window size for recognizing driver behaviors, and 3) To analyze the effectiveness of several deep learning classifiers using the benchmark dataset.

The remaining parts of the work are arranged as follows. New research of relevance is included in Sect. 2. The study's underlying model, a branch of CNN, is described in Sect. 3. The results of our studies are presented in Sect. 4. The report finishes with a consideration of necessary future studies (Sect. 5).

2 Related Works

The deep learning method has seen widespread implementation to overcome machine learning's shortcomings. When using deep learning, feature extraction is efficient, meaning fewer people need to be involved. Many deep learning models have been presented for identifying human activities, presenting promising findings and a unique learning technique [8, 12]. The majority of suggested models use standard CNNs.

According to [18], a CNN model is meant to analyze three-dimensional accelerometer data without considerable preprocessing. Before sending the input to the initial convolution layer, all information is preprocessed using the sliding window approach, and the accelerometer data is normalized. The normalized data are then given to the one-dimensional convolution and max-polling layers. The researcher proposes performing model evaluation using the WISDM standard dataset. Experimental findings indicated that the presented model could achieve significant precision while preserving reasonable computing costs. A CNN with several channels was proposed to unravel the motion detection issue in exercise programs' environment [1]. This study implements a self-collected dataset of 16 events from the Otago training schedule. Multiple sensors are installed on body parts to collect inactivity data for different movements, with individual sensors feeding a distinct CNN channel. After CNN functions, the findings from all sensors will be analyzed individually to establish the optimal placement of sensors for improved lower-limb action recognition. Their findings suggest that many sensor configurations could be more efficient than just one.

A deep HAR network is developed, transforming movement-sensing input to a series of spectrum images before passing these images to two CNN models that have been separately trained [7]. Individually CNN representative incorporates the image sequencing produced by the accelerometer and gyroscope. An ensemble of trained CNNs is used to make an informed guess about the kind of human behavior being observed. This research employs the Real-world Human Activity Recognition (RWHAR) dataset. This dataset includes eight actions: descending and ascending stairs, laying, standing, seated, running, leaping, and walking. Using the proposed model, an F-score of 0.78 is possible during static and dynamic activities and 0.87 during vigorous activity. The researchers furthermore concluded that the model could effectively process image information. The model generalization is promising, but its accuracy performance is not equivalent to that of the other standard deep learning model. In [2], three ways for using the temporal features of a series of windows are provided. The first technique involves calculating the CNN model's average of the input windows. In another technique, the window series is given to a coincident CNN, which determines the action category established on the intermediate scores. The last approach resembles the second approach, and the learned characteristics are blended using a global intermediate pooling layer to obtain the last forecast.

Compared to using a single CNN classifier, it has been hypothesized that using an ensemble of CNN might improve the accuracy of motion recognition. Zhu et al. [21] introduced a CNN-based framework for HAR by combining several smartphone-based sensors, including a magnetometer, accelerometer, and gyroscope. The suggested technique is an ensemble of two different CNN standards. The first model of CNN is prepared to forecast action categories, and the second CNN is conditioned to concentrate on activity classes with many misclassifications. Employing weighted polling, the result of separate CNN models is then merged to forecast unexpected behaviors. The testing outcome reveals that this suggested model could attain an accuracy of 96.20%.

Also, [19] recommended using an ensemble model with three separate CNN models. The ensemble model computes the final result by averaging the results of the three CNN models. Before assembling each CNN for actual interpretation assessment, researchers investigated the effectiveness of every CNN model. The experimental outcome suggests that the ensemble model outperforms the three CNNs with a precision of 94.00%. This finding demonstrated that this learning approach could generalize how the weak learner's learning influence can be enhanced to increase the overall model. A two-channel model of CNN for action recognition is presented in [14]. The presented approach improves identification accuracy using sensor inputs' frequency and power characteristics. The model's accuracy was 95.30% when experimented on the publicly available UCI-HAR dataset. This technique has the disadvantage of requiring the extraction of specific characteristics to enhance movement detection from sensor data. Applying the attention mechanism module to identify the importance of the features enhances the effectiveness of the CNN model [20]. In order to capture the local features, the three acceleration inputs are transmitted concurrently to three convolutional layers with varying filter sizes. The attention mechanism then calculates how important each feature is to select the most useful ones. The model was validated using the public WISDM dataset, which performed with a 96.40% success rate.

3   Sensor-Based HAR Methodology

Data acquisition, preprocessing, data generation, model training, and evaluation are the four main operational phases in the sensor-based HAR methodology used in this investigation (see Fig. 1).

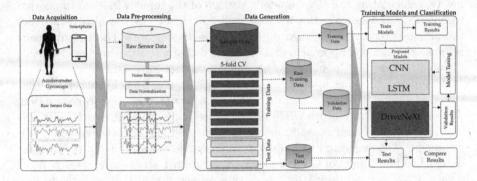

Fig. 1. The proposed HAR methodology

3.1   Driver Activity Dataset

This study uses a public dataset called "Driver entrance into and leaves from a vehicle using smartphone sensors," which records when a driver enters and leaves an automobile while their phone is in their pocket [3]. Participants performed the driving duties of:

- Grabbing the child safety seat (designated IN).
- Seated for some time (designated SITTING).
- Exit the automobile (designated OUT).
- Waiting a little while, perhaps 2 or 3 s, with the phone in the left pocket and the screen towards the thigh as you stand outside the automobile (designated STANDING).

Xiaomi Redmi Note6-Pro smartphones running Android 8.1 were utilized to gather data for the dataset. It features many sensors, including the gyroscope and accelerometer which were employed for data collecting. To acquire these signals, we relied on the Android program Sensor Kinetics Pro, which records data from the three-dimensional sensors at a sampling frequency of more than 400 Hz and provides information on the gravitation, linear acceleration, and spinning of the sensors.

This dataset sampled major features including acceleration, gravitation, direction, linear acceleration, and rotational across all three axes at a rate of 50 Hz.

3.2 Data Pre-processing

In data pre-processing, noise removal and data normalization were performed on unprocessed sensor data. The pre-processed data of the sensor were then separated by utilizing fixed-width sliding windows of 1 to 5 s with a 50% overlap ratio.

3.3 The Proposed DriveNeXt Architecture

In this work, we devised a multi-branch aggregation strategy in response to the ResNeXt model [17]. This approach provides kernel feature maps of varying sizes as a contrast to concatenated in the InceptionNet model [6]. This significantly reduced the number of model parameters, enabling these interconnections to be suitable for edge and low-latency processes.

Three convolutional kernel dimensions are represented in the DriveNeXt model's three components. There are three unique kernel dimensions (1×3, 1×5, and 1×7) in each MultiKernel (MK) device. The sophistication of the network and the number of parameters are further reduced by using 1×1 convolutions before implementing these kernels. DriveNeXt specifications are shown in Fig. 2.

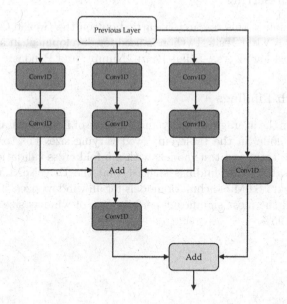

Fig. 2. An overview of MultiKernel component architecture

The DriveNeXt architecture has a minimal number of trainable parameters – just 23,653. The complete model is made up of six MK units, with the number of kernels being reduced to the desired number of classes using a 1×1 convolutional method. The layout of the DriveNeXt model is shown in Fig. 3.

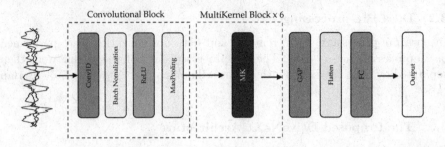

Fig. 3. The DriveNeXt architectural design

4   Experiments and Research Findings

In this section, we discuss the experimental setup and provide the experimental observations used to assess the standard CNN and LSTM models and the proposed DriveNeXt model for driving action detection based on smartphone sensor data.

4.1   Research Setting

Each investigation in this research is carried out on the Google Colab-Pro platform operating a V100 Tesla. Python is used for development in addition to the packages TensorFlow, Keras, Scikit-Learn, Numpy, and Pandas.

4.2   Research Findings

Table 1 displays the average accuracy and F1-score of DriveNeXt and benchmark models. Each model in the table employed varying sizes (1 s to 5 s) of sliding window data to train and test models with a 5-fold cross-validation process.

Based on Table 1, the findings suggest that the DriveNeXt model outperformed CNN and LSTM benchmark models for all window sizes. The DriveNeXt model achieved the most significant performance of window size of 1 s with an accuracy of 96.95%.

Table 1. Identification effectiveness of baseline models compared with the proposed DriveNeXt model

Classifiers	Window size (s)	Identification effectiveness		
		Accuracy	Loss	F1-score
CNN	1	95.49% (±0.411%)	0.29 (±0.058)	95.38% (±0.405%)
	2	94.26% (±1.134%)	0.32 (±0.052)	94.05% (±1.165%)
	3	92.43% (±1.576%)	0.39 (±0.117)	92.09% (±1.607%)
	4	91.63% (±1.047%)	0.41 (±0.072)	90.62% (±1.155%)
	5	90.45% (±2.441%)	0.56 (±0.147)	88.44% (±2.847%)
LSTM	1	96.62% (±0.313%)	0.16 (±0.029)	96.49% (±0.339%)
	2	93.48% (±1.225%)	0.41 (±0.036)	93.27% (±1.225%)
	3	92.74% (±0.793%)	0.32 (±0.070)	92.49% (±0.781%)
	4	92.77% (±1.761%)	0.43 (±0.106)	91.88% (±2.037%)
	5	92.51% (±1.901%)	0.20 (±0.062)	91.12% (±2.086%)
DriveNeXt	1	96.95% (±0.509%)	0.18 (±0.057)	96.82% (±0.549%)
	2	95.57% (±0.446%)	0.21 (±0.089)	95.40% (±0.491%)
	3	95.20% (±1.076%)	0.17 (±0.062)	94.95% (±1.134%)
	4	93.53% (±1.928%)	0.18 (±0.042)	93.09% (±2.141%)
	5	92.81% (±1.779%)	0.37 (±0.127)	91.26% (±2.130%)

5   Conclusion and Future Works

In this study, smartphone sensor-based identification of driving activity was investigated. We proposed the DriveNeXt deep residual model to achieve the study objective for driving behavior identification. Models were trained and tested to measure detection capability using a publicly available benchmark dataset. CNN and LSTM are the two baseline deep learning models used to compare the DriveNeXt model. The experimental findings demonstrate that the DriveNeXt has the most outstanding performance for all sliding window data sizes. The DriveNeXt model is successful at recognizing driver behavior.

In future research, we want to investigate driving action detection using different kinds of deep learning networks, including ResNet, InceptionTime, Temporal Transformer, etc.

Acknowledgment. This research project was supported by the Thailand Science Research and Innovation fund; the University of Phayao (Grant No. FF65-RIM041); National Science, Research and Innovation (NSRF); and King Mongkut's University of Technology North Bangkok with Contract No. KMUTNB-FF-66-07.
The authors also gratefully acknowledge the support provided by Thammasat University Research fund under the TSRI, Contract No. TUFF19/2564 and TUFF24/2565, for the project of "AI Ready City Networking in RUN", based on the RUN Digital Cluster collaboration scheme.

References

1. Bevilacqua, A., MacDonald, K., Rangarej, A., Widjaya, V., Caulfield, B., Kechadi, T.: Human activity recognition with convolutional neural networks. In: Brefeld, U., et al. (eds.) ECML PKDD 2018. LNCS (LNAI), vol. 11053, pp. 541–552. Springer, Cham (2019). https://doi.org/10.1007/978-3-030-10997-4_33

2. Gil-Martín, M., San-Segundo, R., Fernández-Martínez, F., Ferreiros-López, J.: Time analysis in human activity recognition. Neural Process. Lett. **53**(6), 4507–4525 (2021). https://doi.org/10.1007/s11063-021-10611-w

3. Hirawat, A.: Driver entry into and exit from a car using smartphone sensors. https://data.mendeley.com/datasets/3czshz7zpr/1, https://doi.org/10.17632/3czshz7zpr.1. Accessed 01 July 2022

4. Hirawat, A., Bhargava, D.: Enhanced accident detection system using safety application for emergency in mobile environment: SafeMe. In: Das, K.N., Deep, K., Pant, M., Bansal, J.C., Nagar, A. (eds.) Proceedings of Fourth International Conference on Soft Computing for Problem Solving. AISC, vol. 336, pp. 177–183. Springer, New Delhi (2015). https://doi.org/10.1007/978-81-322-2220-0_14

5. Hnoohom, N., Mekruksavanich, S., Jitpattanakul, A.: An efficient resnetse architecture for smoking activity recognition from smartwatch. Intell. Autom. Soft Comput. **35**(1), 1245–1259 (2023). https://doi.org/10.32604/iasc.2023.028290

6. Ismail Fawaz, H., et al.: InceptionTime: finding AlexNet for time series classification. Data Min. Knowl. Discov. **34**(6), 1936–1962 (2020). https://doi.org/10.1007/s10618-020-00710-y

7. Lawal, I.A., Bano, S.: Deep human activity recognition using wearable sensors. In: Proceedings of the 12th ACM International Conference on PErvasive Technologies Related to Assistive Environments, PETRA 2019, pp. 45–48. Association for Computing Machinery, New York (2019). https://doi.org/10.1145/3316782.3321538

8. Mekruksavanich, S., Hnoohom, N., Jitpattanakul, A.: A hybrid deep residual network for efficient transitional activity recognition based on wearable sensors. Appl. Sci. **12**(10), 4988 (2022). https://doi.org/10.3390/app12104988

9. Mekruksavanich, S., Jitpattanakul, A.: Deep learning approaches for continuous authentication based on activity patterns using mobile sensing. Sensors **21**(22), 7519 (2021). https://doi.org/10.3390/s21227519

10. Mekruksavanich, S., Jitpattanakul, A.: Multimodal wearable sensing for sport-related activity recognition using deep learning networks. J. Adv. Inf. Technol. **13**(2), 132–138 (2022). https://doi.org/10.12720/jait.13.2.132-138

11. Mekruksavanich, S., Jitpattanakul, A.: Sport-related activity recognition from wearable sensors using bidirectional GRU network. Intell. Autom. Soft Comput. **34**(3), 1907–1925 (2022). https://doi.org/10.32604/iasc.2022.027233

12. Mekruksavanich, S., Jitpattanakul, A., Sitthithakerngkiet, K., Youplao, P., Yupapin, P.: ResNet-SE: channel attention-based deep residual network for complex activity recognition using wrist-worn wearable sensors. IEEE Access **10**, 51142–51154 (2022). https://doi.org/10.1109/ACCESS.2022.3174124

13. Noppitak, S., Surinta, O.: dropCyclic: snapshot ensemble convolutional neural network based on a new learning rate schedule for land use classification. IEEE Access **10**, 60725–60737 (2022). https://doi.org/10.1109/ACCESS.2022.3180844

14. Sikder, N., Chowdhury, M.S., Arif, A.S.M., Nahid, A.A.: Human activity recognition using multichannel convolutional neural network. In: 2019 5th International Conference on Advances in Electrical Engineering (ICAEE), pp. 560–565 (2019). https://doi.org/10.1109/ICAEE48663.2019.8975649

15. Silla, C., Freitas, A.: A survey of hierarchical classification across different application domains. Data Min. Knowl. Disc. **22**, 31–72 (2011). https://doi.org/10.1007/s10618-010-0175-9
16. White, J., Thompson, C., Turner, H., Dougherty, B., Schmidt, D.: WreckWatch: automatic traffic accident detection and notification with smartphones. Mob. Netw. Appl. **16**, 285–303 (2011). https://doi.org/10.1007/s11036-011-0304-8
17. Xie, S., Girshick, R., Dollár, P., Tu, Z., He, K.: Aggregated residual transformations for deep neural networks. In: 2017 IEEE Conference on Computer Vision and Pattern Recognition (CVPR), pp. 5987–5995 (2017). https://doi.org/10.1109/CVPR.2017.634
18. Xu, W., Pang, Y., Yang, Y., Liu, Y.: Human activity recognition based on convolutional neural network. In: 2018 24th International Conference on Pattern Recognition (ICPR), pp. 165–170 (2018). https://doi.org/10.1109/ICPR.2018.8545435
19. Zehra, N., Azeem, S.H., Farhan, M.: Human activity recognition through ensemble learning of multiple convolutional neural networks. In: 2021 55th Annual Conference on Information Sciences and Systems (CISS), pp. 1–5 (2021). https://doi.org/10.1109/CISS50987.2021.9400290
20. Zhang, H., Xiao, Z., Wang, J., Li, F., Szczerbicki, E.: A novel IoT-perceptive human activity recognition (HAR) approach using multihead convolutional attention. IEEE Internet Things J. **7**(2), 1072–1080 (2020). https://doi.org/10.1109/JIOT.2019.2949715
21. Zhu, R., et al.: Deep ensemble learning for human activity recognition using smartphone. In: 2018 IEEE 23rd International Conference on Digital Signal Processing (DSP), pp. 1–5 (2018). https://doi.org/10.1109/ICDSP.2018.8631677

Sentence-Level Sentiment Analysis for Student Feedback Relevant to Teaching Process Assessment

Orathai Chantamuang[1], Jantima Polpinij[1(✉)], Vorakit Vorakitphan[1], and Bancha Luaphol[2]

[1] Faculty of Informatics, Mahasarakham University, Mahasarakham 44155, Thailand
{64011253004,jantima.p,vorakit.v}@msu.ac.th
[2] Faculty of Administrative Science, Kalasin University, Kalasin 46230, Thailand
bancha.lu@ksu.ac.th

Abstract. In the academic area, teaching process assessment conducted by students can be used as the main information to improve the teaching and learning process. However, when examination or consideration of the student feedback is conducted by teachers, the outcome may be a biased analysis. In the last decade, sentiment analysis has been applied to automatically evaluate the teaching process because it may help to reduce the problem of biased analysis when the sentiment analysis is performed by humans. This work presents a method of automatically analyzing student feedback relevant to teaching process assessment. The proposed method is called sentence-level sentiment analysis, and it is driven by processing steps such as pre-processing student comments and text representation, identifying aspect class for each sentence using the aspect analyzer, assigning sentence polarity for each sentence using the sentiment analyzer, and summarizing the overall sentiment polarity by considering student comments, respectively. The proposed method returns the recall, precision, F1, and accuracy scores of 0.835, 0.825, 0.825, and 0.825, respectively. These were satisfactory results.

Keywords: Sentiment analysis · Sentence level · Text classification · Aspect analyzer · Sentiment analyzer

1 Introduction

Teaching process assessment done by students is a crucial aspect of the educational process to recognize teacher performance and implement constructive strategies in order to benefit students in their academic progress. Also, it may affect the improvement of the teaching and learning process. Teachers typically allow students to evaluate their own teaching process at the end of each semester's teaching. The purpose is to analyze the opinion and satisfaction of learners with the teacher's teaching process. However, teachers may be biased when examining or considering the student feedback from their teaching process assessments. As a result, this could produce insufficient and erroneous information that cannot be used to improve the teaching process.

© The Author(s), under exclusive license to Springer Nature Switzerland AG 2022
O. Surinta and K. Kam Fung Yuen (Eds.): MIWAI 2022, LNAI 13651, pp. 156–168, 2022.
https://doi.org/10.1007/978-3-031-20992-5_14

In the last decade, sentiment classification has been applied to automatically evaluate the teaching process, with automatic sentiment analysis potentially helping to reduce the problem of biased analysis when the sentiment analysis is performed by humans [1–4]. However, almost all of the previous studies that have been proposed for teaching process assessment were documented-based sentiment analysis [2–6]. Document-level sentiment analysis aims to determine and express the overall sentiment (or opinion) of a document on a single entity. That is, this task inputs documents and classifies them into predefined suitable opinion classes. Some of sentiment analysis studies for student feedback in the educational domain can be illustrated as follows. Zhao et al. [2] proposed a method of sentiment classification for automatically analyzing teaching evaluation texts. Their proposed method of teaching evaluation analysis has been driven on the sentiment dictionary. Esparza et al. [3] applied a support vector machine to model a sentiment classifier, called SocialMining. This model was used to determine the sentiment of student comments that are relevant to teacher performance assessment into positive, negative, or neutral categories. The researchers believed that the results of this study could inform future research on how to better classify student comments while the results of their analysis could be utilized to make suggestions to teachers for improving teacher performance. Recently, Peng et al. [4] also proposed a method of sentiment analysis for teaching evaluation texts. They utilized a CNN-BLSTM model for their analysis. In this study, the CNN was used to set up convolution windows of different sizes to extract the binary and ternary features of the text, while the BLSTM was used to extract feature sequences in order to provide trustworthy text features for the ensuing classification.

However, analysis for determining the overall sentiment of the document may be inaccurate because the importance of each sentence in the document is not considered [4, 5]. To increase the effectiveness in determining the sentiment polarity of a document, each sentence in the document needs to deal with different sentiments and degrees of importance [6–8]. This becomes a challenge in this study, where it aimed to present a solution to identify the sentiment of a review based on considering the sentiment of each sentence before summarizing the overall sentiment (or opinion) of the document by voting. The proposed method is a combination of supervised and unsupervised methods to identify the sentiment of student feedback relevant to teaching process assessment in the domain of the secondary school. This method is driven on the concept of sentence-level sentiment analysis to determine the suitable sentiment of each student feedback to the greatest extent possible. The Natural Language Toolkit (NLTK) in Python (e.g. PyThaiNLP, and scikit-learn) is used in this study.

This paper is organized as follows. Section 2 describes the dataset and Sect. 3 presents the preliminaries. Section 4 covers the proposed method. Section 5 shows the experimental results, including a comparison with a baseline method. Finally, the summary of this paper was concluded in Sect. 6.

2 Datasets

The datasets used in this study were collected from 660 junior high school students by using our questionnaires. Three schools located in Roi-Et province, Thailand, are the sources of our datacollection. We collected two datasets. These datasets gathered student comments in Thai for ten subjects over two semesters. Both datasets were the student comments based on three aspects as comments for the teacher, comments for the lesson context, and comments for the learning environment. Linguists who have no stake in this study also helped us in selecting student comments that were reasonably complete (e.g., correct and complete sentences and without incorrect words). Furthermore, they helped us to assign the sentiment polarity (i.e., positive or negative) for each sentence in a student comment, including giving the summarized polarity sentiment for that student comment. The first dataset was used to generate a corpus of keywords that are relevant to each aspect. Furthermore, this dataset was used for modeling the sentiment analyzer. However, student comments used for generating the corpus of keywords and student comments used for modeling the sentiment analyzer were different. Meanwhile, the second dataset was a set of student comments used for our experiment stage. An example of our datasets can be seen in Fig. 1 and the summary of our datasets is presented as Table 1.

```
<student comments>
    <std_ID> 0001
        <full_comment> คุณครูน่ารักและสอนดีมาก เนื้อหาในบทเรียนค่อนข้างยากแต่ก็สนุกดี (Teacher is cute and very well
        teaching. The content of the lesson is a bit difficult but it's fun.) </full_comment>
        <comment_polarity> pos </comment_polarity>
        <sentencesID> 01
            <sentence_content> คุณครูน่ารักและสอนดีมาก (Teacher is lovely and very well teaching.) </sen-
            tence_content>
            <aspect> Teacher </aspect >
            <sentence polarity> pos </sentence polarity>
        </sentencesID>
        <sentencesID> 02
            <sentence_content> เนื้อหาในบทเรียนค่อนข้างยากแต่ก็สนุกดี (The content of the lesson is a bit difficult but
            it's fun) </sentence_content>
            <aspect> lesson </aspect >
            <sentence polarity> pos </sentence_polarity>
        </sentencesID>
    </std_ID>
    ...
    ...
</student_comments>
```

Fig. 1. An example of student comments.

Consider the number of sentences in the positive class and negative class in Table 1. It can be seen that there is an imbalance and many students did not comment for the aspect of learning environment. With the problem of imbalance in the data, we applied the concept of under-sampling for handling this problem in the stage of modeling the sentiment classifier.

Table 1. The summary of our datasets

Dataset	Usage objectives	Total of student comments		Comment aspects	Total of sentences	
		Positive	Negative		Positive	Negative
1	To generate a corpus of keywords	500	500	Teacher	650	350
				Lesson	600	400
				Learning Environment	480	140
	To model the aspect analyzer and the sentiment analyzer	500	500	Teacher	700	300
				Lesson	650	350
				Learning Environment	332	170
2	To experiment	300	300	Teacher	450	150
				Lesson	378	222
				Learning Environment	280	120

3 Preliminaries

3.1 Aspect-Based Keyword Corpus Development

The first dataset that aimed to be used for generating a corpus of keywords relating to each comment aspect is utilized. With written student comments in Thai, Thai word segmentation technique, called the dictionary-based maximal matching method [9], was used to break down all Thai sentences in the comment related to each comment aspect into "words". This method scans an input sentence from left to right to generate all possible segmentations for a sentence, and then chooses the one that contains the fewest words that match with Thai dictionary forms. Consider the following Thai sentence: "คุณครูน่ารัก (Teacher is nice)". By using this method, two possible segmentations are generated as follows.

> Pattern #1: คุณ (you) / ครู (teacher) / น่ารัก (nice)
> Pattern #2: คุณครู (teacher) / น่ารัก (nice)

As the results above show, the final result of segmenting the sentence "คุณครูน่ารัก (Teacher is nice)" should return as "คุณครู (teacher)" and "น่ารัก (nice)".

Afterwards, all stop-words are removed [10], and then all pre-processed sentences relating to each comment aspect are represented as a vector, called the vector space model (VSM) [11]. Here, we obtain three vectors, namely the vectors representing all pre-processed sentences relating to teacher aspect, lesson aspect, and learning environment aspect.

Later, the Word2Vec was used to extract all terms embedded in student comments that were pertinent to each comment aspect. In general, Word2Vec consists of two major elements, i.e. skip-gram and continuous bag-of-words (CBOW) [12, 13]. The skip-gram is utilized to generate word embeddings, and the surrounding words are predicted depending on the center word. The CBOW is employed to anticipate the word in the center of the window by analyzing the distributed representation of the input word. Here, the maximum vector dimension is used as 300 because it requires a large training set if dimensions are larger than 300 [13]. Finally, three corpuses of keywords relevant to comment aspects (i.e., teacher, lesson, and learning environment) were obtained, called the Keywords of Comment Aspects corpus (KCA corpus). The summary of each corpus can be presented as Table 2.

Table 2. The summary of three corpuses of keywords relevant to specific aspects.

Comment Aspects	Keyword Examples	Total Number of Keywords
Teacher	คุณครู (teacher), น่ารัก (nice)	90
Lesson	เนื้อหา (content), วิชา (subject)	86
Learning environment	ร้อน (hot), ห้องเรียน (classroom)	65

3.2 Development of the Aspect Analyzer and the Sentiment Analyzer Using the Text Classification Technique

In this stage, the first dataset that was to be used for the modeling of the aspect analyzer and the sentiment analyzer was utilized. With using the small dataset, k-fold cross-validation was applied to split the dataset. This technique for splitting the data may help to evaluate the generalization ability of the predictive sentiment analyzer and to prevent overfitting. In this study, k was provided as 10. The summary of each dataset relating to each comment aspect that was used for modeling the sentiment analyzer can be presented as in Table 3 and the overview method of the aspect analyzer and the sentiment analyzer modeling can be seen in Fig. 2.

Table 3. The summary of each dataset for modeling the aspect analyzer and the sentiment analyzer

Comment aspect	Total number of sentences		Training set per round		Validation set per round	
	Positive	Negative	Positive	Negative	Positive	Negative
Teacher	700	300	270	270	30	30
Lesson	650	350	315	315	35	35
Learning environment	332	170	153	153	17	17

For modeling the aspect analyzer, the training set per round for each aspect should be 450 sentences and the validation set per round for each aspect should be 50 sentences. For modeling the sentiment analyzer for each specific aspect, the training set and the validation set per round are already described in Table 3.

In the pre-processing of the training set, word segmentation is the initial step in separating student comment phrases into "words" using the dictionary-based maximal matching method. After segmenting words from the text, all obtained words relating to each comment aspect should be consistent with the words in the word corpus of each comment aspect that was mentioned in Sect. 3.1.

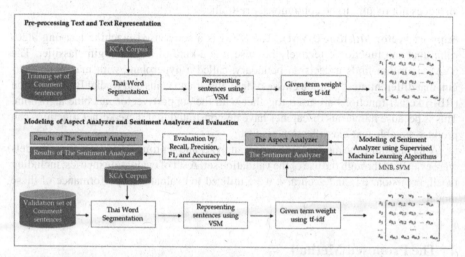

Fig. 2. The overview method of the aspect analyzer and the sentiment analyzer modeling.

After pre-processing the training set, the training set was formatted as VSM, and each word was given its weighting using a simple term weighting scheme, called *term frequency–inverse document frequency* (*tf-idf*) [14]. The equation of *tf-idf* can be written as Eq. (1).

$$tf - idf(t, d, D) = tf(t, d) \times idf(t, D)$$
$$= freq(t, d) \times \log\left(1 + \frac{N}{df(t)}\right) \tag{1}$$

where $freq(t, d)$ is the frequency of term t in a considered document. In this study, a document is considered as a sentence. For the $idf(t, D)$ component, N is the total number of sentences in a comment aspect set, while $df(t)$ is the number of sentences having term t.

Later, these vectors are used for modeling the aspect analyzer and the sentiment analyzer using the text classification technique. The aspect analyzer is used to assign the considered sentence into a specific aspect class (i.e., teacher, lesson, or learning environment), while the sentiment analyzer is used to assign the considered sentence into a specific sentiment class (i.e., positive or negative).

When dealing with small datasets, many previous works suggested low-complexity models like Multinomial Naïve Bayes (MNB) [14] and Support Vector Machines (SVM) [14]. We compared these algorithms to obtain the most appropriate predicative sentiment analyzer. Each algorithm can be described briefly as follows.

Multinomial Naïve Bayes (MNB). The MNB algorithm is a probabilistic learning method based on the Bayes theorem. It is frequently used in text classification tasks. It calculates the probability as 'likelihood' of each class label for a given sample and then gives the class label with the highest likelihood as output. The MNB algorithm offers an ability to perform the text classification using small training sets, and this algorithm also does not require to be continuously re-trained.

Support Vector Machine (SVM). The SVM is a supervised machine learning algorithm that can function effectively because it is a kind of large-margin classifier. The SVM algorithm finds a decision boundary, called a hyperplane with maximum margin, that differentiates between classes. Here, linear and Gaussian Radial Base Function (RBF) kernel functions are used together with the support vector machine algorithm. This is because numerous researches have demonstrated that these kernel functions can produce suitable text classification results.

After obtaining the model of the aspect analyzer and sentiment analyzer, these models were evaluated through the use of the validation set. A set of evaluation metrics, including recall, precision, F1, and accuracy, were utilized to evaluate the performance of these models.

4 The Proposed Method

In this stage, the second dataset was utilized for the experiment. The proposed method consists of four main components. The first component was used to pre-process the student comments and represent student comments in the VSM format, while the second component was to identify a specific aspect label using the aspect analyzer. The third component was to utilize the sentiment analyzer to assign the sentiment polarity for each sentence. Finally, the fourth component was used to summarize the overall sentiment polarity of a student comment by voting. The overview picture of the proposed method can be seen in Fig. 3. Each processing step is discussed below.

4.1 Pre-processing Student Comments and Text Representation

In the pre-processing stage, the proposed method will read incoming student comments one by one. Sentence separation is the first process used to separate student comments into "sentences" using white space. Later, word segmentation based on the dictionary-based maximal matching method was used to separate a considered student comment sentence into "words". After removing stop-words, the rest of the words of the considered sentences were represented as the VSM format. Here, the weighting of each word was calculated by *tf-idf*. However, it is noted that if a sentence did not contain any word from the KCA corpus, that sentence was ignored.

4.2 Identifying Aspect Class for Each Sentence Using the Aspect Analyzer

After obtaining the vector of the sentences, this vector was passed to the aspect analyzer to arrange each sentence in the vector into the suitable aspect class. Then, the possible aspect classes can be teacher, lesson, and learning environment. After each sentence of a considered student comment was assigned its suitable aspect class, these sentences were passed to the next stage, called assigning sentiment polarity for each sentence using the sentiment analyzer.

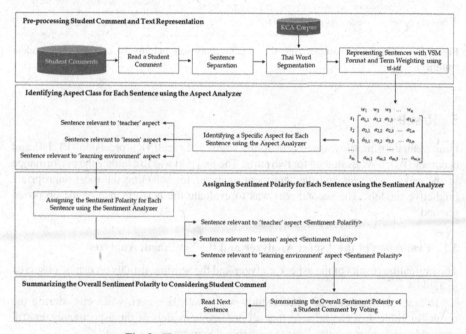

Fig. 3. The overview of the proposed method.

4.3 Assigning Sentence Polarity for Each Sentence Using the Sentiment Analyzer

In this stage, after each sentence of a considered student comment was assigned its suitable aspect class, we utilized the sentiment analyzer to predict its sentiment polarity. The possible sentiment polarities were positive or negative polarity.

4.4 Summarizing the Overall Sentiment Polarity of a Student Comment

After all sentences with aspect class labels were assigned their suitable sentiment polarity, we summarized the overall sentiment polarity of the considered student comments by voting. Here, possible sentiment polarities could be positive, neutral, or negative. If the number of positive comments was equal to the number of negative comments, it means that the sentiment polarity of the considered student comment should be neutral. If the number of positive comments was greater than the number of negative comments, it means that the sentiment polarity of the considered student comment should be positive. In contrast, if the number of positive comments was lower than the number of negative comments, it means that the sentiment polarity of the considered student comment should be negative. An example of summarizing the overall sentiment polarity of a considered student comment can be seen in Fig. 4.

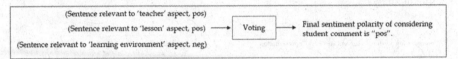

Fig. 4. An example of summarizing the overall sentiment polarity of a considered student comment.

5   Results

Four evaluation metrics were used in this study, i.e. recall (R), precision (P), F1, and accuracy (Acc). We evaluated for two parts. The first part was to evaluate the performance of the aspect analyzer and the sentiment analyzer for selecting the most appropriate predictive models. The second part was to evaluate the performance of the proposed method.

5.1   Evaluation of the Aspect Analyzer and the Sentiment Analyzer

The evaluation results of the aspect analyzer and the sentiment analyzer can be observed in Table 4.

In fact, our dataset used in this study was small. However, when considering the results in Table 4, it can be seen that all predictive models of the aspect analyzer still returned satisfactory results. This is probably due to two main reasons.

Firstly, our features that were generated by Word2Vec might be truly significant to each aspect in the domain of teaching process assessment. These features allowed the construction of useful and effective predictive models in this study. Secondly, it might be the selection of suitable algorithms. However, it can be seen that the predictive models based on the SVM algorithm along with the linear kernel were more likely to perform slightly better than the predictive models based on the SVM algorithm along with the RBF kernel. This is because most text classification problems are linearly separable; therefore, many previous studies have mostly preferred the SVM with the linear kernel. In addition, when modeling predictive models with the SVM with linear kernel, it required less computational time than modeling predictive models with the SVM with RBF. However, both predictive models based on the SVM algorithm along with the linear and RBF kernels returned the performance that was better than the predictive models based on the MNB algorithm because the MNB algorithm can return good performance when the features are independent of each other, which often does not happen in the real world.

As a result, the aspect analyzer and the sentiment analyzer built by SVM with the linear kernel were selected for experimentation with the second dataset.

5.2 Comparison of Proposed and Baseline Methods: In the Case of Modeling the Aspect Analyzer

As we mentioned, a main cause could help us to obtain a good predictive model, but this may be due to its having suitable word features. In our work, we utilized Word2Vec to collect the relevant words of each aspect. Therefore, we would like to compare our technique to another technique applied to obtain the relevant words of each aspect proposed by [15]. They proposed a method for extracting implicit and explicit aspects. The researchers have been advised that an implicit aspect could not be expressed by any particular word, while an explicit aspect generally has a word that can indicate the specific aspect class. Consider this review: *"The app design is attractive. But it is buggy."* The word *"design"* was considered as an explicit term and the word *"attractive"* becomes its opinion word in the first sentence. This sentence indicates a positive sentiment toward an aspect category, called *"User Interface"*. Therefore, their algorithm first searches for opinion words that directly denote aspect according to the lexicon. If the opinion word cannot identify the aspect class, their algorithm will look for the nearest aspect word in the same sentence with a maximum window size of two, and with greater priority to the right side, since the adjective word typically comes before the considered word. Finally, the pair of extracted opinion word and aspect word will be searched in the lexicon in order to define the aspect class.

Table 4. The results of the aspect analyzer and the sentiment analyzer.

Algorithm	Iteration	The aspect analyzer				The sentiment analyzer			
		R	P	F1	Acc	R	P	F1	Acc
MNB	1	0.80	0.79	0.79	0.79	0.82	0.81	0.81	0.81
	2	0.79	0.78	0.78	0.78	0.81	0.80	0.80	0.80
	3	0.79	0.77	0.78	0.78	0.80	0.79	0.79	0.78
	4	0.79	0.78	0.78	0.78	0.80	0.78	0.79	0.78
	5	**0.81**	**0.79**	**0.80**	**0.80**	0.82	0.80	0.81	0.80
	6	0.80	0.77	0.78	0.78	**0.83**	**0.81**	**0.82**	**0.82**
	7	0.80	0.79	0.79	0.79	0.81	0.78	0.79	0.79
	8	0.79	0.77	0.78	0.78	0.80	0.78	0.79	0.78
	9	0.79	0.78	0.78	0.78	0.80	0.78	0.79	0.78
	10	0.79	0.77	0.78	0.78	0.81	0.79	0.80	0.80
SVM with linear kernel	1	0.82	0.80	0.81	0.82	0.83	0.82	0.82	0.82
	2	0.80	0.79	0.79	0.79	0.81	0.80	0.80	0.80
	3	0.83	0.82	0.82	0.81	0.84	0.82	0.83	0.83
	4	0.79	0.77	0.78	0.78	0.80	0.80	0.80	0.80

(continued)

Table 4. (*continued*)

Algorithm	Iteration	The aspect analyzer				The sentiment analyzer			
		R	P	F1	Acc	R	P	F1	Acc
	5	**0.84**	**0.83**	**0.83**	**0.83**	0.80	0.79	0.79	0.79
	6	0.80	0.79	0.79	0.79	**0.85**	**0.84**	**0.84**	**0.84**
	7	0.83	0.82	0.82	0.81	0.80	0.80	0.80	0.80
	8	0.79	0.77	0.78	0.79	0.80	0.79	0.79	0.79
	9	0.79	0.78	0.78	0.79	0.80	0.79	0.79	0.79
	10	0.82	0.80	0.81	0.81	0.83	0.81	0.82	0.82
SVM with RBF kernel	1	0.81	0.80	0.80	0.80	0.82	0.81	0.81	0.81
	2	0.79	0.79	0.79	0.79	0.81	0.80	0.80	0.80
	3	0.81	0.80	0.80	0.80	0.83	0.82	0.82	0.82
	4	0.79	0.77	0.78	0.78	0.80	0.80	0.80	0.80
	5	**0.83**	**0.82**	**0.82**	**0.82**	0.80	0.79	0.79	0.79
	6	0.80	0.78	0.79	0.79	**0.84**	**0.82**	**0.83**	**0.83**
	7	0.81	0.80	0.80	0.80	0.80	0.80	0.80	0.80
	8	0.79	0.76	0.77	0.77	0.80	0.79	0.79	0.79
	9	0.79	0.77	0.78	0.78	0.80	0.79	0.79	0.79
	10	0.80	0.80	0.80	0.80	0.82	0.80	0.81	0.81

In the comparison stage, after obtaining opinion words and aspect classes using the method proposed by [15], those opinion words were used for modeling the aspect analyzer. It is noted that the first dataset and the SVM algorithm with linear kernel function were utilized to model the aspect analyzer. The results of the comparison are presented in Table 5.

Table 5. The results of comparison between the proposed and baseline methods.

Techniques of generating opinion word and aspect class	The aspect analyzer			
	Avg. of recall	Avg. of precision	Avg. of F1	Avg. of accuracy
The baseline	0.802	0.789	0.793	0.793
The proposed method	0.811	0.797	0.801	0.802

The results in Table 5 showed that our proposed method could give slightly improved average scores of recall, precision, F1, and accuracy at 1.11%, 1.00%, 1.00%, and 1.12% respectively. This may be due to the use of specific keywords for each aspect. Thus, the proposed method was able to identify sentences that correspond to the specific aspect better than the baseline method. However, although our proposed method returned better results than the baseline method, it was not superior to the baseline method from every viewpoint. It might be possible that if we utilized the same dataset and algorithms as the baseline method, this would impact the experimental results.

6 Conclusion

Students' feedback for teaching process assessment can be utilized to improve the teaching and learning process. However, teachers may be biased when examining or considering the student feedback for their teaching process assessments. As a result, it could produce insufficient and erroneous information that cannot be used to improve the teaching process. An automatic analysis method is required to evaluate the students' feedback on the teaching process; therefore, automatic sentiment analysis is applied because this may help to reduce the problem of biased analysis when the sentiment analysis is performed by humans. In this work, the method of sentence-level sentiment analysis was proposed. This method is driven by processing steps detailed as pre-processing student comments and text representation, identifying the aspect class for each sentence using the aspect analyzer, assigning sentence polarity for each sentence using the sentiment analyzer, and summarizing the overall sentiment polarity of the considered student comment, respectively. The proposed method returned the recall, precision, F1, and accuracy scores of 0.835, 0.825, 0.825, and 0.825, respectively. In addition, we compared our aspect analyzer to the baseline. Our proposed method could give slightly improved average scores of recall, precision, F1, and accuracy at 1.11%, 1.00%, 1.00%, and 1.12%. However, although our proposed method returned better results than the baseline method, it was not superior to the baseline method from every viewpoint. It might be possible that if we utilized the same dataset and algorithms as the baseline method, this would impact the experimental results.

References

1. Berardinelli, N., Gaber, M.M., Haig, E.: SA-E: Sentiment analysis for education. Front. Artif. Intell. Appl. **255**, 353–362 (2013)
2. Zhao, H., Ji, X., Zeng, Q., Jiang, S.: A teaching evaluation method based on sentiment classification. Int. J. Comput. Sci. Math. **7**(1), 54–62 (2016)
3. Esparza, G.G., et al.: A sentiment analysis model to analyze students reviews of teacher performance using support vector machines. In: 14th International Conference Distributed Computing and Artificial Intelligence, vol. 620, pp. 157–164 (2017)
4. Peng, H., Zhang, Z., Liu, H.: A sentiment analysis method for teaching evaluation texts using attention mechanism combined with CNN-BLSTM model. Sci. Programm. **2022**, 1–9 (2022)
5. Choi, G., Oh, S., Kim, H.: Improving document-level sentiment classification using importance of sentences. Entropy **22**(12), 1–11 (2020)
6. Liu, Y., Yu, X., Liu, B., Chen, Z.: Sentence-level sentiment analysis in the presence of modalities. In: Gelbukh, A. (ed.) CICLing 2014. LNCS, vol. 8404, pp. 1–16. Springer, Heidelberg (2014). https://doi.org/10.1007/978-3-642-54903-8_1
7. Jagtap, V.S., Pawar, K.: Analysis of different approaches to Sentence-Level Sentiment Classification. https://citeseerx.ist.psu.edu/viewdoc/summary?doi=10.1.1.278.4931. Accessed 21 May 2022

8. Lutz, B., Pröllochs, N., Neumann, D.: Sentence-level sentiment analysis of financial news using distributed text representations and multi-instance learning. In: The Hawaii International Conference on System Sciences (HICSS). pp. 1–10. Hawaii, USA (2018)

9. Meknavin, S., Charoenpornsawat, P., Kijsirikul, B.: Feature-based Thai word segmentation. http://www.cs.cmu.edu/~paisarn/papers/old/nlprs97.pdf. Accessed 21 May 2022

10. Kaur, J., Buttar, P.: Stopwords removal and its algorithms based on different methods. Int. J. Adv. Res. Comput. Sci. **9**(5), 81–88 (2018)

11. Erk, K., Padó, P.: A structured vector space model for word meaning in context. In: Proceedings of the 2008 Conference on Empirical Methods in Natural Language Processing, pp. 897–906. Honolulu, Hawaii (2008)

12. Polpinij, J., Srikanjanapert, N., Sopon, P.: Word2Vec approach for sentiment classification relating to hotel reviews. In: Meesad, P., Sodsee, S., Unger, H. (eds.) IC2IT 2017. AISC, vol. 566, pp. 308–316. Springer, Cham (2018). https://doi.org/10.1007/978-3-319-60663-7_29

13. Namee, K., Polpinij, J.: Concept-based one-class SVM classifier with supervised term weighting scheme for imbalanced sentiment classification. Eng. Appl. Sci. Res. **48**(5), 604–613 (2021)

14. Polpinij, J., Luaphol, B.: Comparing of multi-class text classification methods for automatic ratings of consumer reviews. In: Chomphuwiset, P., Kim, J., Pawara, P. (eds.) MIWAI 2021. LNCS (LNAI), vol. 12832, pp. 164–175. Springer, Cham (2021). https://doi.org/10.1007/978-3-030-80253-0_15

15. Alqaryouti, O., Siyam, N., Monem, A.A., Shaalan, K.: Aspect-based sentiment analysis using smart government review data. Appl. Comput. Inform. **2210–8327**, 1–20 (2019)

Sentiment Analysis of Local Tourism in Thailand from YouTube Comments Using BiLSTM

Sanya Khruahong[1]([✉]) [iD], Olarik Surinta[2] [iD], and Sinh Cong Lam[3] [iD]

[1] Department of Computer Science and Information Technology, Faculty of Science, Naresuan University, Phitsanulok, Thailand
sanyak@nu.ac.th
[2] Multi-agent Intelligent Simulation Laboratory (MISL), Faculty of Informatics, Mahasarakham University, Mahasarakham, Thailand
olarik.s@msu.ac.th
[3] Faculty of Electronics and Telecommunication, VNU - University of Engineering and Technology, Hanoi, Vietnam
congls@vnu.edu.vn

Abstract. Currently, social networks, where people can express their opinion through content and comments, are fast developing and affect various areas of daily life; Particularly, some research on YouTube travel channels found that almost tourists and audiences leave comments about their attitudes to that place. Thus, mining the emotional recognition of comments through artificial intelligence can bring knowledge about the tourists' general view. This article analyzes the relationship(s) between social media use and its effect on community-based tourism in Thailand using the Social Media Sensing framework (S-Sense) as sentiment analysis and the Bidirectional Long Short-Term Memory (BiLSTM) methods to analyze the text comments. This research collected 51,280 comments on 114 Youtube Videos, which are tourist attractions in various provinces in Thailand. The approach categorizes attractions based on sentiment analysis of 60% or more, including restaurants, markets, historical sites, temples, or natural attractions. The results show that 67.51% of the 19,391 clean-processed comments were satisfied with those attraction places. Therefore S-Sense and BiLSTM models can be sufficient to analyze the attitude of comments about attraction places with from 43 to remain 33 keywords of 1,603 comments. Furthermore, the offered sentiment analysis method has higher precision, recall, and F1 scores.

Keywords: Social media analytics · Sentiment analysis · Text classification · Social media sensing · Bidirectional long short-term memory

1 Introduction

Tourism is considered an essential economic factor in Thailand since it can contribute a significant part in gross domestic product. In the past, the Thai government had the policy to attract many foreign tourists, but during the past year, a coronavirus epidemic brought a big problem. Thus, the govermonet encourage Thai to have more domestic

O. Surinta and K. Kam Fung Yuen (Eds.): MIWAI 2022, LNAI 13651, pp. 169–177, 2022.
https://doi.org/10.1007/978-3-031-20992-5_15

travels tostimulate the domestic economy. In addition, the government has policies to support local or community-based tourism [1, 2]. Local tourism [3, 4], or Tourism in the community, focuses on local lifestyles which the residents invite travelers to attend their location. Thus, tourism must adhere to environmental sustainability principles, society, and community culture, which can be broadcast through social media.

A Social Networking Site (SNS) [5, 6] is a website that connects people over the Internet and establishes an auxiliary channels for people to communicate easier over large distances. It can create a personal space, for example, Facebook, YouTube, or Twitter. The number of users has increased dramatically in the last ten years. Users primarily use for different purposes such as to show their thoughts and feelings on that moment [7, 8], and may be their new stories, places, or experiences. All of these personal thoughts and feelings are posted on the social media in the forms of texts, images, and videos. Mining comments' emotional propensity in the big data domain is valuable for learning network public sentiment. The analysis results may provide suitable guidance for tourist development.

Social Media Analytics (SMA) [9, 10] is one of data analytics that organizes different sections of evidence or information into categories according to purpose and the assumptions set. Social media analytic is one of the most popular forms of social media that can timely provide knowledge about different situations. SMA process consists of three following steps 1) collecting data, 2) analyzing the obtained interpretations, and 3) displaying the results in an easy-to-understand format.

Deep learning is a method of automating learning by simulating the behavior of human neural networks by overlapping multiple layers of neural networks [11]. The deep learning method is key to learning from data using a general-purpose learning procedure. Thus, deep learning can be developed for various tasks.

Therefore, the researchers are interested in applying social media analytics techniques and sentiment analysis (S-Sense) [12] to analyze local tourism data. The purpose is to use comments from YouTube channels to analyze attitude patterns in community tourist attractions. Moreover, deep learning is applied with Bidirectional Long Short-Term Memory (BiLSTM) models [13] to find relevant factors to recommend entrepreneurs in online marketing with data analysis for local tourism. The results mentioned will be both the process and the resulting form. The researchers hope it can be applied to other community attractions and lead to tourism industry development.

This paper proposes a sentiment analysis of YouTube's comments based on BiLSTM. The paper is organized as follows. Section 2 describes the related works of this research. After that, Sect. 3 introduces the methodology of Social Media Analytics. Section 4 shows the discussion and results. Finally, Sect. 5 concludes the paper and describes the future direction.

2 Related Work

This section describes the data analytics methods investigated in this paper. These methods are the most popular in the literature.

2.1 Big Data Analytics

Data analytics is a method that analyzes and extracts the raw data to make the conclusion which is the information. Big Data Analytics (BDA) [14, 15] is increasingly growing as a trending method that generates extensive data and provides a new opportunity for decision-making. Moreover, it can produce new understandings to improve results in many domains. Big data analytics systems [16] can provide proactive action for strategic decision-making to predict future volumes. Predictive analytics uses previous information to forecast user behavior and trends. Machine learning is applied to analyze data and make predictions. Although BDA is an excellent technique that can be used to analyze data, it may also require big data technology, which is costly.

2.2 Deep Learning

Deep learning is significantly advancing in artificial intelligence problems, which can be divided into feedforward neural network and recurrent neural network [11, 17, 18]. The performance of deep learning systems can usually be dramatically improved by merely scaling them up. With a lot more data and a lot more computation, they generally perform a lot better. Some deep learning techniques are applied to the text to understand the content of a sentence or article. So, it needs to understand in natural language processing.

2.3 Social Media Analytics (SMA)

SMA [19] collects information from websites, social media, and blogs, after which the data is analyzed to be used in business decision-making. Many people may not realize that this process includes fundamental analysis like retweets or likes, highlighting consumer insights on social media. The main objective of using SMA is to analyze the user-generated content and spread speed from social media [20].

SMA is the process of analyzing, measuring, and predicting of digital interaction, relationships, topics, ideas, or content. The primary SMA process has three-stage: 1) Capture, 2) Understand 3) Present, which is called the "CUP framework [21, 22]." This research presents social media commentary on automobiles to adapt to the automobile industry and is suitable for use with other businesses. Some framework [23] describes two data collection approaches (semantically driven and user-driven) and two analytic methods (temporal analysis and corpus analysis). However, it may take more tools to access information, which may take too long to implement this technique.

2.4 Sentiment Analysis

Sentiment analysis [10, 24–27], which is a part of artificial intelligence, is clarified as the task of finding the opinions of users, attitudes, and emotions about specific information. Sentiment analysis is the core method of many social media monitoring systems and trend-analysis applications. Sentiment analysis is a specific text analysis task for valence identification and subjectivity analysis. In comparison, text analysis and text mining aim to analyze textural data and extract machine-readable facts. Social Media Sensing (S-Sense) [12] is a sentiment analysis model consistent with natural language processing, text mining, and sentiment analysis techniques. It can help a business or organization to recognize the various activities related to their organization such as monitoring satisfaction and public attitudes towards their product brands or services. Thus, the business and organization can better understand their customers' needs.

Sentiment analysis can be proposed in three levels: document, sentence, and aspect-based [25]. Document sentiment analysis aims to resolve the overall opinion on a particular entity and express positive or negative sentiments, such as a product and service. Next, sentence-level aims to classify the sentiment expressed in each sentence. Finally, Aspect-level seeks to organize the views concerning the specific aspects of entities. However, data sets are vital for review analysis, especially the primary sources that can support the efficiency of sentiment analysis. These reviews are essential to business holders because they can make business decisions based on analyzing user feedback about their products.

Sentiment analysis was developed in three ways: 1)sentiment analysis based on sentiment dictionary, 2)machine learning, and 3)deep learning. However, using the dictionaries technique need to find sufficient coverage of sentimental words and lack of domain words which is the big problems. Thus, much research used machine learning and deep learning methods in sentiment analysis and achieved good results.

The deep BiLSTM is used as the representation of the comment texts [13, 26, 28]. BiLSTM is an extension version of the LSTM methods in which two LSTMs are applied to the input data. In the first step, the sequence input is fed to the first LSTM. In the second step, the reverse of the input sequence is transferred into the second LSTM. The BiLSTM method improves the learning of long-term dependencies and accuracy performance. Text classification is one of the essential factors for sentiment analysis. Some languages with constraints used text classification, such as Arabic [29]. Significantly, Thai has a complicated pattern; therefore, this article uses BiLSTM technique to improve Text classification in Thai Sentiment analysis.

3   Methodology

This section presents the research methodology with the following steps. The framework has the following principles: 1) Data collection, 2) Sentiment analysis, and 3) Summarizing results as shown in Fig. 1.

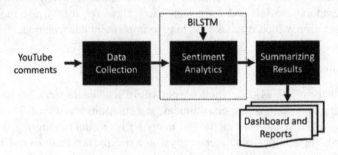

Fig. 1. Social media analytics framework

3.1 Data Collection

This research collected comment data from 114 clips on YouTube, which are tourist attractions in various provinces in Thailand. The 51,280 comments were collected with the service website for importing comments in Thai. We only collected those posts posted from April 17th, 2017, to May 15th, 2022. Text cleansing can be performed using simple Python code with "*AI for Thai*" API [30]. After being cleaned, the valuable comments reduces to 19,391 (Fig. 2).

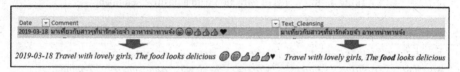

Fig. 2. Original comment and text cleansing

3.2 Sentiment Analysis

Sentiment analysis further classified each text based on its sentiment, positive or negative, as shown in Fig. 3. S-Sense was applied with our comments data in the Thai language, which is analyzed as shown in Table 1. They display 13,091 positive comments and 6,300 negative comments. However, this paper only focuses on positive comments with a sentiment score of 60–100%.

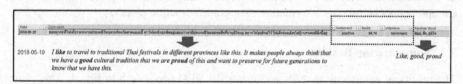

Fig. 3. Sentiment analysis results

Table 1. Number of sentiments from the collection by S-Sense

Sentiments	Comments	Score (Min)	Score (Max)
Positive	13,091	60%	100%
Negative	6,300	−99.99%	−52.63%
Total	19,391		

After S-Sense processing, 43 keywords categories were grouped from 2,631 comments, and we translated them from Thai into English shown in Table 2. The results show that some words may be exact and not present the attraction places, such as " ท่องเที่ยว" or " เที่ยว," they mean travel. Although this term is related to tourism, it does not reflect places or elements that can promote tourism. Those words should represent what tourists like, perhaps a place or something that can be considered a travel destination. Therefore, this paper needs to improve to get more suitable categories.

Table 2. Keywords of attraction with a positive sentiment

Keywords (English)
"Temple", "Travel", "Coffee", "food", "Travel", "Green tea", "Cave", "Forest", "Waterfall", "Tradition", "Places", "Market", "Review", "Atmosphere", "Temple", "Nature", "Travel", "Dam", "Huay", "Travel", "Village", "pagoda", "Cafe", "River", "Mountain", "Festival", "History"," Buddha statues, "Tourists", "Tourist Places", "Local People", "Culture", "Floating Markets", "Festive Places", "Ancient", "Relics", "Attractions", "Museums", "Weekend Markets", "View Points" ,"Archaeological site"

This article uses BiLSTM in Text classification of sentiment analysis to improve the result. BiLSTM can be summarized by concatenating the forward and backward states as $ht = [- \rightarrow h\,t, \leftarrow - h\,t]$. It treats all inputs equally. For sentiment analysis, the sentiment contradiction of the text primarily relies on the terms with sentiment data.

In this paper, using BiLSTM can specific group tourism categories from 43 remain to 33 categories with 1,603 comments representing attraction places, and tourism entrepreneurs can use this information to upgrade attraction places.

3.3 Summarizing Results

The results of sentiment analysis and using BiLSTM are shown in Fig. 4. This chart presents that travelers commented positively on the top four places of interest categories: temples (353), food (335), coffee (154), and green tea (142), respectively. The temples praised the beauty of the architecture, the refinement, and the peaceful atmosphere of the village. As for the food, most tourists will comment on its deliciousness. Both temple and food are considered to be highly positive compared to other keywords. As for coffee and green tea, tourists are expected to like the taste and atmosphere of the cafes where they visit, with the number of restaurants growing in popularity, resulting in many positive reviews. Therefore, as a result, if entrepreneurs focus on these four keywords, they can be used to develop tourist attractions, such as developing temples into essential tourist attractions or developing restaurants that focus on delicious taste, good coffee, and good green tea. Or a good atmosphere in the restaurants can increase customers to travel there. Moreover, the graph also shows that unique markets are essential, so perhaps pulling that market up into a niche market can further increase tourism.

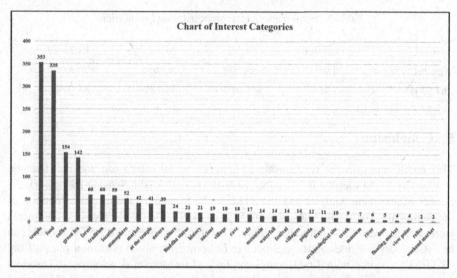

Fig. 4. Tourism categories using BiLSTM

4 Evaluation

In this research, the effectiveness of our proposed model is evaluated by extracting four parameters from the confusion matrix: precision, recall, accuracy, and F1 score. The metrics contain four terms: True Positive (T_P), False Positive (F_P), True Negative (T_N), and False Negative (F_N). *Precision* is the ratio of correctly predicted reviews (T_P) to the total number of expected reviews ($T_P + F_P$) in any class, where the class may be positive or negative. *Recall* is the ratio of correctly predicted reviews (T_P) to the total number of actual reviews ($T_P + F_N$) in any class, where the class may be positive or negative. *Accuracy* is the ratio of correctly predicted to the total number of reviews, and *F1 score* represents the harmonic mean of precision and recall. These four metrics are described briefly below:

$$Precision = \frac{T_P}{(T_P + F_P)} \tag{1}$$

$$Recall = \frac{T_P}{(T_P + F_N)} \tag{2}$$

$$Accuracy = \frac{(T_P + T_N)}{(T_P + T_N + F_P + F_N)} \tag{3}$$

$$F1Score = \frac{2 \times (Precision \times Recall)}{(Precision + Recall)} \tag{4}$$

All the performances of our proposed approach are shown in Table 3.

Table 3. Performance of the proposed text classification

Method	Precision	Recall	Accuracy	F1 Score
Non-BiLSTM	*78.95%*	*80.29%*	*80.40%*	*79.61%*
BiLSTM	*83.25%*	*87.01%*	*85.78%*	*85.08%*

5   Conclusion

This article analyzes the relationship(s) between social media use and its effect on community-based tourism in Thailand using the Social Media Sensing framework (S-Sense) as sentiment analysis and BiLSTM model to analyze the text classification of the comments. The results show that 67.51% of the 19,391 clean-processed comments were satisfied with those attraction places. Therefore S-Sense and BiLSTM models can be satisfactory considering the perspective of comments about attraction places from 43 to 33 keywords with 1,603 comments to lead to tourism development. Travelers commented positively on the top four places of interest categories: temples (353), food (335), coffee (154), and green tea (142), respectively. Therefore, entrepreneurs can focus on these four categories to develop tourist attractions. The evaluation results show that the proposed sentiment analysis approach has heightened precision, recall, and F1 scores. It can enhance to be valuable with increased accuracy on statements.

In the future, we should collect more comments to improve precision in the analytics. The limitation of this article is that the datasets are all in Thai. It would be interesting to execute a parallel study on other languages, such as English or Chinese.

References

1. Lee, T.H., Jan, F.-H.: Can community-based tourism contribute to sustainable development? Evidence from residents perceptions of the sustainability. Tourism Manag. **70**, 368–380 (2019)
2. Melphon Mayaka, W., Croy, G., Cox, J.: A dimensional approach to community-based tourism: Recognising and differentiating form and context. Ann. Tourism Res. **74**, 177–190 (2019). https://doi.org/10.1016/j.annals.2018.12.002
3. Gu, X., Wu, J., Guo, H., Li, G.: Local tourism cycle and external business cycle. Ann. Tourism Res. **73**, 159–170 (2018)
4. Laparojkit, S., Suttipun, M.: The influence of customer trust and loyalty on repurchase intention of domestic tourism: a case study in Thailand during COVID-19 crisis. The J. Asian Finance, Econ. Bus. **8**(5), 961–969 (2021)
5. de Vries, D.A., Peter, J., de Graaf, H., Nikken, P.: Adolescents' social network site use, peer appearance-related feedback, and body dissatisfaction: testing a mediation model. J. Youth Adolesc. **45**, 211–224 (2016)
6. Saiphoo, A.N., Halevi, L.D., Vahedi, Z.: Social networking site use and self-esteem: a meta-analytic review. Pers. Individ. Differ. **153**, 109639 (2020)
7. Kolokytha, E., Loutrouki, S., Valsamidis, S., Florou, G.: Social media networks as a learning tool. Procedia Econ. Financ. **19**, 287–295 (2015)
8. Havakhor, T., Soror, A.A., Sabherwal, R.: Diffusion of knowledge in social media networks: effects of reputation mechanisms and distribution of knowledge roles. Inform. Syst. J. **28**(1), 104–141 (2018)

9. Lee, I.: Social media analytics for enterprises: Typology, methods, and processes. Bus. Horiz. **61**(2), 199–210 (2018)
10. Fan, W., Gordon, M.D.: The power of social media analytics. Commun. ACM **57**(6), 74–81 (2014)
11. Bengio, Y., LeCun, Y., Hinton, G.: Deep learning for AI. Commun. ACM **64**(7), 58–65 (2021)
12. Haruechaiyasak, C., Kongthon, A., Palingoon, P., Trakultaweekoon, K.: S-sense: a sentiment analysis framework for social media Monitoring Applications. Inform. Technol. J. **14**(1), 11–22 (2018)
13. Xu, G., Meng, Y., Qiu, X., Yu, Z., Wu, X.: Sentiment analysis of comment texts based on BiLSTM. IEEE Access **7**, 51522–51532 (2019)
14. Saggi, M.K., Jain, S.: A survey towards an integration of big data analytics to big insights for value-creation. Inform. Process. Manage. **54**(5), 758–790 (2018)
15. Olivera, P., Danese, S., Jay, N., Natoli, G., Peyrin-Biroulet, L.: Big data in IBD: a look into the future. Nat. Rev. Gastroenterol. Hepatol. **16**, 312–321 (2019)
16. Zakir, J., Seymour, T., Berg, K.: Big data analytics. Issues Inform. Syst. **16**(2), 81–90 (2015)
17. LeCun, Y., Bengio, Y., Hinton, G.: Deep learning. Nature **521**, 436–444 (2015)
18. Phiphitphatphaisit, S., Surinta, O.: Deep feature extraction technique based on Conv1D and LSTM network for food image recognition. Eng. Appl. Sci. Res. **48**(5), 581–592 (2021)
19. Stieglitz, S., Mirbabaie, M., Ross, B., Neuberger, C.: Social media analytics – Challenges in topic discovery, data collection, and data preparation. Int. J. Inform. Manag. **39**, 156–168 (2018)
20. Holsapple, C., Hsiao, S.-H., Pakath, R.: Business social media analytics: Definition, benefits, and challenges. In: Twentieth Americas Conference on Information Systems (AMCIS), pp. 1–12. Savannah (2014).
21. Khruahong, S., Asawasakulson, A., Krom, W.N.: Social media analytics in comments of multiple vehicle brands on social networking sites in Thailand. In: Luo, Y. (ed.) Cooperative Design, Visualization, and Engineering (CDVE). Lecture Notes in Computer Science, vol. 12341, pp. 357–367. Springer, Cham (2020)
22. Andryani, R., Negara, E.S., Triadi, D.: Social media analytics: data utilization of social media for research. J. Inform. Syst. Informatics **1**(2), 193–205 (2019)
23. Brooker, P., Barnett, J., Cribbin, T.: Doing social media analytics. Big Data Soc. **3**, 205395171665806 (2016)
24. Feldman, R.: Techniques and applications for sentiment analysis. Commun. ACM **56**(4), 82–89 (2013)
25. Medhat, W., Hassan, A., Korashy, H.: Sentiment analysis algorithms and applications: a survey. Ain Shams Eng. J. **5**(4), 1093–1113 (2014)
26. Liu, B.: Sentiment Analysis: Mining Opinions, Sentiments, and Emotions. Cambridge University Press (2020). https://doi.org/10.1017/9781108639286
27. Darwich, M., Noah, S.A.M., Omar, N.: Minimally-supervised sentiment lexicon induction model: a case study of malay sentiment analysis. In: Phon-Amnuaisuk, S., Ang, SP., Lee, Sy. (eds.) Multi-disciplinary Trends in Artificial Intelligence (MIWAI). Lecture Notes in Computer Science(), vol. 10607, pp. 225–237. Springer, Cham (2017).
28. Siami-Namini, S., Tavakoli, N., Namin, A.S.: The performance of LSTM and BiLSTM in forecasting time series. In: IEEE International Conference on Big Data (Big Data), pp. 3285–3292. IEEE, CA, USA (2019)
29. Maghfour, M., Elouardighi, A.: Standard and dialectal Arabic text classification for sentiment analysis. In: Abdelwahed, E., Bellatreche, L., Golfarelli, M., Méry, D., Ordonez, C. (eds.) Model and Data Engineering (MEDI). Lecture notes in Computer Science(), vol. 11163, pp. 282–291. Springer, Cham (2018)
30. Tapsai, C., Meesad, P., Unger, H.: An overview on the development of Thai natural language processing. Inform. Technol. J. **15**(2), 45–52 (2019)

Stable Coalitions of Buyers in Real World Agriculture Domain

Chattrakul Sombattheera[✉]

Multiagent, Intelligent and Simulation Laboratory (MISL),
Faculty of Informatics, Mahasarakham University,
Khamreang, Kantarawichai, Mahasarakham, Thailand
chattrakul.s@msu.ac.th

Abstract. The Department of Agricultural Extension, Ministry of Agriculture, Thailand, has developed and deployed an AI-based system, namely, Personalized Data (PD), to help millions of Thai farmers to make better decisions with regards to growing and selling crops. One of the AI module equipped with the system applies cooperative game theoretic principles, namely Kernel, a stability concept, as important part of the system. While most applications of game theory in real world domains concentrate on one game setting, this system may have to scan for much larger search space to ensure stability. This paper examines how much time it take and how large the search space can be in order to examine stability in practice. Although there are several algorithms involved, we present only ones for generating coalitions and examining whether the given payoff configuration is in Kernel. The former repeatedly generates all coalitions of a given set of agents. The latter compares between each pair of agents in every coalition of the given configuration payoff whether one of the agent's payoff outweighs the other's. For the search space of 15–30 agents, we find that it can range from 11 to 20 °C of magnitude. For execution time, we find that it takes minutes for up to 18 agents and it takes hours for 19 agents. For larger number of agents, it can take days or months and will require a much more powerful computer to reduce the execution time.

Keywords: Stable · Kernel · Coalition formation · Agriculture

1 Introduction

As part of its strategic plan for the next 20 years, the government of Thailand has launched the national policy on deploying modern technologies to help drive the nation to prosperity. One of the technologies being mentioned in the plan is artificial Intelligence. As it has been seen world wide that the adoption of AI has been widely successfully in many areas. Agriculture has been a successful area where AI has been increasingly deployed world wide. Based on this fact,

Supported by the Department of Agriculture Extension of Thailand.

the Thai government has been driving and hoping for the development on this area with the country.

The Department of Agricultural Extension (DOAE), Ministry of Agriculture, of Thailand has been quick to react to this call. DOAE has been maintaining large databases, collecting data from thousands of its personnel and millions of farmers all over the country for more than 40 years. It is keen to adopt AI technologies to utilize this massive amount of data to be personalized to help farmers make better decisions based on their interests. There are two main AI modules: machine learning-based for predicting prices, yields and costs of crops, and game theoretic modules, both cooperative and non-cooperative, for analyzing the derived data and help make better decision for both DOAE personnel and farmers. For cooperative game theory, there are three important solution concepts, namely, optimal coalition structure for global and individual optimality, Shapley value for fairness among coalition members, and Kernel for stability among coalition members.

This paper focuses on the stability issue of coalition formation among farmers. The Kernel is, one of, if not, the most widely adopted stability concepts. In general, the payoff configuration, a vector specifying how farmers form coalitions and their respective payoffs, will be provided. Then it will be examine whether the payoff configuration is in Kernel. This is not very easy to examine because the algorithm has to go to almost each coalition, out of 2^n coalitions for n farmers, for each agent. This makes it almost 2^{2n}, which can be very large for small n. Although optimal coalition structure is likely to guarantee stability in most cases, particularly for superadditive environment, it is still important that we have to thoroughly examine to ensure stability. We thoroughly analyze the size of the search space and empirically investigate to ensure how large can n be such that the result can be achieved in reasonable, taking into account the reality that farmers and DOAE personnel are awaiting for the results. This paper's contribution is to practically show how large search space can be and how long it takes to ensure stability among agents.

The paper is structured as follow. We review for progress in coalition formation in agricultural domain. We then briefly discuss the circumstance of this project. We discuss in details for fundamental concept of coalition formation and Kernel. We then discuss about experiments and results, then conclude, lastly.

2   Related Works

Game theory [5], both non-cooperative [4] and cooperative, has been widely adopted in AI research. Cooperative game, also known as coalition formation [3,17], provides fundamental concepts for cooperation among decision making. Important solution concepts include efficiency (core [2] and optimal coalition structure [6]), stability [1], and fairness [7]. Here we shall review related work being deployed in agriculture and related domains.

Bistaffa et al. [8] consider coalition formation among energy consumers in the smart grid applying stability concept. The peaks of demands are flatten.

Blankernburg et al. [9] investigate safety and privacy preservation in forming stable coalitions among informative agents. Yamamoto et al. [10] propose a coalition formation scheme in e-commerce to buy as a group on a category of items. This system allows for buyers to post their needs and the system combine these needs a bunch. Sellers then bids for the request. Guthula et al. [11] model a specific troubled agricultural sub-system in India as a Multi-Agent System and use it as a tool to analyze the impact of policies and recommend some policies based on simulation result. Zaryouli et al. [12] help establish a predictive analysis on the impact of climatic change on red fruits by proposing solutions to optimize crop growth decisions by increasing yields and profitability of production for the farmer. Perez-ponz et al. [13] help make decisions in the purchase of sustainable agricultural products by proposing a multiagent system choosing a supplier for agricultural future market price forecast. Chevalier et al. [14] help achieve precision agriculture, combining quadrotor and tracked robots, by using coalition formation concept. Gonzalez et al. [15] help reduce water usage and increase efficiency and effectiveness in automotive irrigation processes in rural areas by using cooperative game concept.

As we can see, there is almost none of stability concept has been deployed in agricultural domain in recent years. The concept has been used in theoretical work or e-commerce domain. Therefore, this Personalized Data is among the first to apply this concept to help farmers make better decisions.

3   Real World Domain

One of the reasons DOAE wants to use AI to help farmers is to leverage their hidden collective power on both producing and negotiating for higher prices when selling and lower prices when buying. This system allows for farmer to specify their needs for fertilizers, seeds, etc. and collectively gain discounts, which to be distributed among participating agents. Any farmer can submit her/his need for buying as a group to other farmers to participate. Interested farmers can choose to participate. Not interested agents can insist to be the group leader. Participating agents specify their needs and constraints, for example, 5 tons of fertilizers of a reserved price maximum. There could be many farmers submitting requests at the same time. The system will scan for farmers looking for the same thing and are located in close proximity. Figure 1 shows a set of screen snapshots of farmers.

3.1   Computing Values for a Group of Farmers

Farmers looking for values accruing from joining a group. The values can be discounts achieved from bulk buy, Typically bulk buy help save a fair amount of expenses for sellers. From sellers perspective, the saved amount can be shared to buyer in order to attract them. On the other hand, farmers can also sell as a group and ask for higher prices because they can save buyers, who look for a large amount of crops, time and expenses in order to collect the crops up to their

Fig. 1. Screen snapshots of farmers looking for available groups (left), existing members (center), and confirming joining a group (right.)

need. From buyers perspective, the time and expenses they can save are to be shared to farmers in order to attract them. From the system point of view, with respect to cooperative game theory, the saved amount to be shared to farmers is the value of forming a group, or coalition, of farmers. This value is yet to be distributed to farmers. There are two steps involved in computing values: i) is to find coalition center, and ii) to find the net value for the group. For selling crops, there must be a center of the coalition where the crops will be collected from members. For buying goods, the center of the coalition is where the goods will be delivered to and distributed to members. The center is the location of farmer where the collective distances to other agents is minimal. This ensures that the cost for delivering goods/crops is collectively the cheapest. The net value is the discounted or increased total price subtracted by the collective cost.

3.2 Computing Payoffs for Farmers

There another very important step involved, computing payoffs for farmers. There are multiple solution concepts in cooperative game that can be adopted, for example, efficiency, fairness, stability, etc. This Personalized System is equipped with these features. From farmer perspective, efficiency is the discounted or increased price they will receive. However, they simply keen to know whether their shared value is fair. With this regard, the system adopts Shapley value. We have discuss in details about this in another work. The last one is stability, which can be ensured by Kernel solution concept. We shall discuss in details in section below.

4   Stability in Coalition of Farmers

This system adopts the concept of cooperative game, also known as *coalition formation*. Below, we shall discuss the fundamental concept of coalition formation and Kernel stable concept.

4.1   Coalition Formation

Foundation of Coalition. A set of n agent is denoted by $A = \{a_1, a_2, \ldots, a_n\}$. A *coalition*, denoted by S of A, $S \subseteq A, S \neq \emptyset$, is a non-empty subset of of A. Therefore, the size of coalition, or the number of agents in S, also known as *cardinality*, $1 \leq |S| \leq n$, ranges between 1 and n. In practice, a coalition is formed once agents agree to cooperate and are abiding to their respective coalitions. The smallest coalition, $|S| = 1$, is the *singleton* coalition. Obviously, there are n singleton coalitions. The set A itself is the largest coalition, $|S| = n$, namely the *grand* coalition, The power set of A is the set of all coalitions, denoted by $\mathbf{S}$, where $\mathbf{S}$ is $2^n - 1$.. Given a set of 3 agents, $A = \{a_1, a_2, a_3\}$, there are $2^3 - 1 = 7$ coalitions. All the coalition $\{a_1\}, \{a_2\}, \{a_3\}, \{a_1, a_2\}, \{a_1, a_3\}, \{a_2, a_3\}$ and $\{a_1, a_2, a_3\}$. Once all agents in a give game agree to form coalitions, they are regarded as being mutually exclusive and exhaustive partitioned to m coalitions. Such a partitioned set of agents, A, is known as a *coalition structure*, denoted by $CS = \{S_1, S_2, \ldots, S_m\}$. The following mathematical definition defines mutual and exhaustive conditions: 1) $S_j \neq \emptyset, j = 1, 2, \ldots, m,$, 2) $S_i \cap S_j = \emptyset$ for all $i \neq j$, and 3) $\bigcup S_j = N$. For example, given $A = \{a_1, a_2, a_3\}$, all CS in $\mathcal{CS}$ are $\{\{a_1\}, \{a_2\}, \{a_3\}\}, \{\{a_1, a_2\}, \{a_3\}\}, \{\{a_1, a_3\}, \{a_2\}\}, \{\{a_2, a_3\}, \{a_1\}\}, \{\{a_1\}, \{a_2\}, \{a_3\}\}$. We denote the set of all CSs of A by $\mathcal{CS}$. The benefit jointly accruing from a coalition is known as *coalition value*. In general, coalition value can be anything valuable to agents. In game theory, coalition values are mostly money value, which can be dollars, pounds, etc. Whereas coalitions in real world need to do real business to achieve their values, we assume the *characteristic function*, $v : S \to \mathbb{R}^+$, associates to each coalition a non-negative value as its coalition value. The coalition value of a coalition S is denoted by $v(S)$. A coalitional game defined by a characteristic function is known as a *characteristic function* game. Here is an example of such a game of three agents defined by a characteristic function: $v(\{a_1\}) = v(\{a_2\}) = v(\{a_3\}) = 0$; $v(\{a_1, a_2\}) = 90; v(\{a_1, a_3\}) = 80; v(\{a_2, a_3\}) = 70; v(\{a_1, a_2, a_3\}) = 105$.

Payoff and Payoff Configuration. The ultimate reason each agent decides to join a coalition is the share of the joint benefit it receives from that coalition. This share is known as the *payoff* of the agent. Mathematically, agent a_i in its respective coalition is given a *payoff*, U_i. The *payoff vector*, $U = (U_1, U_2, \ldots, U_n)$, specifies the payoff for each agent. Generally, the payoff of each agent and the coalition structure are always associated to decide for the outcome. This association is known as the *payoff configuration* [16], $(U; CS)$ specifying payoffs of agents and how agents form coalitions. Considering the game mention above, the payoff configuration, $(45, 0, 35; \{a_1, a_3\}, \{a_2\})$ specifies that agents decide to form two coalition $\{a_1, a_3\}$ and a_1, a_1 receives payoff 45, a_2 receives payoff 0, and a_3 receives payoff 35, respectively.

Solution Concept. The state which leads to the final and stable state of each game is known as *equilibrium*. The principles which agents can use to decide for equilibrium of each game is known as *solution concept*. There are three important solution concepts in coalition formation: $i)$ **fairness** which helps agents receive fair payoffs based on agents' contribution to the coalition values, $ii)$ **efficiency** which helps agents receive highest possible payoffs both individually and globally, and $iii)$ **stability** which helps agents receive satisfactory payoffs such that there is no need for agents to deviate from their current payoffs for higher payoffs. In the next solution, we shall discuss a stability solution concept, namely, the Kernel.

4.2 Kernel Solution Concept

Principle. To help define a stable condition, Davis et al. [1] propose that agents do not need to deviate from their respective coalitions for higher payoffs if they have already achieved the highest possible payoffs. This solution concept is named the Kernel. that stabilizes coalition structure by balancing each pair of agents payoffs in every coalition. Given a payoff configuration $(U; CS)$ for a game $(N; v)$, there may be a group of agents contemplate leaving their respective coalitions to form a new coalition R for more payoff. The *excess*: $e(R; U) = v_R - U_R$ is difference between the value of R and the sums of the collective payoffs, U_R, of the agents. Considering any pair of agents $a_i \in S$ and $a_j \in S$, and $S \in CS$. Agent a_i may join R alone, $R \notin CS$ and $a_j \notin R$. Coalition R, any similar coalitions, will have excess (U, CS). The largest excess is the *maximum surplus* of a_i over a_j with respect to $(U; CS)$, e.g., $S_{i,j} = max_{R|i \in R, j \notin R} \ e(R; U)$. Agent, a_i can potentially gain that higher payoff. Similarly, a_j can do the same, with maximum surplus S_{a_j, a_i}. If both a_i's maximum surplus is greater than that of a_j and a_j's payoff is greater than its singleton coalition's value, $S_{i,j} > S_{j,i}$ and $U_j > v_j$, then a_i **outweighs** a_j, with regards to $(U; CS)$ [1]. Agent a_i ask for compensation from a_j because of its higher maximal surplus otherwise it could join R for higher payoff. However, a_i can ask for up to a certain value because a_j can only accept payoff at least v_j It is said that an equilibrium between each pair of agents exists when one of the following holds: $i)$ $S_{i,j} = S_{j,i}$; each agent cannot ask for compensation be their maximum surpluses are equal, $ii)$ $S_{i,j} > S_{j,i}$ and $U_j = V_j$; agent a_i cannot ask for compensation from a_j because agent a_j can be in its $\{a_j\}$ $iii)$ $S_{j,i} < S_{i,j}$ and $U_i = V_i$; agent a_j cannot ask for compensation from a_i because agent a_i can be in its $\{a_i\}$. The global equilibrium is defined as the set **K** [1] of all payoff configurations $(U; CS)$, namely "Kernel", such that every pair of agents $a_i, a_j \in S \in CS$ are in equilibrium. Given this global equilibrium, it is said that the coalitions are stable.

Example. Let us consider the game defined in Sect. 4.1. Suppose we are given payoff configuration $(U; CS) = (45, 0, 35; \{1, 3\}, \{2\})$ to examine if it is in Kernel. Firstly, we consider coalition $\{a_1, a_3\}$. For a_1, it may join, excluding a_3, two coalitions, e.g., $\{a_1\}$ and $\{a_1, a_2\}$. The excesses and maximum surplus are $e(a_1; U) = v_1 - U_1 = 0 - 45 = -45$, $e(\{a_1, a_2\}; U) = v_{1,2} - U_1 = 90 - 45 = 45$, and $mathcal{S}_{1,3} = max(-45, 45) = 45$. Similarly, $\mathcal{S}_{a_3, a_1} = 35$. Hence, a_1 outweighs a_3 because $\mathcal{S}_{a_1, a_3} = 45 > \mathcal{S}_{a_3, a_1} = 35$. Therefore, payoff configuration $(U; C) = (45, 0, 35 : \{a_1, a_3\}, a_2)$ is not in the Kernel. Consider another payoff configuration $(U; CS) = (50, 30, 25; \{a_1, a_2, a_3\})$. The excesses and maximum surplus between agent a_2 and a_3 are: $\mathcal{S}_{2,3} = max(v_2 - U_2, v_{1,2} - U_2) = max(0 - 30, 90 - 30) = 60$ and $\mathcal{S}_{3,2} = max(v_3 - U_3, v_{1,3} - U_3) = max(0 - 25, 80 - 25) = 55$. Hence, a_2 outweighs a_3, or $(50, 30, 25; \{a_1, a_2, a_3\})$ is not in Kernel. Given another payoff configuration $(U; C) = (45, 35, 25; \{a_1, a_2, a_3\})$, we consider balance between each pair of them. Agent a_1 and a_2 are in equilibrium because $\mathcal{S}_{1,2} = max(0 - 45, 80 - 70) = 10 = max(0 - 35, 70 - 60) = \mathcal{S}_{2,1}$. Agent a_1 and a_3 are in equilibrium because $\mathcal{S}_{1,3} = max(0 - 45, 90 - 80) = 10 = max(0 - 25, 70 - 60) = \mathcal{S}_{3,1}$. Agent a_2 and a_3 are in equilibrium because $\mathcal{S}_{2,3} = max(0 - 35, 90 - 80) = 10 = max(0 - 25, 80 - 70) = \mathcal{S}_{3,2}$. Therefore, the $(U; C) = (45, 35, 25; \{1, 2, 3\})$ is in the Kernel.

5   Algorithms

5.1   Overview

As presented above, it takes a payoff configuration to determine whether the payoffs for agents are in the Kernel. There are three algorithms involved in verifying stability of coalitions. *i)* **Generate Coalitions** Since a coalition is merely a subset, any algorithm for generating subset can be applied for this purpose. The additional requirement is to associate a coalition value to each coalition. *ii)* **Generate Coalition Structure** This is quite a complex algorithm. There are two strong constraints, i.e. exclusiveness and exhaustiveness. *iii)* **Verify Kernel** This is also a complex algorithm because it has to iterate through a lot of coalitions. Because of limited space, we choose to demonstrate only algorithms for generating coalitions and verifying Kernel. This is based on the theoretical principle described above that a certain coalition structure is given as the input, along with payoff vector, in the payoff configuration. On the other hand, all coalitions must be repeatedly generated for examining whether it is in the Kernel.

5.2   Algorithm to Generate Coalitions

The coalitions are to be created in lexicographical order as shown in previous section, i.e. the coalition member at the right most position is the highest and the most value of the next member to the left is less by 1. We generate coalitions in form of array of integer, starting from size 1 to n. There is a main for loop where array *coal* of the respective size is created. Each cell of the array is initialized with its corresponding index. The algorithm enters the second loop where array *coal* is output. Another array, *temp*, is then created and initialized with the value of *coal*. For each position in *temp*, the algorithm checks within the current size $i \leq n$ if its value can be increased. If it has reached the maximum value allowed, it moves to the next left position until there is nothing left.

Algorithm 1. Coalition Generation Algorithm

```
for i = 1 to n do
  int array coal[i]
  for j = 1 to i do
    coal[j] = j
  end for
  while coal ≠ null do
    output coal
    int array temp[k]
    for t = 1 to i do
      temp[t] ← coal[t]
    end for
    k ← i
    while k ≥ 1 and coal[k] = n − i + k do
      k ← k − 1
    end while
    if k = 0 then
      return
    else
      for j = k to i do
        temp[j] ← coal[k] + 1 + j − k
      end for
    end if
    for j = 1 to k do
      coal[j] ← temp[j]
    end for
  end while
end for
```

Although there are many ways to generate subsets or coalitions, our algorithm is suitable for verifying if a payoff configuration is in Kernel. According to the principle, each pair of agents in every coalition in the coalition structure of the given payoff configuration must be examined against almost coalitions for stability. Therefore generating a list of coalitions of the given set A and storing it for later referencing is suitable for our purpose.

5.3 Algorithm to Verify Kernel

At presented above, the concept of Kernel requires that we have to explore a lot of possible coalitions, i.e. up to 2^n, for every pair of agents in each coalition. In order to complete the search, at least, the algorithm needs a payoff configuration, a characteristic function (from game theory perspective, or a list of coalition values), of a given game. Firstly, the payoff configuration is assumed to be in Kernel, $inKernel$ is set to true. The algorithm enters the main loop which goes through each S in the CS of the given payoff configuration. The second loop is to goes through each a_i. The third loop is to go through each $a_j, i \neq j$, checking for each pair a_i, a_j in the coalition. The forth loop is to go through all possible coalitions R, then determine their excesses and maximum surpluses. After that, the algorithm verifies the three conditions. If one of them is violated, the algorithm returns $false$. It is required by the principle that the verification must be done exhaustively. While the algorithm proceeds, the algorithm returns false whenever it finds that the one the three conditions is violated. We illustrate the algorithm below.

Algorithm 2. Kernel Algorithm

---

for each $S \in CS$ **do**
  $S_{i,j}$
  for each $a_i \in S$ **do**
    for each $a_j \neq a_i$ and $a_j \in S$ **do**
      for each $R \subset A$ and $R \neq S$ **do**
        $U \leftarrow 0$
        for each $a_k \in R$ **do**
          $U \leftarrow v_k$
        end for
        $e(R;U) \leftarrow v_R - U_R$
        if $S_{i,,j} < \quad e(R;U)$ **then**
          $S_{i,,j} \leftarrow e(R;U)$
        end if
      end for
      if $!(S_{i,j} = S_{j,i})$ or $!(S_{i,j} > S_{j,i}$ and $U_j = V_j)$ or $!(S_{i,j} > S_{j,i}$ and $U_j = V_j)$
      then
        $InKernel \leftarrow false$
        return $false$
      end if
    end for
  end for
end for
return $true$

As mentioned, this algorithm strictly follow the principle of examining Kernel. One may use the figures provided in the previous section to learn and further understand Kernel algorithm.

6   Experiments and Results

There are two parts we consider about using the solution concept Kernel in real world setting. The first part is to analyze how large the search space can be. Due to the fact that the algorithm has to exhaustively search for all possible cases whether any agent can deviate for better payoffs, it is important to know how large the search space can be. As we have already mentioned in the review, Kernel is hardly adopted. We therefore present statistical results of our experiments. We conducted the experiments on a Ryzen 9 CPU, 16 core 32 thread and 32GB ram computer. Since coalition values can be varied, we divide the search space into 10 ranges, i.e. 10%, 20%, ..., 100%, of the number of coalitions. We consider cases, where $10 \leq n \leq 30$, whose number of coalitions are defined by 2^n, e.g., $1,024, 2,048, \ldots; 1,073,741,824$. Then we calculate, how large is the search space by multiply the number of coalitions for each n by $10\%, 20\%, \ldots, \%100$, respectively.

n	2^n	Percentage for Iteration									
		10	20	30	40	50	60	70	80	90	100
10	1024	1E+07	2.1E+07	3.1E+07	4.2E+07	5.2E+07	6.3E+07	7.3E+07	8.4E+07	9.4E+07	1E+08
11	2048	4.2E+07	8.4E+07	1.3E+08	1.7E+08	2.1E+08	2.5E+08	2.9E+08	3.4E+08	3.8E+08	4.2E+08
12	4096	1.7E+08	3.4E+08	5E+08	6.7E+08	8.4E+08	1E+09	1.2E+09	1.3E+09	1.5E+09	1.7E+09
13	8192	6.7E+08	1.3E+09	2E+09	2.7E+09	3.4E+09	4E+09	4.7E+09	5.4E+09	6E+09	6.7E+09
14	16384	2.7E+09	5.4E+09	8.1E+09	1.1E+10	1.3E+10	1.6E+10	1.9E+10	2.1E+10	2.4E+10	2.7E+10
15	32768	1.1E+10	2.1E+10	3.2E+10	4.3E+10	5.4E+10	6.4E+10	7.5E+10	8.6E+10	9.7E+10	1.1E+11
16	65536	4.3E+10	8.6E+10	1.3E+11	1.7E+11	2.1E+11	2.6E+11	3E+11	3.4E+11	3.9E+11	4.3E+11
17	131072	1.7E+11	3.4E+11	5.2E+11	6.9E+11	8.6E+11	1E+12	1.2E+12	1.4E+12	1.5E+12	1.7E+12
18	262144	6.9E+11	1.4E+12	2.1E+12	2.7E+12	3.4E+12	4.1E+12	4.8E+12	5.5E+12	6.2E+12	6.9E+12
19	524288	2.7E+12	5.5E+12	8.2E+12	1.1E+13	1.4E+13	1.6E+13	1.9E+13	2.2E+13	2.5E+13	2.7E+13
20	1E+06	1.1E+13	2.2E+13	3.3E+13	4.4E+13	5.5E+13	6.6E+13	7.7E+13	8.8E+13	9.9E+13	1.1E+14
21	2E+06	4.4E+13	8.8E+13	1.3E+14	1.8E+14	2.2E+14	2.6E+14	3.1E+14	3.5E+14	4E+14	4.4E+14
22	4E+06	1.8E+14	3.5E+14	5.3E+14	7E+14	8.8E+14	1.1E+15	1.2E+15	1.4E+15	1.6E+15	1.8E+15
23	8E+06	7E+14	1.4E+15	2.1E+15	2.8E+15	3.5E+15	4.2E+15	4.9E+15	5.6E+15	6.3E+15	7E+15
24	2E+07	2.8E+15	5.6E+15	8.4E+15	1.1E+16	1.4E+16	1.7E+16	2E+16	2.3E+16	2.5E+16	2.8E+16
25	3E+07	1.1E+16	2.3E+16	3.4E+16	4.5E+16	5.6E+16	6.8E+16	7.9E+16	9E+16	1E+17	1.1E+17
26	7E+07	4.5E+16	9E+16	1.4E+17	1.8E+17	2.3E+17	2.7E+17	3.2E+17	3.6E+17	4.1E+17	4.5E+17
27	1E+08	1.8E+17	3.6E+17	5.4E+17	7.2E+17	9E+17	1.1E+18	1.3E+18	1.4E+18	1.6E+18	1.8E+18
28	3E+08	7.2E+17	1.4E+18	2.2E+18	2.9E+18	3.6E+18	4.3E+18	5E+18	5.8E+18	6.5E+18	7.2E+18
29	5E+08	2.9E+18	5.8E+18	8.6E+18	1.2E+19	1.4E+19	1.7E+19	2E+19	2.3E+19	2.6E+19	2.9E+19
30	1E+09	1.2E+19	2.3E+19	3.5E+19	4.6E+19	5.8E+19	6.9E+19	8.1E+19	9.2E+19	1E+20	1.2E+20

Fig. 2. Progresses of contribution values of 24 (left) and 25 (right) agents

As shown in Fig. 2, the search space can be very large. Since the search space is large, we herein will consider the degree of magnitude. The largest one is degree 20, existing in two cases, 90% and 100%, where $n = 30$. There are Given that most CPUs existing today runs at a few GHz. Let us assume, at the very best case, that it completes one case per a clock cycle. We may complete cases of magnitude degree 9 in a matter of seconds. In the worst case scenarios, to complete cases of magnitude degree 12, it may take minutes or hours. To complete cases of magnitude degree 13, 14, and 15, it will take hours, days, weeks and months, respectively. If we use 10 CPUs to handle magnitude degree 13, it will approximately bring down the search time to hours. If we use 100 CPUs to handle magnitude degree 14 (or 15), it will approximately bring down the search time to hours. Magnitude degree 15 is found in when $n = 24(10\%-30\%)$, $n = 23(20\%-100\%)$, and $n = 22(60\%-100\%)$. These are the worst cases where we can finish the search at the best possibile within hours, using hundreds of CPUs. Note that we are not searching the maximal or minimal points. Instead we must be able to exhaustively search the whole search space to ensure the correct results should the worst case scenario exist (Fig. 3).

n	size					Search Space					
		[10%]	[20%]	[30%]	[40%]	[50%]	[60%]	[70%]	[80%]	[90%]	[100%]
10	1,024	6	3	24	2	1	3	3	2	3	4
11	2,048	13	3	5	6	9	8	11	12	14	15
12	4,096	6	15	19	27	34	40	46	54	62	65
13	8,192	29	57	85	114	140	168	196	226	260	293
14	16,384	130	247	367	488	729	757	861	991	1,155	1,297
15	32,768	551	1,065	1,593	2,117	2,629	3,115	3,659	4,374	4,819	5,256
16	65,536	2,286	4,425	6,865	8,845	11,456	13,326	15,993	18,064	20,175	22,717
17	131,072	9,738	19,460	28,774	39,335	47,806	55,365	64,454	73,840	83,834	91,304
18	262,144	38,644	77,369	115,863	155,160	195,340	231,334	268,763	308,315	346,511	383,752
19	524,288	161,533	323,065	495,370	671,719	818,702	982,994	1,186,361	1,301,344	1,463,397	1,626,389

Fig. 3. Elapsed time of exhaustive search through 10–19 agents.

The second part is to carry out a set of experiments to investigate the execution time it might take to exhaustively examine stability, given the above analysis, in the best case scenarios. According to the definition of Kernel that for each agent in each coalition of a given payoff configuration, we have to exhaustively search by constructing nested loops to cover all the possibilities. Note that we assume that the actual elapsed time for comparison for each pair of coalitions is minimal. We have completed the experiment of 18 agents, all ranges, 10%–100% with magnitude degree 11–12. It took 383,752 milliseconds, over 6 min, to complete the -100% range. For the cases of 19 agents, range 100%, and magnitude degree 13, it took 1,626,389 milliseconds or almost 30 min to complete. At the time of writing this report, we can finish 60% range of 20 agents with magnitude degree 13 by 5,028,333 milliseconds, over 83 min, or 1 h and 23 min. This means the 100% range of 10 agents with magnitude degree 14 could easily takes days. If we take the problems of 15 °C of magnitude, 30% of 24 agents, 20%–100% of 23 agents, and 60%–100% of 22 agents, it may take up to months. In this case, we might need hundreds of CPUs to finish the search in hours.

7   Conclusion

Based on the Personalized Data system, developed by the Department of Agricultural Extension, Ministry of Agriculture, Thailand. Among many AI libraries and concepts used, the stability concept, Kernel, is needed when farmers cooperate and do not deviate for other alternative groups for better payoffs. We must be ensured that given any worst case scenario in real world environment, we can still deliver the answer in reasonable time This means the number of agents participating in forming coalitions must not be too large. We firstly analyze how large the search space can be. We found that with up to 30 agents, the largest space is 1.2×10^{20}. By approximation with typical GHz CPUs, we may finish the search with minutes for 18 agent, hours for 19 agents, and days for 20 agents. We may bring down these figures by adding more CPUs by 10 s or 100 s of them. We have also carried out the approximate search time, assuming that the exact comparison between each pair of coalitions can be done at minimal time, for up to 60% of 20 agents. This takes almost an hour and a half. This implies that by using single CPU for 20 agents we may need merely hours. For 21 and 22 agents it might take days or weeks for a single CPU. By adding 10 s or 100 s CPUs, it may take hours or days for 23 or 24 agents. Therefore, we can use this system in practice to verify if a payoff configuration is in Kernel. In the future, more advanced techniques can be developed to search for a payoff configuration that is in Kernel.

References

1. Davis, M., Maschler, M.: The kernel of a cooperative game. Naval Res. Logist. Q. **12**(3), 223–259 (1965)
2. Gillieszz, D.B.: Some Theorems In N-person Games. Princeton University, New Jersey (1953)
3. Kahan, J.P., Rapoport, A.: Theories of Coalition Formation. Psychology Press, New York (1984)
4. Nash, J.F.: Equilibrium Points in N-person Games. Proc. Nat. Acad. Sci. U.S.A. **36**(1), 48–49 (1950)
5. Von Neumann, J., Morgenstern, O.: Theory of Games and Economic Behavior, 3rd edn. Princeton University Press, Princeton (1953)
6. Sandholm, T.W., Larson, K.S., Anderson, M.R., Shehory, O., Tohme, F.: Anytime Coalition Structure Generation with Worst Case Guarantees. In: Proceedings of the AAAI 1998, WI, pp. 46–53. AAAI (1998)
7. Shapley, L.S.: Notes on the n-Person Game - II: The Value of an n-Person Game. RAND Corporation, Santa Monica (1951)
8. Bistaffa, F., Farinelli, A., Vinyals, M., Rogers, A.: Decentralised stable coalition formation among energy consumers in the smart grid. In: Proceedings of the 11th International Conference on Autonomous Agents and Multiagent Systems - Volume 3. International Foundation for Autonomous Agents and Multiagent Systems, Richland, SC, pp. 1461–1462 (2012)
9. Blankenburg, B., Klusch, M.: On safe kernel stable coalition forming among agents. In: Proceedings of the Third International Joint Conference on Autonomous Agents and Multiagent Systems, vol. 2, pp. 580–587. IEEE Computer Society, New York (2004)
10. Yamamoto, J., Sycara, K.: A stable and efficient buyer coalition formation scheme for E-marketplaces. In: Proceedings of the Fifth International Conference on Autonomous Agents, Montreal, Quebec, Canada, pp. 576–583. Association for Computing Machinery, New York (2001)

11. Guthula, S., Simon, S., Karnick, H.: Analysis of agricultural policy recommendations using multi-agent systems. Comput. Res. Repository (CoRR) **1**(1), 1–13 (2020)

12. Zaryouli, M., Fathi, M.T., Ezziyyani, M.: Data collection based on multi-agent modeling for intelligent and precision farming in Lokoss region Morocco. In: 2020 1st International Conference on Innovative Research in Applied Science, Engineering and Technology (IRASET), pp. 1–6 (2020)

13. Pérez-Pons, M.E., Alonso, R.S., García, O., Marreiros, G., Corchado, J.M.: Deep Q-learning and preference based multi-agent system for sustainable agricultural market. Sensor **21**(16), 1–16 (2021)

14. Chevalier, A., Copot, C., De Keyser, R., Hernandez, A., Ionescu, C.: A multi agent system for precision agriculture. In: Buşoniu, L., Tamás, L. (eds.) Handling Uncertainty and Networked Structure in Robot Control. SSDC, vol. 42, pp. 361–386. Springer, Cham (2015). https://doi.org/10.1007/978-3-319-26327-4_15

15. González-Briones, A., Mezquita, Y., Castellanos-Garzón, J.A., Prieto, J., Corchado, J.M.: Intelligent multi-agent system for water reduction in automotive irrigation processes. Proc. Comput. Sci. **151**, 971–976 (2019)

16. Kahan, J., Rapoport, A.: Theories of Coalition Formation. Lawrence Erlbaum Associates, Hillsdale (1984)

17. Shehory, O., Kraus, S.: Feasible formation of coalitions among autonomous agents in non-super-additive environments. Comput. Intell. **15**(3), 218–251 (1999)

The Analysis of Explainable AI
via Notion of Congruence

Naruson Srivaro[✉] and Nguyen Duy Hung

Sirindhorn International Institute of Technology, Thammasat University,
Khlong Luang, Thailand
naruson.sri@gmail.com, hung@siit.tu.ac.th

Abstract. Explainable AI has become a popular topic that draws the
attention of many researchers, and since the inception of this field, the
most popular method of model explanation is undoubtedly using Decision Tree to approximate black box model. However, Decision Tree is
single-dimensional model without any nuance in the decision making
which may be intrinsic to the behaviors of the black box model itself.
With this, we propose using a structured framework in the form of Probabilistic Assumption-based Argumentation (PABA) framework in place
of Decision Tree. This paper will demonstrate an application of the aforementioned framework in model explanation problem by establishing the
notion of congruence between an example black box model and its structured argumentation framework predictor counterpart.

Keywords: Argumentation · Explainable · AI · Congruence ·
Assumption-based · PABA

1   Introduction

In recent years, the popularity of complex AI models have risen and are becoming
increasingly integral to the field of AI studies itself. However, these models are
created as black boxes, where a black box is a system in which its internal
logic cannot be seen by the user. This poses many issues and thus the field of
Black Box Explanation has been established to tackle this problem by providing
methodology to create an explainable predictor mimicking black box model's
behaviors. Among many methods available, the usage of Decision Tree (DT),
or Single Tree, for "single-tree approximation" technique is undoubtedly the
most widely used due to its ease of interpretation in both global explanations
and local explanations applications [2]. However, the problem arise from the fact
that Decision Tree as a lone argument system would naturally be a generalization
of logic in comparison to human decision making.

We propose an improvement to this approach by using a structured model in
place of Decision Tree to approximate a black box model. Firstly, the following
is the current definition of black box explanation problem:

© The Author(s), under exclusive license to Springer Nature Switzerland AG 2022
O. Surinta and K. Kam Fung Yuen (Eds.): MIWAI 2022, LNAI 13651, pp. 191–203, 2022.
https://doi.org/10.1007/978-3-031-20992-5_17

Given a black box predictor b and a set of instances X, the model explanation problem consists in finding an explanation E, belonging to a human-interpretable domain ε, through an interpretable global predictor $C_g = f(b, X)$ derived from black box b and the instances X using some process f(,). An explanation E is obtained through C_g if $E = \epsilon_g(C_g, X)$ for some explanation logic $\epsilon_g(,)$ which reasons over C_g and X.

This definition defines that, if given a black box model (b), and a predictor (C_g) which were made as a transparent substitute of black box (b), then an "explanation" of this predictor, and in turn; the black box, must be extracted in some way from the predictor (C_g) over the valid instance (X) of the predictor via a consistent explanation logic (ϵ_g). Valid instance in this definition would be the type of data in which the predictor can interpret (text, image, tree, etc.).

Faithfulness of single-tree approximation can be measured by comparing single value output of the predictor directly to that of the black box model. But If we were to extend the definition of explainability from Decision Tree to structured model, there exist the problem of how best do we measure the similarity between a structured model and its black box counterpart once the structural properties are involved. Our proposal to remedy this issue is by establishing notion of congruence ϵ_c which defines as a measurement of congruence correlating similarities between a structured predictor and its black box, as follows:

Some notion of congruence $\epsilon_c(, ,)$, where notion of congruence states the congruence between global predictor C_g and black box model b over Instances X via explanation E.

The application of model explanation via aforementioned notion of congruence shall be demonstrated in this paper.

2   Background

2.1   Abstract Argumentation

An AA framework is a pair $F = (AR, Att)$ where AR is a set of arguments, $Att \subseteq AR \times AR$ and $(A, B) \in Att$ means that A attacks B. $S \subseteq AR$ attacks $A \in AR$ iff $(B, A) \in Att$ for some $B \in S$. $A \in AR$ is acceptable wrt S iff S attacks everyargument attacking A. S is *conflict-free* iff S does not attack itself; *admissible* iff S is conflict-free and each argument in S is acceptable wrt S; *complete* iff S is admissible and contains every argument acceptable wrt S; a *preferred* (aka. credulous) extension iff S is a maximal (wrt set inclusion) complete set; the *grounded* extension iff S is the least complete set; the *ideal* extension iff it is the maximal admissible set contained in every preferred extension. An argument A is accepted under semantics $sem \in \{cr, gr, id\}$, denoted $F \vdash_{sem} A$, iff A is in a *sem* extension.

2.2 Assumption-Based Argumentation

As AA ignores the internal structure of argument, an instance of AA called Assumption-Based Argumentation (ABA) defines arguments by deductive proofs based on assumptions and inference rules. Assuming a language L consisting of countably many sentences, an ABA framework is a triple $F = (R, A, \bar{\ })$ where R is a set of inference rules of the form $r : l_0 \leftarrow l_1, \ldots, l_n$ ($n \geq 0$), $A \subseteq L$ is a set of assumptions, and $\bar{\ }$ is a (total) one-to-one mapping from A into L, where $\bar{x}$ is referred to as the *contrary* of x.

A *(backward) deduction* of a conclusion π supported by a set of premises Q is a sequence of sets $S_1, S_2, \ldots, S_n$ where $S_i \subseteq L, S_1 = \{\pi\}, S_n = Q$, and for every i, where σ is the selected proposition in $S_i : \sigma \notin Q$ and $S_{i+1} = S_i \backslash \{\sigma\} \cup body(r)$ for some inference rule $r \in R$ with $head(r) = \sigma$.

An argument for $\pi \in L$ supported by a set of assumptions Q is a dediction d from π to Q and denoted by (Q, d, π). an argument (Q, d, π) attacks an argument (Q', d', π') if π is the contrary of some assumption in Q'. For simplicity, we often refer to an argument (Q, d, π) by (Q, π) if there is no possibility for mistake.

A proposition π is said to be accepted under semantics $sem \in \{cr, gr, id\}$, denoted $F \vdash_s em\pi$ if in the AA framework consisting of above defined arguments and attacks, there is an argument for π accepted under pi accepted under sem semantics. A set of assumptions is admissible/preferred/grounded/ideal if it is the union of all sets of assumptions supporting the arguments in an admissible/preferred/grounded/ideal set of arguments.

2.3 Probabilistic Argumentation

A DT's PAA framework is a triple (F, W, P) where $F = (AR, Att)$ is a standar AA framework, W is a set of possible worlds such that each $\omega \in W$ defines a subset of arguments $AR_\omega \subseteq AR$, and $P : W \to [0, 1]$ is a probability distribution over W with $\sum_{\omega \in W} P(\omega) = 1$. The probability that argument $X \in AR$ is accepted under the grounded semantics, denoted $Prob_{gr}(X)$, is defined as the sum of probabilities of possible worlds in which X is groundedly accepted, concretely

$$Prob_{gr}(X) \triangleq \sum_{\substack{\omega \in W \\ F_\omega \vdash_{gr} X}} P(\omega)$$

where $F_\omega = (AR_\omega, Att \cap (AR_\omega \times AR\omega))$, i.e. the restriction of F on the set of arguments actually occurring in ω and construction of AR_ω and $P(\omega)$. Probabilistic Assumption-based Argumentation (PABA) instantiates DT's PAA using ABA.

Definition 1. A PABA framework has the form (A_p, R_p, F) where

1. $F = (R, A, \bar{\ })$ is an ABA framework.
2. A_p is a finite set of **positive probabilistic assumptions**. Elements of $\neg A_p = \{\neg p | p \in A_p\}$ are called **negative probabilistic assumptions**.

3. R_p is a set of probabilistic rules in the form $[\alpha : x] \leftarrow \beta_1, \ldots, \beta_n$ $n \geq 0, x \in [0,1], \alpha \in A_p \cup \neg A_p$, where $[\alpha : x]$, called a **probabilistic proposition**, represents that the probability of probabilistic assumption α is x.

Definition 2. A PABA framework $P = (A_p, R_p, F)$ is **well-formed** if it satisfies the four constraints below.

1. For each $\alpha \in A_p \cup \neg A_p, \alpha$ does not occur in A or in the head of a rule in R, and $[\alpha : x]$ does not occur in the body of a rule in $R \cup R_p$.
2. If R_p contains $[\alpha : x] \leftarrow \beta_1, \ldots, \beta_n$, then it also contains a complementary rule $[\neg \alpha : 1 - x] \leftarrow \beta_1, \ldots, \beta_n$.
3. For each $\alpha \in A_p$, there exists $Pa_\alpha \subseteq A_p$ s.t. for each maximal consistent subset $\{\beta_1, \ldots \beta_m\}$ of $Pa_\alpha \cup \neg Pa_\alpha$, R_p contains a rule $[a : x] \leftarrow \beta_1, \ldots, \beta_m$ (and the complementary rule $[\neg \alpha : 1 - x] \leftarrow \beta_1, \ldots, \beta_m)$.
4. If R_p contains two rules r_1, r_2 with heads $[\alpha : x]$ and $[\alpha : y]$, $x \neq y$, then either of the conditions below holds.
   (a) $body(r_1) \subset body(r_2)$ or $body(r_2) \subset body(r_1)$
   (b) $\zeta \in body(r_1)$ and $\neg \zeta \in body(r_2)$ for some $\zeta \in A_p$.

3   Procedure

In this paper, we will achieve the objective of introducing the notion of congruence via an example. For that purpose, we will be using a pre-made Bayesian Network model [4], and a pre-made Argumentation Tree model [3] by assuming that the BN model is a black box, and AT model is its predictor. These two models were synthesized in their original publications to represent a criminal case (the Simonshaven Case), and thus would represent the same knowledge base. For ease of demonstration, we chose to translate stated models locally to the same framework, Probabilistic Assumption-Based Argumentation (PABA). Afterward, we will be analyzing both models for possible congruence, then derive a method in which the degree of congruence can be expressed.

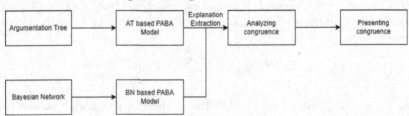

Furthermore, only certain parts of each models will be mentioned for demonstration, which may result in the calculation being different from their original publications.

3.1   Translating BN Model to PABA Framework

To translate the Bayesian Network Model, each Bayesian node is converted to inference rules in accordance to the probabilistic table such as this example:

Table 1. Example of Bayesian network probabilistic table.

motive+capability	motive	¬motive
capability	1.0	0.0
¬capability	0.0	0.0

Would be converted into four rules as follows:

[motive+capability : 1.0] ← motive, capability

[motive+capability : 0.0] ← ¬motive, capability

[motive+capability : 0.0] ← motive, ¬capability

[motive+capability : 0.0] ← ¬motive, ¬capability

Translation of BN model from [4] resulted in the following PABA model:

$A_p = \{$

[defendant_capability : 0.2] ←

[defendant_motive : 0.1] ←

[police_credibility : 0.9] ←

[defendant_motive_and_capability : 1.0]←
defendant_motive, defendant_capability

[defendant_motive_and_capability : 0.0]←
¬defendant_motive, defendant_capability

[defendant_motive_and_capability : 0.0]←
defendant_motive, ¬defendant_capability

[defendant_motive_and_capability : 0.0]←
¬defendant_motive, ¬defendant_capability

[effective_police_handling_of_crime_scene_and_search : 0.9]←
police_credibility

[effective_police_handling_of_crime_scene_and_search : 0.01]←
¬police_credibility

[number_of_people_in_wood(10) : 0.9]←
effective_police_handling_of_crime_scene_and_search

[number_of_people_in_wood(20) : 1.0]←
effective_police_handling_of_crime_scene_and_search,
¬number_of_people_in_wood(10)

[number_of_people_in_wood(10) : 0.0625]←
¬effective_police_handling_of_crime_scene_and_search

[number_of_people_in_wood(20) : 0.3333]←
¬effective_police_handling_of_crime_scene_and_search,

¬number_of_people_in_wood(10)

[number_of_people_in_wood(100) : 1.0]←
¬effective_police_handling_of_crime_scene_and_search ,
¬number_of_people_in_wood(10), ¬number_of_people_in_wood(20)

[defendant_killed_her : 0.5]← number_of_people_in_wood(100),
defendant_motive_and_capability

[defendant_killed_her : 0.8]← number_of_people_in_wood(20),
defendant_motive_and_capability

[defendant_killed_her : 0.9]← number_of_people_in_wood(10),
defendant_motive_and_capability

[defendant_killed_her : 0.01]← number_of_people_in_wood(100),
¬defendant_motive_and_capability

[defendant_killed_her : 0.05]← number_of_people_in_wood(20),
¬defendant_motive_and_capability

[defendant_killed_her : 0.0]← number_of_people_in_wood(10),
¬defendant_motive_and_capability

[defendant_criminal_background : 0.8]← defendant_capability

[defendant_criminal_background : 0.1]← ¬defendant_capability

[man_in_bushes_killed_her : 0.99]← number_of_people_in_wood(100)

[man_in_bushes_killed_her : 0.95]← number_of_people_in_wood(20)

[man_in_bushes_killed_her : 0.9]← number_of_people_in_wood(10)

[defendant_killed_her : 1.0]← ¬man_in_bushes_killed_her

[man_in_bushes_killed_her : 1.0]← ¬defendant_killed_her

[defendant_confused_from_assault : 0.8]← man_in_bushes_killed_her

[defendant_confused_from_assault : 0.01]← ¬man_in_bushes_killed_her

[defendant_credibility : 0.01]← defendant_killed_her,
defendant_criminal_background, defendant_confused_from_assault

[defendant_credibility : 0.01]← defendant_killed_her,
defendant_criminal_background, ¬defendant_confused_from_assault

[defendant_credibility : 0.1]← defendant_killed_her,
¬defendant_criminal_background, defendant_confused_from_assault

[defendant_credibility : 0.1]← defendant_killed_her,
¬defendant_criminal_background, ¬defendant_confused_from_assault

[defendant_credibility : 0.4]← ¬defendant_killed_her,
defendant_criminal_background, defendant_confused_from_assault

```
[defendant_credibility : 0.9] ← ¬defendant_killed_her,
defendant_criminal_background, ¬defendant_confused_from_assault

[defendant_credibility : 0.5] ← ¬defendant_killed_her,
¬defendant_criminal_background, defendant_confused_from_assault

[defendant_credibility : 0.9] ← ¬defendant_killed_her,
¬defendant_criminal_background, ¬defendant_confused_from_assault

[defendant_says_man_in_bushes_killed_her : 1.0] ←
man_in_bushes_killed_her

[defendant_says_man_in_bushes_killed_her : 0.0] ←
defendant_credibility, ¬man_in_bushes_killed_her

[defendant_says_man_in_bushes_killed_her : 0.99] ←
¬defendant_credibility, ¬man_in_bushes_killed_her

[man_in_bushes_is_perry_sultan : 0.5] ← man_in_bushes_killed_her

[man_in_bushes_is_perry_sultan : 0.0] ← ¬man_in_bushes_killed_her

[perry_fits_description_man_in_wood : 0.9] ←
man_in_bushes_killed_her

[perry_fits_description_man_in_wood : 0.1] ←
defendant_credibility, ¬man_in_bushes_killed_her

[perry_fits_description_man_in_wood : 0.5] ←
¬defendant_credibility, ¬man_in_bushes_killed_her

[attack_style_similar : 0.7] ← man_in_bushes_is_perry_sultan

[attack_style_similar : 0.3] ← ¬man_in_bushes_is_perry_sultan

[marks_on_map_represent_murder_or_assault_location : 0.6] ←
man_in_bushes_is_perry_sultan

[marks_on_map_represent_murder_or_assault_location : 0.4] ←
¬man_in_bushes_is_perry_sultan

[pits_in_woods : 0.7] ← man_in_bushes_is_perry_sultan

[pits_in_woods : 0.3] ← ¬man_in_bushes_is_perry_sultan
}
```

3.2 Translating Argumentation Tree to PABA Framework

The translation of PABA framework from Argumentation Tree can be achieved by converting the attacking vectors directly from [3], and using method of translating undermining attacks proposed in [10]. Due to the limitation of PABA Framework, preferences stated in [3] cannot be translated directly, and preferred argument in each symmetrical attacks have been selected during translation instead. This affect the flexibility of the model but not the result for our demonstration.

Translation of AT [3] resulted in the Following PABA Framework:

$$F = (R, A, \bar{})$$

```
R = {
r1: pr1 ← pr1.1, pr1.2, pr1.3, pr1.4
r2: pr1.1 ← pr1.1.1, pr1.1.2
r3: pr1.2 ← pr1.2.1
r4: pr1.3 ← pr1.3.1, pr1.3.2, pr1.3.3
r5: pr1.4 ← pr1.4.1, pr1.4.2
r6: pr1.1.1 ← pr1.1.1.1, pr1.1.1.2, ab_d1
r7: pr1.1.2 ← pr1.1.2.1, f8.2.2
r8: u1 ← u1.1
r9: u1.1 ← u1.1.1, u1.1.2
r10: v2 ← v2.1, v2.2
r11: v1 ← v1.1
r12: n_ab_d1 ← u1
r13: n_u1.1.2 ← v1
r14: n_u1 ← v2
r15: n_pr1 ← pr2.1, pr2.2, pr2.3
r16: pr2.3 ← pr2.3.1, pr2.3.2, pr2.3.3}
```

$$\bar{} = \{$$

```
pr1 = n_pr1
pr1.1 = ¬pr1.1
pr1.2 = ¬pr1.2
pr1.3 = ¬pr1.3
pr1.4 = ¬pr1.4
pr1.1.1 = ¬pr1.1.1
pr1.1.2 = ¬pr1.1.2
u1 = n_u1
u1.1 = ¬u1.1
v1 = ¬v1
v2 = ¬v2
n_ab_d1 = ab_d1}
```

where the overline notation applies to each left-hand side term.

3.3   Establishing Notion of Congruence

To establish the notion of congruence, we will first need to establish semantically equivalent arguments to act as reference points between both models. The following pairs of arguments shall be defined as semantically equivalent:

pr1 (The argument for f14 strictly defeats the argument for f13)
= defendant_killed_her

pr1.1 (The suspect's statements on the alternative scrnario are not credible)
= ¬defendant_credibility

pr1.3.1 (Only one of the crosses on the map relates to crimes committed by Perry S.) AND pr1.3.3 (Perry S. has also been convicted of crimes at locations that do not correspond with crosses on the map)
=¬marks_on_map_represent_murder_or_assault_location

pr1.3.2 (The pit near the crime scene is not suitable for long-term use) ·
= ¬pits_in_woods

pr2.2 (No proper investigation was done into traces of an alternative attacker)
= ¬effective_police_handling_of_crime_scene_and_search

pr2.3 (The description evidence is weak)
= ¬perry_fits_description_man_in_wood

pr2.3.1 (The suspect cannot be expected to give an accurate description of an attacker of such a shocking event)
= defendant_confused_from_assault

After which, we will need to examine the possible sets of evidence in which the central claim could be reached (Explanation (E)). Furthermore, structured models are able to derive a set of argument into multiple unique forms, which may result in multiple seemingly unique sets of argument referring simply to derivations of the same set. This shall be defined as a *"Perfect Congruence"*.

Definition C.1. Given A = {a,b, ...} and B = {c,d, ...} be sets of evidence, containing a,b,c,d, ... as inference rules. If $A \models_p B$, and $B \models_p A$, under some predictor p, then A is perfectly congruence to B.

Bayesian Network Based PABA Model. However, there is still the question of how best to define "Acceptability" for probabilistic models such as one that were derived from Bayesian Network. For this, we decided to simply set acceptability threshold, where a set of evidence is considered accepted if the probabilistic value given said evidence is above the threshold. To select this threshold, we shall refer to the evidence used in the original publication for the BN model and using only the evidences present in our truncated model.

{
defendant_motive_and_capability,
¬effective_police_handling_of_crime_scene_and_search,
pits_in_woods,
attack_style_similar,
defendant_says_man_in_bushes_killed_her,
perry_fits_description_man_in_wood
}

This set of evidence result in the probabilistic value "defendant killed her" of 0.3241838. Due to this result, we chose our acceptability threshold to be 0.3, Which result in the following acceptable sets of evidence:

BN0) {defendant_killed_her}: accepted (1.0)

BN1) {defendant_motive_and_capability,
¬effective_police_handling_of_crime_scene_and_search}:accepted (0.33751422)

BN2) {¬perry_fits_description_man_in_wood}:accepted (0.32377292)

BN3) {¬defendant_says_man_in_bushes_killed_her}:accepted (1.0)

BN4) {defendant_motive_and_capability,
¬defendant_confused_from_assault}:accepted(0.35173202)

BN5) {¬defendant_credibility, ¬defendant_confused_from_assault}
:accepted(0.804384244)

BN6) {¬defendant_confused_from_assault}:accepted(0.30849329)

BN7) {¬defendant_credibility,
¬marks_on_map_represent_murder_or_assault_location,
¬pits_in_woods,¬attack_style_similar,
effective_police_handling_of_crime_scene_and_search,
¬man_in_bushes_is_perry_sultan} :accepted(0.30581578)

Argumentation Tree Based PABA. For AT based PABA, we can simply use sets of evidence which result in argument p1 being accepted. The sets of argument derived from Argumentation Tree based model are as follows:

AT0) { pr1 } (The argument for f14 strictly defeats the argument for f13)

AT1) { pr1.1, pr1.2, pr1.3, pr1.4, ¬pr2.1 }
(The suspect not credible, hearsay testimony is weak, map evidence is weak, sound in the bush evidence is weak, the suspect statement on alternative scenario did not come before evidence concerning Perry S. came to light)

AT2) { pr1.1, pr1.2, pr1.3, pr1.4, ¬pr2.2 }
(The suspect not credible, hearsay testimony is weak, map evidence is weak, sound in the bush evidence is weak, proper investigation was done into traces of alternative attacker).

AT3) { pr1.1, pr1.2, pr1.3, pr1.4, ¬pr2.3 }
(The suspect not credible, hearsay testimony is weak, map evidence is weak, sound in the bush evidence is weak, the description evidence is not weak)

The following sets of evidence can be derived into evidence AT3)
AT3.1) { pr1.1, pr1.2, pr1.3, pr1.4, ¬pr2.3.1 }
(The suspect not credible, hearsay testimony is weak, map evidence is weak, sound in the bush evidence is weak, the suspect was not shocked)

AT3.2) { pr1.1, pr1.2, pr1.3, pr1.4, ¬pr2.3.2 }
(The suspect not credible, hearsay testimony is weak, map evidence is weak, sound in the bush evidence is weak, the look of persons stay the same over time)

AT3.3) { pr1.1, pr1.2, pr1.3, pr1.4, ¬pr2.3.3 }

(The suspect not credible, hearsay testimony is weak, map evidence is weak, sound in the bush evidence is weak, police used identification parade).

By **Definition C.1** which establishes the notion of perfect congruence, we can extend that definition to define the degree of congruence between two sets of argument via reference points established previously as fraction.

$$\epsilon_{A,B} = \frac{n(A \cap B)}{n(A \cup B)}$$

For example, let us compare BN5 and AT1:
  { ¬defendant_credibility, ¬defendant_confused_from_assault}
  { pr1.1, pr1.2, pr1.3, pr1.4, ¬pr2.1}
We have established that pr1.1 and ¬defendant_credibility is equivalent. Which mean $\epsilon_{BN5,AT1} = 1/6 \approx 0.17$.

Applying this to all evidences (omitting the assumption AT0 and BN0) results in the following tables:

Table 2. Degree of congruence between AT and BN based models (left).

	AT1	AT2	AT3'
BN1	0.00	0.00	0.00
BN2	0.00	0.00	0.17
BN3	0.00	0.00	0.00
BN4	0.00	0.00	0.17
BN5	0.17	0.17	0.40
BN6	0.00	0.00	0.20
BN7	0.43	0.50	0.43

Table 3. Degree of congruence between BN model and AT3 sub-arguments (right).

	AT3	AT3.1	AT3.2	AT3.3
BN1	0.00	0.00	0.00	0.00
BN2	0.17	0.00	0.00	0.00
BN3	0.00	0.00	0.00	0.00
BN4	0.00	0.17	0.00	0.00
BN5	0.17	0.40	0.00	0.00
BN6	0.00	0.20	0.00	0.00
BN7	0.43	0.43	0.43	0.43

As AT3, AT3.1, AT3.2, AT3.3 are perfectly congruence, the results of column AT3' were calculated by finding the MAX value among them.

Table 4. Maximum congruence (left).

	BN1	BN2	BN3	BN4	BN5	BN6	BN7
MAX	0.00	0.17	0.00	0.17	0.40	0.20	0.50

Table 5. Faithfulness Table (right).

	Faithfulness
MIN	0.00
MAX	0.50
AVG	0.206

In this paper, we will be calculating faithfulness from this notion of congruence firstly by finding MAX value of each row. This can be understood as measurement of faithfulness of using AT (assumed predictor) to represent BN (assumed black box). Furthermore, we propose that overall faithfulness of a structured model with respect to its black box counterpart be measured in MIN MAX and Average value of its local faithfulness. This table can represent the worst case scenario where evidence given is not well represented in the structured model, the best case scenario where evidence given is represented faithfully in the structured model, and finally the average value of faithfulness across the entire model. This result in the following tables:

4   Conclusion

In order to demonstrate the usability of structured model for model explanation, we were able to establish a faithfulness measurement method by using explanation via notion of congruence between both models by first discussing what would be considered a perfect congruence, that is, the arguments can be derived into the same argument, and then extending that notion to a more generalized scenario by calculating the degree of congruence between both arguments instead, using it to explain the similarity involving a structured model via simple fraction. While attempting to use a more complex framework for model explanation may allow us to push the boundary of this subject, further studies into both the method in which the degree of congruence can be calculated and application of other structured model frameworks may yield more insight into this approach.

References

1. Guidotti, R., Monreale, A., Ruggieri, S., Turini, F., Giannotti, F., Pedreschi, D.: Revealed preference in argumentation: algorithms and applications. ACM Comput. Surv. **51**(5) (2018)
2. Fenton, N., Neil, M., Yet, B., Lagnado, D.: Analyzing the Simonshaven case using Bayesian networks. Top. Cogn. Sci. **12**, 1092–1114 (2019)

3. Prakken, H.: An argumentation-based analysis of the Simonshaven case. Top. Cogn. Sci. **12**, 1068–1091 (2019)

4. Dung, P.M., Kowalski, R.A., Toni, F.: Dialectic proof procedures for assumption-based, admissible argumentation. Artif. Intell. **170**, 114–159 (2006)

5. Hung, N.D., Huynh, V.N.: Revealed preference in argumentation: algorithms and applications. Int. J. Approx. Reason. **131**, 214–251 (2021)

6. Dung, P.M., Thang, P.M.: Fundamental properties of attack relations in structured argumentation with priorities. Artif. Intell. **255**, 1–42 (2017)

7. Hung, N.D.: Inference procedures and engine for probabilistic argumentation. Int. J. Approx. Reason. **90**, 163–191 (2017)

8. Guidotti, R., Monreale, A., Ruggieri, S., Pedreschi, D., Turini, F., Giannotti, F.: Local rule-based explanations of black box decision systems. arXiv (2018)

9. Dung, P.M., Kowalski, R.A., Toni, F.: Assumption-based argumentation. In: Simari, G., Rahwan, I. (eds.) Argumentation in Artificial Intelligence, pp. 199–218. Springer, Boston (2009). https://doi.org/10.1007/978-0-387-98197-0_10

10. Modgil, S., Prakken, H.: The ASPIC+ framework for structured argumentation: a tutorial. Argument Comput. **5**, 31–62 (2013)

Using Ensemble Machine Learning Methods to Forecast Particulate Matter (PM$_{2.5}$) in Bangkok, Thailand

Patchanok Srisuradetchai$^{(\boxtimes)}$ and Wararit Panichkitkosolkul

Department of Mathematics and Statistics, Faculty of Science and Technology, Thammasat University, Pathum Thani 12120, Thailand
{patchanok,wararit}@mathstat.sci.tu.ac.th

Abstract. Many areas of Bangkok and its environs are currently blanketed with fine dust with dangerous levels of PM$_{2.5}$. High levels of PM$_{2.5}$ have a negative impact on human health. In this study, support vector regression, begged regression tree, random forest, gradient boosted models, neural networks, neural networks autoregressive, seasonal autoregressive moving average with exogenous covariates, k-nearest neighbor, Bayesian additive model, Prophet, and general additive models are used to anticipate PM$_{2.5}$. The usefulness of adopting an ensemble model for forecasting is investigated. A thorough evaluation of standalone algorithms and ensemble techniques was performed using the root-mean-square error, mean absolute error, and Pearson correlation coefficient. According to the results, hybrid models are effective in the forecasting of PM$_{2.5}$ concentrations.

Keywords: Ensemble machine learning · Predictive performance · PM$_{2.5}$

1 Introduction

All life on Earth depends on air, making it one of the most essential components. Over the last half-century, human activity, industry, automobiles, power plants, chemical plants, and other natural phenomena like agricultural burning, earthquakes, and fires have all contributed to an increase in pollution [1]. It is the fourth most common cause of death in the world. About 6.67 million people died in 2019 as a result of pollution, the most lethal of which scientists call PM$_{2.5}$ (particles measuring less than 2.5 μm in aerodynamic diameter) [2]. Breathing in PM$_{2.5}$ is harmful because it can reach the bloodstream and the lungs. For 24-h exposure to PM$_{2.5}$ both outdoors and indoors, most studies indicate that PM$_{2.5}$ of 12 μg/m^3 (micrograms per cubic meter) or less is considered healthy. Asthmatics and people who already have respiratory problems, such as those who live in areas with high levels of ozone in the air, should seek medical assistance if their symptoms worsen [3]. PM$_{2.5}$ has been related to an increase in respiratory and cardiovascular hospitalizations, emergency room visits, and mortality. Exposure to fine particles for a long time has been linked to chronic bronchitis, poor lung function, and death from lung cancer and heart disease [4].

© The Author(s), under exclusive license to Springer Nature Switzerland AG 2022
O. Surinta and K. Kam Fung Yuen (Eds.): MIWAI 2022, LNAI 13651, pp. 204–215, 2022.
https://doi.org/10.1007/978-3-031-20992-5_18

Many areas of Bangkok and its environs are currently shrouded in fine dust with lethal PM$_{2.5}$ levels. According to the Pollution Control Department (PCD), the maximum allowable level of air dust in the environment is 50 μg/m^3, and this limit was exceeded numerous times in February 2022, with PM$_{2.5}$ levels ranging from 40 to 146 μg/m^3 [5]. Due to poor air quality, the PCD has expanded its list of Bangkok province areas and districts where people should wear protective gear and stay indoors.

Emissions from a variety of sources constantly change the quality of the air we breathe. As a result, things can appear normal one day and then take an unexpected turn the next. This emphasizes the importance of developing a tool for forecasting future air quality accurately. Machine learning techniques like artificial neural networks and regression trees can make predictions faster, more accurate, and easier to do with more than one type of data.

To forecast PM$_{2.5}$ in this paper, we utilize techniques of support vector regression (SVR) with linear and polynomial (degrees of 2 and 3) kernel functions, bagged regression trees (BRT), random forest (RF), gradient boosted models (GBM) with different loss functions, extreme gradient boosted (XGBoost) trees using L2 regularization, artificial neural networks (ANN) having 1 and 2 hidden layers and different activation functions, neural network autoregressive (NNAR), ANN using model averaging, seasonal ARIMAX (SARIMAX), k-nearest neighbor (KNN) regression with Epanechnikov and rectangular kernels, Prophet model, boosted generalized additive model (Boosted GAM), and Bayesian additive model (BAM). Finally, the "great" models will be included in the ensemble models to better forecast PM$_{2.5}$ concentration, and they will be compared to standalone algorithms. Following this introduction, the structure of the study is as follows: literature review; dataset overview and preparation; research methods; findings and conclusions, accordingly.

2 Literature Review

Because of the volatile nature of PM$_{2.5}$, accurate prediction has become challenging. Several models for predicting particulate matter emissions have been developed in the last several years in an effort to monitor air quality around the world.

Catalano [6] looked at the relationship between the hourly mean NO$_2$ concentration and factors that explain the NO$_2$ mean level one hour before, as well as traffic and weather conditions like the number of cars on the road, the speed of the wind, the direction of the wind, and the temperature. To model pollution peaks, the ANN, ARIMAX, and SARIMAX models were used.

Masood and Ahmad [7] looked at the possibilities of ANN and SVM in creating reliable and accurate PM$_{2.5}$ predictions for New Delhi. Carbon monoxide (CO), sulfur dioxide (SO$_2$), nitrogen oxide (NO), toluene (C$_7$H$_8$), nitrogen dioxide (NO$_2$), wind speed, relative humidity, and temperature are studied.

Suleiman et al. [8] evaluated and compared three air quality management techniques for predicting and managing roadside PM$_{10}$ and PM$_{2.5}$, including SVM, ANN, and BRT. It has been found that the ANN and regression tree-based models perform marginally better than the SVM model for PM$_{10}$ forecasting but significantly worse for PM$_{2.5}$ forecasting.

Doreswamy et al. [9] employed RF, XG Boost, BRT, and MLP Regression to forecast Taiwan $PM_{2.5}$. In both training and testing datasets, XG Boost obtained the best R^2 and lowest MSE. Sharma et al. [10] evaluated many air contaminants and utilized a time series regression model with extraneous factors to predict SO_2, NO_2, O_3, CO, and $PM_{2.5}$.

Qiao et al. [11] proposed a new model based on WT (wavelet transform)-SAE (stacked autoencoder)-LSTM (wavelet transform-stacked autoencoder-LSTM). To begin, WT is used to break down the $PM_{2.5}$ time series into numerous low- and high-frequency components based on different data from six Chinese research sites. SAE-LSTM is then used to forecast the deconstructed components.

Biancofiore et al. [12] analyzed three years of continuous measurements of PM and CO concentration in central Italy using a multiple linear regression model and ANN models with and without recursive architecture. One to three days in the future, an ANN was used to predict the concentrations of PM_{10} and $PM_{2.5}$ in the air. The ANN used meteorological and chemical factors as input.

Mahajan et al. [13] utilized the NNAR, an additive version of the Holt-Winters method, and the ARIMA model to forecast hourly $PM_{2.5}$ in Taiwan. For comparison, root-mean-square error (RMSE) and mean absolute error (MAE) were the criteria. The results show that the NNAR model has the lowest values for both RMSE and MAE.

Ejohwomu et al. [14] used ARIMA, exponential smoothing, prophet, NNAR, ANN based on multiple variables, SVM, XG Boost, and RF. $PM_{2.5}$, relative humidity, and temperature were measured every 15 min and converted to hourly time-series data. Accuracy of forecast model predictions was evaluated using metrics such as RMSE and MAE.

Gupta et al. [15] used NASA's Modern-Era Retrospective analysis for Research and Applications, Version 2 (MERRA2) aerosols and meteorology reanalysis data to estimate the surface $PM_{2.5}$ concentration in Thailand. The RF was used to validate and train the data. Furthermore, the RF can estimate hourly and daily mean PM2.5 with a high degree of precision. The mean bias is near to zero, with correlation coefficients above 0.90 in the majority of cases.

3 Dataset Overview and Preparation

The $PM_{2.5}$ air pollution index (API) data utilized in this study are secondary data obtained from the website of the World Air Quality Index (WAQI) project, https://aqicn.org/city/Bangkok/. Bangkok's API database in WAQI is retrieved from the Division of Air Quality Data, Bureau of Air Quality and Noise Management, Pollution Control Department. The daily AQI is based on the 24-h average of hourly readings from all stations from January 1, 2019 to December 31, 2021. Also, some variables are obtained from the World Meteorological Organization (WMO) via the webpage https://meteostat.net/en/place/th/bangkok. The database contains pollutants and meteorological variables such as ozone (O_3), nitrogen dioxide (NO_2), average temperature (Temp.avg), precipitation (PRCP), wind speed (Wspd), and pressure.

In data cleaning and preparation processes, the missing data can be accessed in aggregation plots as shown in Fig. 1. The missing proportion of PRCP is 1.09%, and $PM_{2.5}$, NO_2, and O_3 are all the same, at 0.36%, while the other covariates have no missing values. Two different types of blocks are shown on the right of Fig. 1: one for observed (blue) values and one for missing (red) data. There are 1,078 days with complete covariates, 12 days with only missing PRCP, 2 days with only missing PM$_{2.5}$, 2 days with missing NO$_2$ and O$_3$, and 2 days with missing PM$_{2.5}$, NO$_2$, and O$_3$. Multiple imputation by chained equations (MICE) was utilized to replace missing values in the gathered data. The MICE approach is based on the premise that multiple imputation is best accomplished in distinct steps, each of which may require diagnostic examination. Multiple imputation, analysis of imputed data, and pooling of analysis outcomes are MICE's main steps. This task can be achieved by using the R package "mice" [16].

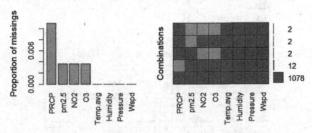

Fig. 1. Aggregation plots for missing values

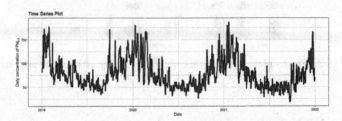

Fig. 2. Time-series plot of PM$_{2.5}$

Table 1. Descriptive statistics of cleaned data from 1 January 2019 to 31 December 2021

Covariates	Unit	Range	Mean	S.D	Min	Max
PM$_{2.5}$	μg/m^3	169.0	78.84	31.927	18.0	187.0
O3	μg/m^3	93.0	12.79	7.114	1.0	94.0
NO$_2$	μg/m^3	37.0	9.886	6.109	1.0	38.0
Temperature	Celsius	12.9	29.28	1.736	21.6	34.5
Precipitation	inches	117.1	3.967	10.625	0.0	117.1
Humidity	percent	51.8	71.19	9.063	44.0	95.8
Pressure	Hg	0.4	29.80	0.085	29.6	30.0
Wind Speed	km/hour	5.0	2.074	0.842	0.2	5.2

After preprocessing data, the time-series data on $PM_{2.5}$ concentration is illustrated in Fig. 2, and descriptive statistics of $PM_{2.5}$ concentration and metrological data are shown in Table 1. To quantify relationship, Pearson's values are calculated and presented in Fig. 3 along with scatter plots. It is observed that $PM_{2.5}$ concentration is correlated with NO_2 the most, followed by pressure, O_3, and humidity. These factors correlate moderately to strongly with $PM_{2.5}$. Precipitation and average temperature have low correlations with $PM_{2.5}$, and wind speed has the lowest correlation.

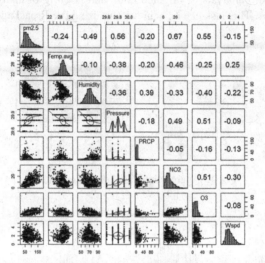

Fig. 3. Scatter plots and Pearson correlations among all pairs of variables

4   Research Methods

4.1   Seasonal ARIMA with Exogenous Covariates

The autoregressive moving average (ARMA) model is a combination of the AR and MA models. The AR model of order p can be written as,

$$\left(1 - \phi_1 L - \cdots \phi_p L^p\right)y_t = c + \varepsilon_t, \tag{1}$$

where L^i is a lag operator that converts a variable at time t into its ith-order lagged form, and the MA model of order q is defined as

$$y_t = c + \left(1 + \theta_1 L + \cdots + \theta_q L^q\right)\varepsilon_t. \tag{2}$$

The AR component represents the connection between the dependent variable and its previous expression, while the MA term combines the effect of a limited series of random disturbances on the dependent variable. Incorporating differencing and exogenous variables to ARMA model, we obtain a non-seasonal ARIMAX model:

$$\phi(L)\nabla^d y_t = x_t^T \beta + \theta(L)\varepsilon_t, \tag{3}$$

where $\phi(L)$ is called the autoregressive operator, $\theta(L)$ is called the moving average operator, β is a vector of coefficients, x_t^T is a vector of covariate at time t, and ε_t is a disturbance characterized by a normal distribution with a mean of zero and a constant variance. To describe Eq. (3), notation ARIMAX(p, d, q) is usually used.

The ARIMAX models can also be used to model a variety of seasonal data. Additional seasonal terms are added to the ARIMAX model to create a seasonal ARIMAX model, Eq. (3). It is written as follows:

$$\phi_p(L)\Phi_P(L^S)\nabla^d\nabla^D y_t = x_t^T\beta + \theta_q(L)\Theta_Q(L^S)\varepsilon_t, \tag{4}$$

where $\Phi_P(L^S)$ corresponds to a seasonal AR component, $\Theta_Q(L^S)$ corresponds to a seasonal MA component, and S is the duration of the recurring seasonal pattern. The corresponding notation for Eq. (4) is SARIMAX(p, d, q)(P, D, Q)$_S$ [17].

In the R package "forecast", there is a function called auto.arima() that can fit a regression model with ARIMA errors. It employs a variant of the Hyndman-Khandakar method [18] that combines unit root testing, Akaike information criterion (AICc) reduction, and MLE to get the ARIMA model.

4.2 Prophet Model

Facebook [19] created the Prophet model to forecast daily data with weekly and yearly seasonality, as well as holiday influences. It was later extended to incorporate other seasonal data sources. It is effective with time series with strong seasonality and data from many seasons. Prophet is a nonlinear regression model of the following form:

$$y_t = g(t) + s(t) + h(t) + \varepsilon_t, \tag{5}$$

where $g(t)$ represents a piecewise-linear trend, $s(t)$ denotes the various seasonal patterns, $h(t)$ determines the holiday effects, and ε_t is a random error term.

4.3 Regression Tree

Since Breiman [20] proposed decision trees in 1984, statistical learning approaches based on them have grown in popularity. A binary regression tree T divides the space X into many regions as there are leaf nodes, as stated by W. The total prediction function g associated with the tree may be represented as

$$g(x) = \sum_{w \in W} g^w(x)I(x \in \mathbb{R}_W), \tag{6}$$

where I represents the indicator function and $\mathbb{R}_W$ is the region built in the regression tree using logical criteria. The goal of building a tree using a training set $\tau = \{(x_i, y_i)\}_{i=1}^n$ is to minimize the training squared-error loss,

$$l_\tau(g) = \frac{1}{n}\sum_{w \in W}\sum_{i=1}^n I(x_i \in \mathbb{R}_W)\big[y_i - g(x_i)\big]^2. \tag{7}$$

Cost-Complexity Pruning. Let $\tau = \{(x_i, y_i)\}_{i=1}^n$ be a data set and $\gamma \geq 0$ be a real number. For a given tree T, the cost-complexity measure $C_\tau(\gamma, T)$ is defined as:

$$C_\tau(\gamma, T) = \frac{1}{n} \sum_{w \in W} \sum_{i=1}^n I(x_i \in \mathbb{R}_W)[y_i - g(x_i)]^2 + \gamma |W|, \tag{8}$$

where W denotes the set of terminal nodes of T and $|W|$ denotes the total number of leaves on the tree, which provides insight into its intricacy.

Bootstrap Aggregation. One of the ensemble methods is bootstrap aggregation, commonly known as bagging. There are bootstrap samples $\mathfrak{I}_1^*, \mathfrak{I}_2^*, ..., \mathfrak{I}_B^*$ and the matching B independent models giving learner $g_{\mathfrak{I}_1^*}, g_{\mathfrak{I}_2^*}, ..., g_{\mathfrak{I}_B^*}$ from the training set $\mathfrak{I}$ with n observations. The bootstrapped aggregated estimator or bagged estimator is obtained by model averaging as follows:

$$g_{bag}(x) = \frac{1}{B} \sum_{b=1}^B g_{\mathfrak{I}_b^*}(x). \tag{9}$$

In an idealized situation, the average prediction function converges to the expectation prediction function if $B \to \infty$ and $\mathfrak{I}_1, \mathfrak{I}_2, ..., \mathfrak{I}_B$ are identically and distributed. However, $\mathfrak{I}_1, \mathfrak{I}_2, ..., \mathfrak{I}_B$ are not independent, and for large n, the bootstrap sample $\mathfrak{I}^*$ only contains roughly 0.37 of the points from $\mathfrak{I}$[21].

Random Forest. Suppose there is a feature that gives a very excellent split of the data, it will be chosen and divided for every $\{g_{\mathfrak{I}_b^*}\}_{b=1}^B$ at the root level, and predictions will be highly correlated. Prediction averaging is unlikely to improve in such a case. this problem is addressed by selecting $m \leq p$ features at random and then calculating splitting criteria. Strong predictors have a lower chance of being retained at the root levels [21].

Conditional Inference Forest. Torsten Hothorn et al. [22] created conditional inference forests (Cforest) to identify the conditional distribution of statistics that quantify the relationships between the response variable and the predictor factors. The Chi-square test statistics are used to examine if any predictors have statistically significant correlations with the response. A global null hypothesis is defined as $H_0 : \bigcap_{j=1}^m H_0^j$, where H_0^j indicates that Y is independent of $X_j, j \in \{1, 2, ..., p\}$.

Gradient Boosted Regression Tree. Any learning algorithm may benefit from boosting, especially if the learner is a poor one. Boosting and bagging both use prediction functions, however the two techniques are fundamentally distinct from each other. Bootstrapped data are used in bagging, while in boosting, the prediction functions are learned in sequentially. At each stage of the boosting round b, $b = 1, 2, ..., B$, a negative gradient on n training points $x_1, ..., x_n$ will be calculated. Next, the negative gradient is estimated using a simple tree by solving

$$h_b = \arg\min_{h \in H} \frac{1}{n} \sum_{i=0}^n \left(r_i^{(b)} - [g_{b-1}(x_i) + h(x_i)] \right)^2. \tag{10}$$

The algorithm makes a γ-sized step in the direction of the negative gradient:

$$g_b(x) \leftarrow g_{b-1}(x) + \gamma h_b(x). \tag{11}$$

Approximation tree learning with sparse data was proposed by Chen and Guestrin [23]. They explain how to build a scalable tree boosting system using caching, compression, and sharing techniques. The combination of these findings allows XGBoost to handle billions of instances while using a fraction of the resources.

Bayesian Additive Regression Tree (BART). The BART model is comprised of a sum-of-trees model plus a regularization prior on model parameters. Let $M = \{\mu_1, \mu_2, ..., \mu_b\}$ denote a set of parameter values for each terminal node b in T and Function $f(x; T, M)$ that assigns a $\mu_i \in M$ to a single component in $x = (x_1, x_2, ..., x_p)$ as follows:

$$Y = \sum_{j=1}^{m} g(x; T_j, M_j) + \varepsilon, \tag{12}$$

where $\varepsilon \ N(0, \sigma^2)$ and $g(x; T_j, M_j)$ is the function which assigns $\mu_{ij} \in M_j$ to x. Also, a prior $g(T_1, M_1), ..., g(T_m, M_m)$ and σ must be imposed over all sum-of-trees parameters. BART draws posterior samples using MCMC. Chipman et al. [24] describe in detail an iterative Bayesian backfitting MCMC algorithm.

4.4 Support Vector Regression

Vapnik et al. [25] proposed an SVM for regression. Here, $F(x, w)$ denotes a family of functions parameterized by w, $G(x)$ is an unknown function, and $\hat{w}$ is the value of w that minimizes an error between $G(x)$ and $F(x, \hat{w})$. The representation of $F(x, \hat{w})$ can be defined as

$$F(x, \hat{w}) = \sum_{i=1}^{n} (\alpha_i^* - \alpha_i)\left(v_i^T x + 1\right)^p + b, \tag{13}$$

where there are $2n + 1$ values of α_i^*, α_i, and b. The optimum values for the components of $\hat{w}$ or α depend on a definition of a loss function and the objective function.

4.5 Artificial Neural Network

The artificial neural network (ANN) approach resembles the functioning of human bran, and the algorithm has been based on function:

$$g^*(x) = \sum_{j=1}^{2p+1} h_j\left(\sum_{i=1}^{p} h_{ij}(x_i)\right), \tag{14}$$

where each of the p parts of the input x is expressed as a node in an input layer; there are $2p + 1$ nodes in the hidden layer. The output of a feed-forward neural network with $L + 1$ layers may be expressed as the function composition:

$$g(x) = S_L \circ M_L \circ \cdots \circ S_2 \circ M_2 \circ S_1 \circ M_1, \qquad (15)$$

where $M_l = W_l z + b_l$, $l = 1, 2, ..., L - 1$, S_l is an activation function, W_l is a weight matrix, and b_l is a bias vector.

4.6   K-Nearest Neighbors (KNN) Regression

Let $\tau = \{(x_i, y_i)\}_{i=1}^n$ be a training set and $\{(x_{(i)}, y_{(i)})\}_{i=1}^n$ be a reordering of the data according to increasing distances $\|x_i - x\|$ of the $x_i's$ to x. The usual k-NN regression estimate takes the form $g_n(x) = \sum_{i=1}^n y_{(i)}(x)/k_n$.

5   Results and Conclusions

A total of 1004 data points were used for training and a further 92 for testing. The RMSE, MAE, and Pearson correlation coefficient (PCC) were used to evaluate the forecasts provided by the machine learning models.

Table 2 summarizes and presents the predictive performance indicators for all the 24 models. Based on the training data, the RF has the lowest RMSE and MAE, followed by SARIMAX and trees without pruning; the RF is clearly superior, as its RMSE is only 9.68 and its PCC is close to one. For test data, GBMs with Gaussian and Laplace have the lowest RMSE and MAE, respectively. Based on the PCC, the best three approaches are, respectively, Prophet, NNAR, and GBM with Gaussian distribution.

Considering all the criteria in both the training and test datasets, SARIMAX, trees without pruning, and typical neural networks (except NNAR and ANN using model averaging) tend to be overfitted models, so they are not suitable for $PM_{2.5}$ prediction. The other models are considered "good" and some of them are evaluated for a particular period, as shown in Fig. 4.

To provide superior forecasts, ensemble techniques employ a collection of machine learning methods. There are numerous "great" models here based on a certain criterion for both training and test datasets. For example, GBM with Gaussian, NNAR, SVR (Poly deg. of 2), BRT, and RF all give RMSE values of less than 20, MAE values of less than 16, and PCC values of greater than 0.7 for the test data. These models shown in Fig. 4 are among the top ten and were included in the ensemble models. There are three kinds of ensemble models: (1) average, (2) median, and (3) weighted. The weights (W) are allocated based on predictive performance: $W_{GBM} = 5$, $W_{NNAR} = 4$, $W_{SVR} = 3$, $W_{BRT} = 2$, and $W_{RF} = 1$. The predictive performance is shown in Table 3. When compared to all standalone algorithms, the ensemble (weighted) model gives the lowest RMSE, the lowest MAE, and the highest PCC. The ensemble model produced in this work is a mix of the "great" models, which might explain why it performs better.

Table 2. Predictive performance of the univariate and multivariate models

Models		Training data			Test data		
		RMSE	MAE	PCC	RMSE	MAE	PCC
1	SARIMAX (3,1,2)(2,0,0) [7]	13.2309	9.8416	0.9135	29.1229	21.0273	0.3017
2	Prophet model	16.4195	12.4349	0.8625	16.8109	12.9635	**0.7852**
3	Boosted GAM	19.6704	14.8718	0.7958	17.3149	13.3911	0.7487
4	Tree without pruning	13.7452	10.0344	0.9059	27.5612	21.2349	0.5096
5	Tree with pruning	19.7211	14.9438	0.7942	19.7729	14.9105	0.7017
6	Bagged regression TREE	16.5598	12.8007	0.8644	17.9855	13.8474	0.7280
7	Random forest (RF)	**9.6836**	**7.1578**	**0.9617**	18.8680	14.7794	0.7065
8	Conditional RF	16.5503	12.2456	0.8626	18.1553	13.8912	0.7169
9	GBM with Gaussian	18.2094	13.6183	0.8288	**16.7995**	12.8349	0.7603
10	GBM with Student-t	20.1617	14.2879	0.7971	17.5609	12.8646	0.7345
11	GBM with Laplace	19.3167	13.5126	0.8122	16.9995	**12.5213**	0.7578
12	XGBoost	16.2301	12.1305	0.8686	17.3822	13.1277	0.7448
13	BART	17.9175	13.5989	0.8346	17.7948	13.5950	0.7357
14	7-11-1 ANN (logistic)	17.4170	13.0207	0.8438	23.6783	19.4137	0.6601
15	7-11-1 ANN (tanh)	17.5802	13.3950	0.8406	31.6012	26.3459	0.2858
16	7-11-4-1 ANN (logistic)	15.9349	11.8504	0.8712	25.7745	21.3557	0.5825
17	7-11-4-1 ANN (tanh)	14.8501	11.1096	0.8892	53.2947	40.3602	0.3647
18	NNAR (29,1,18)[7]	13.5594	9.0555	0.9095	17.3663	12.9768	0.7772
19	ANN using model averaging	19.8413	15.0865	0.7950	18.5319	14.5525	0.7132
20	KNN (Rectangular)	18.4564	13.6578	0.8288	19.5365	15.7029	0.6755

(continued)

Table 2. (*continued*)

Models		Training data			Test data		
		RMSE	MAE	PCC	RMSE	MAE	PCC
21	KNN (Epanechnikov)	19.2517	14.2518	0.8103	19.4960	15.6700	0.6782
22	SVR Linear	21.6400	16.2817	0.7453	17.0003	13.1713	0.7562
23	SVR (Poly deg. of 2)	20.2533	14.5404	0.7848	17.9685	13.9103	0.7277
24	SVR (Poly deg. of 3)	19.2560	13.4661	0.8075	21.9772	16.3793	0.6050

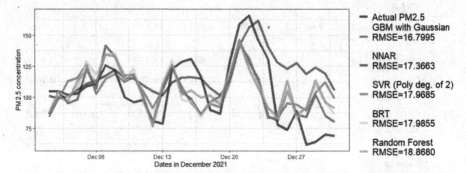

Fig. 4. Forecasts from the selected models compared to the actual values of $PM_{2.5}$

Table 3. Predictive performance on test data for the ensemble models

Model	RMSE	MAE	PCC
Ensemble (mean)	16.3746	12.6136	0.7763
Ensemble (median)	17.1361	13.0713	0.7501
Ensemble (weighted)	15.9516	12.3144	0.7888

References

1. Jung, R., Hwang, F., Chen, T.: Incorporating long-term satellite-based aerosol optical depth, localized land use data, and meteorological variables to estimate ground-level PM 2.5 concentrations in Taiwan from 2005 to 2015. Environ. Pollut. **237**(1), 1000–1010 (2018)
2. Health Effects Institute: State of Global Air 2020. Special Report. Boston, MA (2020)
3. Yiyi, W., et al.: Associations of daily mortality with short-term exposure to PM2.5 and its constituents in Shanghai, China. Chemosphere **233**, 879–887 (2019)
4. Xing, Y.F., et al.: The impact of PM2.5 on the human respiratory system. J. Thorac. Dis. **8**(1), E69–E74 (2016)
5. World Air Quality Index project. https://aqicn.org/city/bangkok/. Last accessed 25 Mar 2022

6. Catalano, M., et al.: Improving the prediction of air pollution peak episodes generated by urban transport networks. Environ. Sci. Policy. **60**, 69–83 (2016)
7. Masood, A., Ahmad, K.: A model for particulate for Delhi based on machine learning approaches. Procedia. Comput. Sci. **167**, 2101–2110 (2020)
8. Suleiman, A., et al.: Applying machine learning methods in managing urban concentrations of traffic-related particulate matter (PM$_{10}$ and PM$_{2.5}$). Atmos. Pollut. Res. **10**(1), 134–144 (2019)
9. Doreswamy, et al.: Forecasting air pollution particulate matter (PM$_{2.5}$) using machine learning regression models. Procedia. Comput. Sci. **171**, 2057–2066 (2020)
10. Sharma, N., et al.: Forecasting air pollution load in Delhi using data analysis tools. Procedia. Comput. Sci. **132**, 1077–1085 (2018)
11. Qiao, W., et al.: The forecasting of PM$_{2.5}$ using a hybrid model based on wavelet transform and an improved deep learning algorithm. IEEE Access **7**, 142814–142825 (2019)
12. Biancofiore, F.: Recursive neural network model for analysis and forecast of PM$_{10}$ and PM$_{2.5}$. Atmos. Pollut. Res. **8**, 652–659 (2017)
13. Mahajan, S.: An empirical study of PM$_{2.5}$ forecasting using neural network. In: 2017 IEEE SmartWorld, Ubiquitous Intelligence & Computing, Advanced & Trusted Computed, Scalable Computing & Communications, Cloud & Big Data Computing, Internet of People and Smart City Innovation, pp. 1–7. IEEE, San Francisco, USA (2017)
14. Ejohwomu, O.A., et al.: Modelling and forecasting temporal PM$_{2.5}$ concentration using ensemble machine learning methods. Buildings **12**(1), 46 (2022)
15. Gupta, P., et al.: Machine learning algorithm for estimating surface PM$_{2.5}$ in Thailand, Aerosol Air Qual. Res. **21**(11), 210105 (2021)
16. Buuren, S.: Karin Groothuis-Oudshoorn: mice: multivariate imputation by chained equations in R. J. Stat. Softw. **45**(3), 1–67 (2011)
17. Box, G.E.P., et al.: Time series analysis: forecasting and control, 4th edn. John Wiley & Sons Inc., Hoboken, New Jersey (2008)
18. Hyndman, R.J., Khandakar, Y.: Automatic time series forecasting: the forecast package for R. J. Stat. Softw. **27**(3), 1–22 (2008)
19. Taylor, S.J., Letham, B.: Forecasting at scale. Am. Stat. **72**(1), 37–45 (2018)
20. Breiman, L., et al.: Classification and Regression Trees, 1st edn. Chapman and Hall/CRC, Boca Raton (1984)
21. Kroese, D.P., et al.: Data Science and Machine Learning: Mathematical and Statistical Methods, 1st edn. Chapman and Hall/CRC, Boca Raton (2020)
22. Hothorn, T., et al.: Unbiased recursive partitioning: a conditional inference framework. J. Comput. Graph. Stat. **15**(3), 651–674 (2006)
23. Chen, T.Q., Guestrin, C.: XGBoost: a scalable tree boosting system. https://arxiv.org/abs/1603.02754. Last accessed 17 Apr 2022
24. Chipman, H.A., et al.: BART: Bayesian additive regression trees. Ann. Appl. Stat. **4**(1), 266–298 (2010)
25. Vapnik, V., et al.: Support vector method for function approximation, regression estimation, and signal processing. Adv. Neural Inf. Process. Syst. **9**, 281–287 (1997)

Wearable Fall Detection Based on Motion Signals Using Hybrid Deep Residual Neural Network

Sakorn Mekruksavanich[1]([✉]), Ponnipa Jantawong[1], Narit Hnoohom[2],
and Anuchit Jitpattanakul[3]

[1] Department of Computer Engineering, School of Information and Communication
Technology, University of Phayao, Mueang Phayao, Phayao, Thailand
`sakorn.me@up.ac.th`
[2] Image, Information and Intelligence Laboratory, Department of Computer
Engineering, Faculty of Engineering, Mahidol University, Nakhon Pathom, Thailand
`narit.hno@mahidol.ac.th`
[3] Intelligent and Nonlinear Dynamic Innovations Research Center,
Department of Mathematics, Faculty of Applied Science,
King Mongkut's University of Technology North Bangkok, Bangkok, Thailand
`anuchit.j@sci.kmutnb.ac.th`

Abstract. There have been several approaches for wearable fall detection devices during the last twenty years. The majority of technologies relied on machine learning. Although the given findings appear that the issue is practically addressed, critical problems remain about feature extraction and selection. In this research, the constraint of machine learning on feature extraction is addressed by including a hybrid convolutional operation in our proposed deep residual network, called the DeepFall model. The proposed network automatically generates high-level motion signal characteristics that can be utilized to track falls and everyday activities. FallAllD dataset, a publicly available standard dataset for fall detection that gathered motion signals of falls and other events, was utilized to analyze the proposed network. We performed investigations using a 5-fold cross-validation technique to determine overall accuracy and F-measure. The experimental outcomes show that the proposed DeepFall performs better accuracy (95.19%) and F-measure (92.79%) than the state-of-the-art baseline deep learning networks.

Keywords: Fall detection · Wearable sensors · Deep learning · Deep residual network

1 Introduction

The importance of fall detection systems (FDSs) for the elderly derives from the concept that serious fall-related problems could well be avoided with prompt and adequate medical care. The FDSs might be classified as either ambient or

O. Surinta and K. Kam Fung Yuen (Eds.): MIWAI 2022, LNAI 13651, pp. 216–224, 2022.
https://doi.org/10.1007/978-3-031-20992-5_19

wearable. The first category is limited to residential use, but the latter benefits following the elderly inside and outside. This article discusses wearable fall detection technologies, and the sensors frequently utilized in this equipment are discussed in the next section.

Micro-Electro-Mechanical Systems (MEMS) permitted the production of a range of sensors, including accelerometers and gyroscopes, in compact and lightweight packaging as wearable technology advanced. These MEMS-based sensors are commonly employed in wearable devices presently. Accelerometers are the most often utilized sensors for fall detection and human activity identification due to their low energy consumption and techniques used to collect important body movement data.

Several FDSs have been designed in the past twenty years. Some of these strategies are threshold-based [12], however the most are machine learning-based [15], to mention just some. In threshold-based approaches, thresholds are determined based on the available data. Correspondingly, with machine learning-based approaches, the training phase depends on the available information.

Based on the interpretation of the findings acquired by wearable inertial sensors, machine learning (ML) techniques have demonstrated remarkable efficacy in differentiating between falls and typical motions or Activities of Daily Living (ADLs). Random forest, Support vector machine, Multi-layer perceptron, and k-nearest neighbors are four well-known and commonly employed ML techniques in FDSs [5]. Nevertheless, the effectiveness of these ML approaches was constrained by manual feature extraction.

Deep learning (DL) has been utilized extensively in the majority of areas throughout the globe [10,11,17]. In recent years, fall recognition has benefited more from the application of DL techniques [1,7] than threshold-based procedures [2]. Designs of DL comprise layers, and each layer extracts the characteristics of the provided data or transforms the data. Typically, the last layers of models consisted of synthetic neurons. The data could be recorded as a vision-based image, raw data from an accelerometer and gyroscope. Several DL approaches are employed to identify autumnal occurrences [8]. Some systems are constructed using a single DL algorithm, while others combine many methods to get a greater detection rate [6]. Convolutional neural networks (CNNs) and recurrent neural networks (RNNs) are the most prevalent DL models for fall detection [9,20].

In this study, we proposed a convolutional and residual block-based deep neural network named DeepFall model. Using the TensorFlow platform, the recommended model has been trained to identify falls and ADLs. The suggested model was assessed and compared on a public benchmark dataset against various baseline DL models (FallAllD dataset).

The article continues with the following outline: New relevant research is included in Sect. 2. The details of the proposed model are outlined in Sect. 3. The outcomes of our investigations can be seen in Sect. 4. The study finishes with a discussion of necessary future studies in Sect. 5.

2   Related Works

2.1   Fall Detection System

Current fall detection technologies may be loosely categorized into vision-based, ambient, and wearable sensors.

Vision-based sensors gather motion information by monitoring systems and extracting a person's body photograph orientation or human skeleton annotations from collected video or image data [21] to detect a fall. Typically, the ambient sensor measures fall by gathering infrared [19], radar [13], and other signals from the scene sensor. Although it does not pose any privacy concerns, it comes at a slightly higher price. It is susceptible to noise and has a somewhat restricted detection range. Multiple low-cost sensors are used by wearable technology to monitor falls [18]. Its detecting abilities depend on the sensor being worn in real-time. However, the elderly may be unable to do so in some situations, such as having a bath. Furthermore, some older individuals may experience pain from their apparel.

Due to the inexpensive cost of sensors in recent times, wearable sensors have gained increasing popularity. To acquire the three-axis acceleration at various points and the three-axis rotation angular velocity in a gyroscope, the most popular locations for wearable sensors are the calf, spine, head, pelvis, and feet [4].

2.2   Automatic Fall Detection by Using DL

Approaches for ML are primarily separated into classical pattern recognition and classification and recognition based on DL. Conventional recognition techniques depend on manually extracted features for identification. Consequently, researchers recommend stricter parameters for fall detection. Initially, it is required to identify the physical components involved in the falling procedure. Second, it is necessary to evaluate how these traits are separated from ADLs such as sitting and leaping; otherwise, the feature selection method will be significantly slowed down. Classification and identification based on DL are being used in fall detection systems that can automatically extract feature data. Due to this benefit, DL approaches have gained increasing popularity among the scientific community. They have been utilized in various fields where they have performed a part equal to that of human specialists. In principle, the stages required in DL approaches using sensor data from wearable devices are to preprocess the received signals, extract features from signal segments, and train a model using these features as input [16]. Thus, current studies in wearable sensor data fall risk assessment concentrate primarily on technical aspects that optimize performance. Various DL methods utilize the retrieved information as input to forecast the occurrence of falls. Klenk et al. [3] built a fall detection system based on long short-term memory (LSTM), which used a long-time sequence as input and extracted temporal features efficiently.

3   Fall Detection Approach

The sensor-based fall detection approach used in this investigation includes four main operational phases, as shown in Fig. 1: data acquisition, data pre-processing, data generation, model construction, and evaluation.

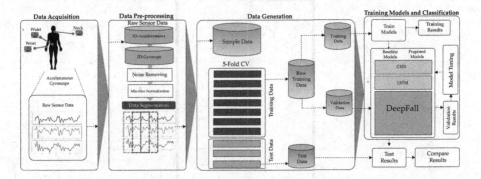

Fig. 1. Sensor-based fall detection approach

3.1   FallAllD Dataset

The FallAllD dataset [14] is a free public standard dataset for fall identification. Motion signal data was collected from 15 healthful people (age 21–53, height 158–187 cm, and weight 48–85 kg) using three types of equipment: an accelerometer, gyroscope, magnetometer, and barometer. The individuals wore the wearable devices on three distinct body locations (neck, wrist, and waist). In this dataset, 44 categories of ADL and 35 categories of falls were conducted.

Each information recorder has an inertial measurement unit, LSM9DS1, built for tracking movement. This module includes 1) a 3D accelerometer (a sampling rate 238 Hz and a broad dynamic scope of 8 g), 2) a 3D gyroscope (a sampling rate 238 Hz and a geometric proportion of 2000 DPS), and 3) a 3D magnetometer (a frequency response 80 Hz). In addition, a separate data recorder is integrated with an MS5607 barometric sensor with 10 Hz sampling rate.

3.2   Pre-processing of Data

Original sensor data of the accelerometer and gyroscope were processed by making the following adjustments. First, the median filter and a third-order low-pass Butterworth filter with a 20-Hz cutoff frequency were employed to reduce noise. Then, the Min-Max method was utilized to normalize the data. Segmentation of the pre-processed sensor data was conducted using fixed-width 1-second of sliding windows with a 50% overlapping, as shown in Fig. 2.

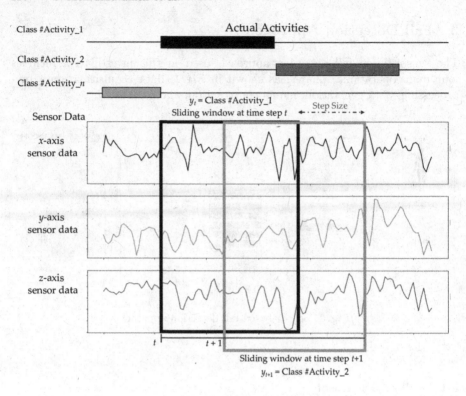

Fig. 2. Fixed-length sliding window

3.3   Hybrid Deep Residual Neural Network

DeepFall model, a hybrid deep residual neural network introduced in this paper, consists of two primary details. The first part is a convolutional block automatically extracting low-level characteristics from unprocessed movement inputs. The second method hierarchically recovers combination characteristics from a mixture of Spatio-temporal and channel-specific data using the residual block. This residual block contained Conv1D, BN, and ReLU layers, including a direct connection to LSTM, as seen in Fig. 3.

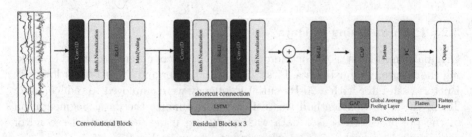

Fig. 3. The proposed DeepFall structure

3.4   Interpretation Measurements

The effectiveness of the proposed DL model is evaluated using four standard evaluation metrics obtained during the 10-fold cross-validation process: accuracy, precision, recall, and F-measure. These four metrics can be calculated using the following formulas:

$$Accuracy = \frac{TP + TN}{TP + TN + FP + FN} \tag{1}$$

$$Precision = \frac{TP}{TP + FP} \tag{2}$$

$$Recall = \frac{TP}{TP + FN} \tag{3}$$

$$F - measure = 2 \times \frac{Precision \times Recall}{Precision + Recall} \tag{4}$$

The four most often used KPIs for fall detection are listed above. The classification is considered true positive (TP) for the group under study, whereas, for all other groups, it is considered true negative (TN). When sensor data from one group is incorrectly assigned to another, this is called a false positive (FP). On the other hand, a false positive (FP) designation could occur if data from an activity sensor that belongs to a different group was wrongly labeled as belonging to that group.

4   Experimental Results

In the Google Colab-Pro+ system, every experiment in this research is conducted. We experiment to assess the recognition interpretation of the offered network and compare the model to benchmark DL algorithms in this study (CNN and LSTM). To assess the efficiency of the algorithm, we divided these laboratory experiments into three scenarios:

- Scenario I: using movement signal data from neck-mounted wearable sensors,
- Scenario II: using movement signal data from wrist-mounted wearable sensors,
- Scenario III: using movement signal data from waist-mounted wearable sensors.

During experiments, movement signal data were acquired employing a 5-fold cross-validation methodology. Several tests were done to assess the identification effectiveness of various standard DL models (CNN and LSTM) and the suggested network. The precision and loss quantify the experimental findings, and F-measure is indicated in Table 1.

The proposed network obtained the maximum accuracy and F-measure in every scenario, according to the data. Incorporating an accuracy of 95.19% and an F-measure of 92.79%, the recommended network with movement signals from the waist position shows the most satisfactory performance.

Table 1. Identification effectiveness of baseline models compared with the proposed DriveNeXt model

Model	Identification effectiveness		
	Accuracy	Loss	F1-score
Scenario I: Neck			
CNN	74.21% (±0.006%)	0.57 (±0.000)	42.60% (±0.002%)
LSTM	81.72% (±0.363%)	0.40 (±0.002)	72.18% (±0.934%)
Hybrid deep residual network	92.13% (±0.938%)	0.28 (±0.028)	89.61% (±1.381%)
Scenario II: Wrist			
CNN	83.02% (±0.004%)	0.46 (±0.001)	45.36% (±0.001%)
LSTM	87.62% (±0.291%)	0.29 (±0.005)	72.70% (±1.383%)
Hybrid deep residual network	93.82% (±0.467%)	0.26 (±0.021)	88.81% (±0.678%)
Scenario III: Waist			
CNN	79.50% (±1.280%)	0.50 (±0.032)	56.91% (±15.846%)
LSTM	86.37% (±0.153%)	0.32 (±0.006)	76.80% (±0.718%)
Hybrid deep residual network	95.19% (±0.353%)	0.24 (±0.033)	92.79% (±0.561%)

5   Conclusion and Future Studies

Applying wearable sensors, we developed a hybrid DL model to address the fall detection challenge in this work effectively. The proposed DL method utilizes some of the benefits of residual blocks. In this study, we investigated the proposed DeepFall network using the FallAllD standard dataset for wearable sensors. Experimental findings revealed that the proposed network surpasses other models with the best accuracy (95.19%) and F-measure (92.79%).

Future research could also include evaluating the proposed DL model using a larger sample size of people with various fall circumstances. The efficacy might be significantly increased with the development of increasingly complex and compact DL networks and specific data representations based on time-frequency analysis.

Acknowledgment. This research project was supported by the Thailand Science Research and Innovation fund; the University of Phayao (Grant No. FF65-RIM041); National Science, Research and Innovation (NSRF); and King Mongkut's University of Technology North Bangkok with Contract No. KMUTNB-FF-66-07.

The authors also gratefully acknowledge the support provided by Thammasat University Research fund under the TSRI, Contract No. TUFF19/2564 and TUFF24/2565, for the project of "AI Ready City Networking in RUN", based on the RUN Digital Cluster collaboration scheme.

References

1. Colón, L.N.V., DeLaHoz, Y., Labrador, M.: Human fall detection with smartphones. In: 2014 IEEE Latin-America Conference on Communications (LATINCOM), pp. 1–7 (2014). https://doi.org/10.1109/LATINCOM.2014.7041879

2. Hsieh, S.L., Yang, C.T., Li, H.J.: Combining wristband-type devices and smartphones to detect falls. In: 2017 IEEE International Conference on Systems, Man, and Cybernetics (SMC), pp. 2373–2377 (2017). https://doi.org/10.1109/SMC.2017.8122977

3. Klenk, J., et al.: The FARSEEING real-world fall repository: a large-scale collaborative database to collect and share sensor signals from real-world falls. Eur. Rev. Aging Phys. Act. **13**, 8 (2016). https://doi.org/10.1186/s11556-016-0168-9

4. Mannini, A., Trojaniello, D., Cereatti, A., Sabatini, A.M.: A machine learning framework for gait classification using inertial sensors: application to elderly, post-stroke and huntington's disease patients. Sensors **16**(1), 134 (2016). https://doi.org/10.3390/s16010134

5. Martínez-Villaseñor, L., Ponce, H., Brieva, J., Moya-Albor, E., Núñez-Martínez, J., Peñafort-Asturiano, C.: UP-fall detection dataset: a multimodal approach. Sensors, 19(9) (2019). https://doi.org/10.3390/s19091988

6. Mekruksavanich, S., Hnoohom, N., Jitpattanakul, A.: A hybrid deep residual network for efficient transitional activity recognition based on wearable sensors. Appl. Sci. **12**(10), 4988 (2022). https://doi.org/10.3390/app12104988

7. Mekruksavanich, S., Jantawong, P., Charoenphol, A., Jitpattanakul, A.: Fall detection from smart wearable sensors using deep convolutional neural network with squeeze-and-excitation module. In: 2021 25th International Computer Science and Engineering Conference (ICSEC), pp. 448–453 (2021). https://doi.org/10.1109/ICSEC53205.2021.9684626

8. Mekruksavanich, S., Jitpattanakul, A.: Deep learning approaches for continuous authentication based on activity patterns using mobile sensing. Sensors **21**(22), 7519 (2021). https://doi.org/10.3390/s21227519

9. Mekruksavanich, S., Jitpattanakul, A.: CNN-based deep learning network for human activity recognition during physical exercise from accelerometer and photoplethysmographic sensors. In: Pandian, A.P., Fernando, X., Haoxiang, W. (eds.) Computer Networks, Big Data and IoT, pp. 531–542. Springer Nature Singapore, Singapore (2022). https://doi.org/10.1007/978-981-19-0898-9_42

10. Mekruksavanich, S., Jitpattanakul, A., Sitthithakerngkiet, K., Youplao, P., Yupapin, P.: ResNet-SE: channel attention-based deep residual network for complex activity recognition using wrist-worn wearable sensors. IEEE Access **10**, 51142–51154 (2022). https://doi.org/10.1109/ACCESS.2022.3174124

11. Noppitak, S., Surinta, O.: dropcyclic: Snapshot ensemble convolutional neural network based on a new learning rate schedule for land use classification. IEEE Access **10**, 60725–60737 (2022). https://doi.org/10.1109/ACCESS.2022.3180844

12. Pierleoni, P., et al.: A wearable fall detector for elderly people based on AHRS and barometric sensor. IEEE Sens. J. **16**(17), 6733–6744 (2016). https://doi.org/10.1109/JSEN.2016.2585667

13. Sadreazami, H., Bolic, M., Rajan, S.: Fall detection using standoff radar-based sensing and deep convolutional neural network. IEEE Trans. Circuits Syst. II Express Briefs **67**(1), 197–201 (2020). https://doi.org/10.1109/TCSII.2019.2904498

14. Saleh, M., Abbas, M., Le Jeannès, R.B.: FallAllD: an open dataset of human falls and activities of daily living for classical and deep learning applications. IEEE Sens. J. **21**(2), 1849–1858 (2021). https://doi.org/10.1109/JSEN.2020.3018335

15. Saleh, M., Jeannès, R.L.B.: Elderly fall detection using wearable sensors: a low cost highly accurate algorithm. IEEE Sens. J. **19**(8), 3156–3164 (2019). https://doi.org/10.1109/JSEN.2019.2891128

16. Saleh, M., Jeannès, R.L.B.: FallAllD: a comprehensive dataset of human falls and activities of daily living (2020). https://doi.org/10.21227/bnya-mn34

17. Shin, H.C., et al.: Deep convolutional neural networks for computer-aided detection: CNN architectures, dataset characteristics and transfer learning. IEEE Trans. Med. Imaging **35**(5), 1285–1298 (2016). https://doi.org/10.1109/TMI.2016.2528162

18. Tongyue, G., Jia, Y., Kaida, H., Qingxuan, H., Fengshou, Z.: Research and implementation of two-layer fall detection algorithm. In: 2018 5th International Conference on Systems and Informatics (ICSAI), pp. 70–74 (2018). https://doi.org/10.1109/ICSAI.2018.8599495

19. Tzeng, H.W., Chen, M.Y., Chen, J.Y.: Design of fall detection system with floor pressure and infrared image. In: 2010 International Conference on System Science and Engineering, pp. 131–135 (2010). https://doi.org/10.1109/ICSSE.2010.5551751

20. Vallabh, P., Malekian, R.: Fall detection monitoring systems: a comprehensive review. J. Ambient. Intell. Humaniz. Comput. **9**, 1809–1833 (2018). https://doi.org/10.1007/s12652-017-0592-3

21. Yao, L., Yang, W., Huang, W.: A fall detection method based on a joint motion map using double convolutional neural networks. Multimedia Tools Appl. 1–18 (2020)

Author Index

Printed in the United States
by Baker & Taylor Publisher Services